BLESSINGS, KICKS AND CURSES

Geoffrey Grigson

BLESSINGS, KICKS AND CURSES

A Critical Collection

Allison & Busby
LONDON / NEW YORK

Blessings, Kicks and Curses

First published 1982 by
Allison and Busby Limited,
6a Noel Street, London W1V 3RB, England
and distributed in the USA by
Schocken Books Inc.,
200 Madison Avenue, New York, NY 10016

Copyright © 1982 by Geoffrey Grigson

British Library Cataloguing in Publication Data

Grigson, Geoffrey
  Blessings, kicks and curses.
  1. English literature – History and criticism
  I. Title
  820′.9   PR83

  ISBN 0-85031-437-2

Printed and bound in Great Britain at
The Camelot Press Ltd, Southampton

Contents

Preface

The items in this critical collection are the work of a writer by profession in search of his cheques, which he has hoped to earn without toadying or temporizing – a writer whose preferred subject has all the while been poems and poets, or rather the essences of the "poetic" in poems and in other shapes as well. Most of them, have been written lately – since, that is to say, I published a last collection of the kind *The Contrary View* (a book sub-titled "Glimpses of Fudge and Gold") in 1974 – and if a few are by now more than twenty years old I hope that in trend these will not be considered now to be too antique.

In general these writings have been welcomed by editors, or literary editors, their hosts on first publication have included the *Listener,* the *London Magazine,* the *New Statesman,* the *New York Review of Books, Encounter,* the *Guardian,* and the *Times Literary Supplement.* A few were written for broadcasting, a few haven't been printed before, editorial discretion not having stretched quite so far. If nearly all these pieces are short, too short to allow for a fullness of affection, appreciation or dismay, that must be put down to the shrinkage of modern periodicals, which encourages the contributor to peremptorary full-stops, to saying *that's that* and *there you are.*

Dogmatism or no, I hope readers will find me consistent enough about I call the "poetic", the deeply, wholeheartedly made, whether in poems or in prose or in paint or in living, towards which I direct myself in these essays, reviews and notes, either by assent or denial.

Broad Town   Geoffrey Grigson
April 1982

To Paul Bailey, from one of
his readers

Apartheid, or in a Class Apart

[The jeu d'esprit which follows was written in 1957, looking forward to a time now past, which then seemed impossibly far ahead. I had forgotten its existence, but now I have read it again it does seem to me a just prologue to more than twenty years' decline in the standards expected of authorship and intellect, or intellectualism. So here it is, with a few footnotes appended to explain the now unfamiliar — unfamiliar, say, to readers under fifty.]

From our Special Correspondent, Kierkegaard Pueblo, Adlestrop, in the Cotswold Reservation. October 1979.

It is twenty-two years since I attended the Enclosing Ceremony of the English Intellectuals Reservation on the windy plateau of the Cotswolds. I have now been allowed to return as a welcome visitor and interested observer.

Allow me, though, as we say in our sacred European parlour games, to re-cap. For a long while, you may remember, passes to visit the Reservation were unobtainable. The Bureau of Intellectual Affairs, under the capable direction of Dr Charles Hill,[1] had the welfare of the then few remaining aborigines truly at heart.

The celebrated Massacre of the Intellectuals in Sloane Square by the shock troopers of the W.V.S. under the joint command of Generals John Gordon[2] and Lady Tweedsmuir[3] had left their morale and their numbers dangerously low. It was the Prime Minister of the time[4] who was instrumental in saving the remnants and ensuring a future for them. He had, I think, no Intellectual blood in his own veins, but due in part to his distant connection with the now forgotten craft of the publication of books other than White Papers and Instruction Manuals, he had a true sympathy with these poor, defeated, decimated and — at that time rightly — detested outcasts; which he was courageous in avowing.

He spoke at the Enclosing Ceremony; and I recall a memorable phrase he employed. The Intellectuals, for their own good and the good of the community upon which they had preyed for so long, were "now being placed in", he

---

1   Chairman of the BBC.
2   Editor of the *Sunday Express*.
3   Politicizing widow of John Buchan.
4   Harold Macmillan.

ventured to declare, "a Class Apart". And the P.M. went on that it must, if so interesting a relic of the Old World were to be preserved, and also rehabilitated, remain, for a long while to come, "truly Apart".

The class remained so indeed — until last week. The huge shabby notices, INTELLECTUALS RESERVATION. KEEP OUT, so long familiar to the passing motorist, have now been removed. It will be recalled that passes out as well as passes in, except to accredited scientists and now and again to Intellectuals from foreign reservations, were refused by the Bureau, with the hearty agreement of successive Governors of the Reservation, all of them, by the way, Intellectuals, self-imposed (since it was Dr Hill's wise anthropological policy to retain the old literary and artistic system) upon the Intellectual enclave.

Only one native Intellectual attempted to leave and re-join our world, so I was assured on my visit last week. This was Kingsley Amis[1] — a name that may be recalled by older readers — who protested that he had been drafted into the Reservation in error after a belated round-up by General Gordon's Vigilantes, who had illegally — and pointlessly — entered a redbrick university.

Amis, though, has long been reconciled and is likely, having reached years of tribal discretion, to succeed the ninety-seven-year-old Sir Herbert Read as next Governor.

Several persons have, I must report, curiously attempted to enter the Reserve, in spite of the severest penalties. A Lowland Scots poet was found in the *ica*, or underground ceremonial chamber, of one of the principal villages, reciting in Lallans; and was at once removed to the Imbecile Section of the Scottish Intellectuals Reserve on St Kilda. Machine-gun posts had to fire several times on Mr Colin Wilson as he was attempting to cut the wire with nail-scissors, having decided that Outside was Inside. Mr John Connell[2] was picked up on the wire disguised as A.J.P. Taylor (or as Henry Fairlie,[3] according to other accounts). Mr A.L. Rowse[4] attempted to sneak in with an inspecting commission of Oxford anthropologists and was carried off — a distressing scene — crying, "But I *am* an Intellectual"; while Mr and Mrs J.B. Priestley managed actually to penetrate all the defences and lurk undetected for some days reading each other's works by candle-light in the

1 An authority on education.
2 A journalist.
3 A more conceited journalist.
4 An historian, known usually as Dr Rowse.

deepest chamber of a Cotswold long barrow.

They were spotted, however, and exposed, by Mrs Arthur Miller, then on a sabbatical from the Reservation of American Intellectuals on Martha's Vineyard. Mrs Miller was searching for a corner where she could read Dostoievsky unmolested.

So much for the past. Now that rehabilitation has so far advanced, and now that the drop in numbers has been reversed by controlled and encouraged inbreeding, let me picture for you today's scene in the tidy pueblo of *Kierkegaard* in the very heart of the Reservation (the site of the former church and village of Adlestrop). I signed the new visitors' book and reported (Governor Sir Herbert Read was too frail to receive me) to the Reservation Sub-Governor, old Mr Philip Toynbee,[1] who had just driven back to Kierkegaard in his official limousine from the brief holiday at Butlin's, which is now allowed to senior Intellectuals. The huts, which had once housed some of the three million refugees from the People's Republic of Ghana, were long ago anachronistically, yet appropriately and accurately rebuilt in the Advanced Style of the Nineteen-twenties.

On the *Waste Land*, as the central square or plaza of each of the pueblos on the Reservation is called in the old teminology, old Mr Toynbee (speaking tolerable European, though with an archaic Intellectual accent) pointed out to me the back-axle of a kiddie car, set in concrete, supporting a cast-iron full-stop — a group by Reg Butler celebrating and symbolizing the *Spirit of the Little Magazines*. Near at hand, indeed, is the tidy office of Mr David Astor, now well-advanced in years, but still editor of the weekly Little Magazine of the whole Reservation, which he sets entirely by hand, on Saturday evenings, in the intervals of weaving, and which is written entirely by the Sub-Governor.

Everything is done by the conscientous Bureau of Intellectual Affairs to keep alive Intellectual arts and crafts. Every pueblo — Kierkegaard, Wittgenstein, Ayer, All Souls, Stearns, Brechtburg, Chatterley, Wystenshaw, Sutherland — has now been given a craft shop or trading-post for the sale of native arts to the expected tourists. In the Kierkegaard trading-post (which now incongruously advertises the outer world's *Daily Mirror*) a neatly dressed young native, who is actually a correspondence graduate of M.I.T., Oxford (Magdalene Institute of Technology) and a great-grandnephew of Kathleen Raine,

1 A metaphysical book-reviewer.

offered me Intellectual poems in autolithography, somewhat, I must admit, in a debased style catching more of Kathleen Raine and Elvis Presley, if you understand my meaning, than of T.S. Eliot; also figurines by leading Intellectual sculptors. These had more of the authentic touch, being plastic representations of characters from *Old Possum's Book of Practical Cats,* keeping, with five legs apiece, something at any rate of the old reckless spirit of Advance.

I remarked to the Sub-Governor that the Waste Land — indeed, the whole pueblo — seemed surprisingly empty.

He told me the Intellectuals, especially their women and their fifty-fifties (a term he did not actually explain) were still understandably shy, being admitted, or re-admitted, so newly to the gaze of Outsiders. Cameras, he added, were forbidden without a permit and a general fee, and no Intellectual might be photographed without his own leave and without being paid an individual fee — "though you may votograf me — for noddings", added the Sub-Governor, with a smile recalling the old publicity itch of Intellectuals.

I made for a circular hole out in the Waste Land, from which protruded the twin horns of an old-fashioned aerial; and was at once restrained — almost fiercely — by the bejewelled hand of the Sub-Governor. "No. Noddings doing. No wide man[1] nod Indellectual go town dere. Dat de *ica*, dat private."

It was indeed the *ica*, the famous subterranean *Institute of Contemporary Arts,* one of which exists below the Waste Land of every pueblo. Sub-Governor Toynbee presented a blank face to all my questions about the ceremonies which take place in the *ica*. They have never been witnessed by a white man. Since no Intellectual would enlighten me, I can neither deny nor confirm tales of their savagery, indelicacy or auto-intoxication.

That the *icas* contain relics does appear to me likely. These are said to include, in the *ica* of this pueblo of Kierkegaard, sundry scraps of T.S. Eliot, a squared fragment of the skin of Piet Mondriaan preserved inside the egg of Brancusi, and a mobile reliquary by Lynn Chadwick supporting, above the actual mobile unit which enshrines a milk-tooth of Ezra Pound, the symbolic Spirit-Level of the Universe. That the relics in the *ica* include, as some reports would have it, either Mr Evelyn

1 The master race of Non-Intellectuals speak of themselves of course as "white men", grouping Intellectuals with the inferior coloured races. Such has been the debasement of the Intellectuals in their reserves that they have accepted both the classification and the terminology (though the model of their reservations has evidently been Red Indian).

Waugh's rosary or Van Gogh's ear seems to me to be improbable.

In the material world, let me conclude by saying, these Intellectual pueblos of the Cotswold plateau, now open to the public under such safeguards as I have mentioned, preserve for our instruction something, at any rate, of the Immaterial. This was confirmed in a striking manner by one other building across the Waste Land of Kierkegaard pointed out to me by Sub-Governor Toynbee. We had paused by a tablet in the wall of the trading-post which recorded the expulsion, in very early days, of Lord Hailsham for signing his letters "Yours very truly, Isaiah Berlin", and of Mr Robert Birley for posing as the Headmaster of Dartington Hall, a school retained for the training of young Intellectuals in an obscure corner of the South-Western Reservation. I now asked the Sub-Governor, as I contemplated the list of rather high fees demanded of Outsiders for entering the pueblos or taking photographs or witnessing such overt ceremonials as the Inner Light Dance and the Dance of Pure Aesthesis (many of which have affinities with the Witch Cult of Cerne Abbas) and as I paid over decidedly hard cash for a debased autolithographic poem in the manner of Dylan Thomas, which can be used for an ashtray, and a dandy figure of MacAvitty the Cat in the manner of Barbara Hepworth, if Intellectuals (surely it could not be so ?) received *money* in the Reservation for their Intellectual Efforts or Creations?

"Tsertanly nods", replied the Sub-Governor with the simplicity of the aboriginal, smiling at my ignorance, and caressing idly with one hand the bonnet of his official Cadillac.

"Tsertanly nods", and with his other hand he pointed to the glass-walled, glass-roofed building on the far side of the Waste Land, which — the light shining through — appeared quite empty. "Dat building," he said, with pride in his tone, "designed by der Boss, Sherbert Read, is der *Bank of Spiridual Reward.*"

"In der," he said slowly, "de money de artists earn musd-a be trans-a-formed indo *Spridual Values.*"

"Are ve nods —" and I wish you could have seen, as I saw, the smile which now spread so gently, so intimately, across the gold-filled tobacco-stained incisors and canines and grinders of that old savage — "in a Glass Apard?"

It was a phrase I had not heard for twenty-two years, though now I am glad to report that the Intellectuals, once more pulling their weight in the community, are so much apart no longer.

Master of Gangrene

The publication of a book in England about Grünewald[1] and his Isenheim Altarpiece poses a situation. I have a vision of Grünewald's devotees (every Germanic art-lover and art-historian in existence) crouching in suspense. Will they like it? No? Then what Philistines the English are; and they leap from ambush with cudgels of abuse. Dr Pevsner actually starts with his own knuckle-duster. Here, he says, is a book to introduce to the English-speaking world "one of the greatest masters of European painting". And what does England, he at once goes on, know of German painting or sculpture about Grünewald's time? And — take care, you English art-admirers — what art could the English show at the time, themselves?

In a monastery transformed to a museum, not in Germany, but in Colmar in Alsace, you will find the large altarpiece, in several wings and panels, which Grünewald finished in 1515. It was for the church of a house of Antonites; hospitallers who looked after the sick — who nursed, says Dr Pevsner, the epileptic, the gangrenous, the syphilitic; and those fevered and inflamed with St Anthony's own Fire (erysipelas).

Go to Colmar in June. Outside this Musée d'Unterlinden there is a scent of lime blossom. Inside, a smell of gangrene. Across the first leaves of the altarpiece is a Crucifixion, stark, gnarled, stiff, highly individual. An enormous Christ rots on a tree out of the forest, his body green and corrupt and jabbed with thorns and spotted and clotted with blood. This was seen on weekdays by such of the patients as could hobble, crawl or be carried into the church. On Sunday the outer leaves were parted, revealing to the sick a Virgin and Child, the Annunciation, and the resurrection of a Christ of pure and spiritualized and shining flesh. On special days the leaves were parted again, upon carvings of St Anthony and other saints by a Strassburg sculptor, flanked by Grünewald's St Anthony and St Paul in the desert, and St Anthony himself tortured, as diseases obscenely tortured the patients, by an obscene bestiary of devils.

How much of this famous work is "occasional", personal, and (if you allow that communities or societies are divided by special ways of thought and feeling) Germanic? First of all, the altarpiece is for a hospital of horrors. That is the occasion, or

1 *Grünewald* by Nikolaus Pevsner and Michael Meier (1958).

commission. As Christ was, you are. As Christ became, you shall become. Secondly, both the horrors of the rotting Christ and the luminous glories of the Virgin and the resurrected Christ are Grünewald's stylization in paint of the detailed ecstatic visions of St Brigitta of Sweden.

Grünewald, though, was obsessed by his rotting Christ, the subject of four of his surviving works. Since these were commissioned altarpieces, his obsession was not his alone; it must have belonged to a Germanic vision of Christ. Yes, say the apologists — in a disturbed period of German cruelty, unreason, sectarianism, individualism, illumination, "enthusiasm", and eccentricity, introducing the Reformation and culminating in the South German savageries of the Peasants' War; a Germany released from an old dispensation and not yet firmly held in a new one.

My own reactions are these: that for all Grünewald's power (*This have I done, This have we done*), his rotting Christs are without that *dignitas* we expect of visions of the Crucifixion, without that unevasive grandeur and worthiness which we are given, shall I say, by Mantegna (or by that magnificent English poem of Grünewald's own day, also perhaps influenced by St Brigitta, in which Christ talks of himself as "woefully arrayed" and speaks of his body "blue and wan"); that for all his power, Grünewald's vision of pain is not balanced by his visions of bliss, in which a fungoid or livid quality of coloured light, found elsewhere in German art, repellently contradicts the lyrical colour tradition of every other school. For all his power, Grünewald's work also exhibits drawing and painting (as in the wing of St Anthony and the devils) of a realism detestable, unmediated, and oddly commonplace or "commercial" in a Victorian or a modern sense. I should add that I make these criticisms as someone intrigued by German painting and sympathetic to its purities.

Dr Pevsner sees a romanticism in German art precisely where others may see, not the mediating overtones of a Mediterranean light and sweetness (transmitted to an England which cleared Grendel and other ancestrally Germanic demons away so long ago with the clearance of the forests), but a morbid licence uneasily and incompletely suppressed. Grünewald, I think, could only be called one of the greatest European masters by a people who can apprehend their own peculiar turmoil in his touch and his compositions. No Italian has had to inquire anxiously: "Will they like Mantegna?"

Shall There be no More Tomato Juice?

[A talk given to the Library élite of Marlborough College, 1963.]

Gentlemen,

Speeches usually begin Ladies and Gentlemen, or Your Highness, My Lords, Ladies and Gentlemen; but here I am, at last, re-entering one of those strange survivals, an English Public School, behind those blank red brick walls, inside a monastery. Perhaps I should begin: "My Lord Abbot, Friars or Lay Brothers." I have a little anxiously wondered what you would be like. I have seen you only from the outside, at your favourite tea-shop, the Polly, having tea with parents, on those occasions of extraordinary blank silence on either side. I have taken foreign friends to the Polly, from Sweden, from America, from Austria, to show them where the strong silent Englishman begins; and this morning I see that the *Observer* refers to "that most Victorian school, Marlborough".

I am here just in time, I feel. The Labour Party seems a little divided on what to do about Public Schools. A very dangerous situation. People *start* by being a little divided, they start by saying *No* publicly to what they really want. And of course the Conservative Party wants to get rid of the Public Schools even more, though they say even less. After all, they send their children to this and to other monasteries; they have to pay the fees. And the very moment when a Labour Government at last abolishes the Public Schools and turns them into much needed remand schools, or extra Borstals, or extra prisons — without a great deal of change — parents of the Conservative Party will be able to go on longer holidays and buy larger cars; and they will have the added pleasure of blaming it all on Mr Gaitskill or Mr Aneurin Bevan.

So tonight I am taking advantage of your kindness in inviting me here as a writer and as your guest to launch my Save the Public Schools Campaign. And not only that, but my campaign for Keeping the Public Schools as They Were, restoring, wherever he has vanished, the Flogging Clerical Headmaster, and doubling the time spent upon compulsory games and O.T.C. parades, and doubling the length and the frequency of runs. And the motto of my campaign, dear

Brothers Minor, on the official notepaper will be, in the interests of literature, *Mens Mediocris in Corpore Sano*.

I cannot conceive what English literature will do without the Public School. I cannot think how English literature will survive without it. If there is to be art, if there is to be poetry, as well as fiction, the human spring must be compressed. The Public School has been for us a great, if not quite the greatest Compressor.

Robert Birley, the present headmaster of Eton, in the days when he was headmaster of the Charterhouse told me that he detested flogging, but did not dare to abolish it, formally, because the Archbishop of Canterbury (and other School Governors) wouldn't approve.

In longer letters to the *Times*

— if I may quote one of my own poems —

> Good men pontificate on crimes
> They were not tempted to commit:
> Flogged we were and proud of it.

So he was forgetting to order canes, and all the old canes were fraying and becoming useless. Also, when he became head master, he found that there was an art school. This art school — quite properly, I shall say — was always closed. No one could find the key. It turned up at last and the art room was discovered to be full of plaster copies of such things as The Dying Gaul. Quite disgracefully, all the casts were piled into a lorry and sold. The Art Room — capital A, capital R — was now always open, pictures could be borrowed, or coloured prints rather, of Bruegel, Cézanne, and Paul Klee. That wasn't all. To the horror of the staff, the school play, in his first or second year at the Charterhouse, was not *She Stoops to Conquer,* but *The Ascent of F 6* by W.H. Auden and Christopher Isherwood; which the friars minor in the cast and in the audience both enjoyed very much.

Now, when I hear that in Marlborough the school play by official consent is Tennessee Williams's *Cat on a Hot Tin Roof,* which in its film version rates an X certificate, I shall know that the end has come, and that the axe of the Labour Party is about to fall; and I shall be inclined to join at that moment, in disguise, the League of Empire Loyalists, in a last effort to rally the defence.

The headmaster of the Charterhouse had no care for English literature, that was the trouble. If he had cared for it, the

Principle of the Great Compressor would have been strengthened, not weakened. The art room would still have been shut, *She Stoops to Conquer* would have been performed, with double dullness. Flogging would have been stepped up, discomfort increased at every point, discipline tightened.

This is a library dinner. Early on at my own school, let me say that the library was a closed affair. Books it contained were recommended by word of mouth; but they were obtained only by putting in a list of books, in order of preference. When you *did* get a book you wanted, the reading of it was about the sweetest thing imaginable in life.

I deduce that the discomfortable Public School is good for literature — subsequently — not only from my own experience but from what I know of other authors and from the experience of my friends. The tedious should always be held up as the desirable, the detestable should be insisted upon. The White House Bookshop should be put out of bounds. Coleridge was so unhappy when he was at Christ's Hospital that he used to sit on the leads and gaze at the Evening Star, which became a symbol for him through life in much of his best poetry. He retreated into books which were not upon the syllabus.

If you look around at present-day authors, the discomforts and repressions, partly from the staff, partly from that dictatorship of the proletariat or the mob, which obtained at Gresham's, Holt, helped to produce the greatest English poet of our time, Wystan Hugh Auden. The repressions of the Charterhouse (before the reforms of Robert Birley) helped to produce Robert Graves. Graham Greene might not have been a novelist, and Evelyn Waugh might never have turned to satire without the repressions of Berkhamsted and Lancing. And when, Friars Minor, I look at your own monastery, at Marlborough, I think of my friends Louis MacNeice, who lay in his dormitory bed and thought of Ireland, and John Betjeman, whose years at Marlborough were the unhappiest of his life, but certainly determined his future as a poet of — in some degree — irreverence. Also I think and wonder about another Marlburian author, whose name you will not find in any list of distinguished Marlburians — because he was sacked: I mean John Meade Falkner, son of a poor clergyman at the head of the Avon valley, who went on to write *Moonfleet,* which I hope has been read by everyone here in this room, to write excellent poems, and to become incidentally a millionaire.

And earlier, wasn't there that hero of English cultural life whom we English still decline to acknowledge properly, William Morris? Wasn't he expelled? No one seems to be quite clear whether he was or wasn't, or whether, hot-tempered red-headed boy, he did or didn't lead a rebellion against Marlborough.

I don't know what happens now, or how far the modifications in the Public Schools have eased and improved life, having sent my own children not to such a school but to that celebrated twentieth-century heterosexual love-nest, Dartington Hall, in Devonshire; but in the past certain aspects of what a bourgeois pseudo-Christian society thought was good for us when young has had, I am sure, negative results in forming the positive virtues of authorship. Many an author has been taught by his public school that authority is frequently pompous, cruel, and foolish, that the majority is frequently wrong and oppressive, that justice is frequently a sham, that stupidity is often exalted, that patriotism and other respectable thoughts are too frequently the first, and not the last, resort of scoundrels, that hypocrisy gets away with it, that snobbery determines far too much in English life, that the eminent talk nonsense, that tolerance and fair play are hypocritical cloaks for easy thinking, that principles are despised, and that mediocrity is the road to advancement.

In other words, many an author has been taught negatively by his public schooling to resist positively: his school has shown him how to be free and independent and civilized, by surrounding him with parodies of freedom, independence and civilized ideals. Negatively it will have helped him to a true and positive scepticism. The mental provinciality of his pastors and masters will have helped him not to be provincial.

So when across the Downs, or in the Vale of Pewsey, or somewhere towards Wootton Bassett, I pass a friar minor, in white shorts and white sweater, on his bicycle, looking a little depressed, I feel like saying to him, "Well, cheer up. If you don't like it, it is all for the good of literature; and if you are not going to be a great author yourself, but only a senior civil servant, or a public relations officer, or a company director or a prime minister, you are still suffering for your own good, because a society cannot do without the writers and poets it despises so much."

Sometimes, of course, I wonder if I am not observing, in this white-shorted figure, a new Shakespeare, a new Donne; and then I recall that the Public School succeeded the even Greater

Compressor, the ancient Grammar School, which if it didn't deal in snobbery and jobbery quite in the same way, offered a scholastic fare so dry, so dull, so alien, that the spring was even more compressed, that the release of the spring produced grandeurs of writing which were grander and more numerous than our own.

Of course, you may think I have been too ironic; and you may, I am pretty certain you will, dislike irony. But I am not altogether getting at you or at Marlborough; and you may allow me to end on rather a more speech-day note. Of course I know, my Lord Abbot, that one's educators are not all scoundrels, that they put into one's hands positive as well as negative aids to the free mind, positive as well as negative aids to avoiding all the lies, all the easy evasions acceptable to what we have come to call the Establishment, in all its forms. But we do need to watch and be aware, to prevent our acquiescence in a society more officially, more completely repressive than our own, more ordered by hypocrisies and toadyings and the dictatorship of approved mass opinion.

From such a society there is a poem by Boris Pasternak saying that his business — and ours as well — is not to live as a pretender, is not to "get away with it":

> How shameful, when you have no meaning,
> To be on everybody's lips.

He tells himself in that poem that in fact we retire into obscurity, and should do so as the countryside disappears on early mornings into the autumn mist:

> Another, step by step, will follow
> The living imprint of your feet;
> But you yourself must not distinguish
> Your victory from your defeat.
>
> And never for a single moment
> Betray your credo or pretend.
> But be alive — this only matters —
> Alive and burning to the end.

For writers, certainly, that is as good advice as can be found, rarely as it is taken.

American and Welsh Dylanists: A Last Word from a Non-Dylanist

I don't think it could be denied that the gushier nonsense about Dylan Thomas has been written because his legend is now so mixed with his poems. In the American Dylanists one may detect, in the gush, a self-defensive attitude, as if they remembered Edgar Allan Poe, and as if Baudelaire were on their mind. Poe died drunk in their America. So did Thomas. And Baudelaire sneered at America for sneering at Poe, for scolding his corpse, for combining a wooden insensibility to genius with the savage hypocrisy of the bourgeois. This time the bourgeois have turned round, and lighted a flame of sanctity from the dead poet's alcoholic breath. How ghastly that in England this time (see Professor William York Tindall's *Reader's Guide to Dylan Thomas*) there isn't a by-law to keep dogs out of the cemetery, how demeaning, in England's Establishment-ridden un-democracy, or non-zoocracy (see Baudelaire on Poe), that Kingsley Amis could have invented in *That Uncertain Feeling* — cruelly, I would agree — an Anglo-Welsh poet emitting sounds "woaded with pit-dirt and sheep-shit" from a mouth with "all the mobility of a partly collapsed inner tube": we Baudelairian zoocrats are now the campus heralds of the anti-social rights of genius.

Study of the gush of exposition makes me suspect it would be fairer to broaden the sense of inadequacy it flows from, to academic pedantry as well as zoocracy, the two combined. The pedants, all so to the fore and so enthusiastic, are evading, or think they are evading, the broader charges of academic conservatism. There is to be no behaving as academics used to behave to Lawrence or Eliot, Joyce or Pound (and let's acquire the manuscripts and the Kleenex tissues of every modern poet, for our unprejudiced, unlagging libraries).

In Wales I would expect a not dissimilar motivation, another active inadequacy which must promote the poems in the glow of the legend. The writers of Anglo-Wales are betwixt. Not entirely Anglo, they are not entirely Wales. They fear contempt from either side. They require, in a milieu notably provincial and mediocre, a genius dependent on neither local nor on English recognition. And Wales having been Non-conformist, narrow, moralistic and enraged by Caradoc Evans, it is necessary to admire — to show that they admire — a poet who farted so contemptuously in the face of that kind of

Welshness. Mr John Ackerman in his book on Dylan Thomas, the newest,[1] doesn't tell where he (Mr Ackerman) is to be located: he signs his preface "Wales, 1963", which is running up the Red Dragon on the doorstep. He says "a knowledge of the country and the culture which produced Dylan Thomas is fundamental to a full understanding of the poet." He doesn't bother ostensibly about Dylan Thomas's public legend (good); but having run up the flag, and sung "Men of Harlech", he ties poet and poems to a Swansea childhood (new details about the school magazine), to the influence of Anglo-Welsh writers (including Margiad Evans) "who helped to create a national consciousness, the sense of a life being lived that was peculiar to Wales", and (as if hoping to satisfy all Welsh parties) to "the tradition of culture existing in and through the Welsh language". Since Dylan Thomas did not know Welsh (and did not care a toffee for that lack of knowledge), the tradition came to him from "Welsh-speaking relatives and friends" and from translations. Claim we our own, bach.

Then follows one of those expected displays of cultural compensation which anyone with an equal-minded neighbourly love for Wales or Ireland finds so depressing. Yeats used to proclaim the Irish genius of William Blake. Two Irishmen producing an *Oxford Book of Irish Verse* a few years ago included Emily Brontë, and Robert Graves (whom the Welsh poach as well). Another not remarkably convincing book on Dylan Thomas[2] adds Donne to its list of "Celtic poets and writers". Mr Ackerman (it doesn't sound such a very Welsh name, Ackerman?) has to say that Dylan "is an ancient Welsh name found in the *Mabinogion*", has to lay down that Dylan Thomas's language and ideas don't derive "to any great extent" from the English romantic poets. No, he is affined (but is he?) to Herbert, who was Welsh, and Vaughan, who was Welsh, and Traherne, who was Welsh; and (true this time, under the special surface) to Mr Vernon Watkins, who is Welsh, though also, one would have thought, the smoothest pasticheur of English romantic diction and sonority; after which you may sift the poetical-environmental portions of Mr Ackerman's book for mention of such patently obvious poetry-uncles of Dylan Thomas as Keats or Hound of Heaven Thompson or Thomson (B. V.), or — as well — Gerard Manley Hopkins. Here the required reading — required snub — is D. T. himself, saying:

1 *Dylan Thomas: His Life and Work* by John Ackerman (1964).
2 *Dylan: Druid of the Broken Body* by Aneirin Talfan Davies (1965).

It's the poetry, written in the language which is most natural to the poet, that counts, not his continent, island, race, class, or political persuasion.

Or saying:

Too many of the artists of Wales spend too much time about the position of the artists of Wales. There is only one position for an artist anywhere: and that is, upright.

Or more shortly again (but this is quoted by Mr Ackerman): "The land of my fathers. My fathers can have it."

The poems matter, or they don't. The goodness of them. That is all about it. Mr Ackerman thinks it matters (taking "consummate artistry" for granted) to explain how Welsh his Welshness was: Mr Aneirin Davies thinks the trick is won if it can be shown that Dylan Thomas's poems are religious — as if either way Welshness or religiousness was a guarantee. Mr Ackerman — not alone: American work-sheet examiners are with him in this — thinks that many drafts for each poem guarantee "craftmanship" (which would leave nothing to say for Pope, by the way, who maintained that his best things were those he had written most quickly). Mr Ackerman and Mr Davies, like American Dylanists, think all is well if they annunciate often enough a number of holy vocables: they say "vision" or "relentless discipline", and adjust the halo. "All in all, 'a beautiful poem' said Dame Edith" — but that is from Professor Tindall. Mr Davies likes to say, or quote, not Dame Edith but Simone Weil, Etienne Gilson, Valéry, St Paul, Archbishop Temple, Dafydd ap Gwilym, without the least demonstration that what he quotes from them can be applied legitimately to his subject. Mr Davies, Mr Ackerman and American Dylanists think the job done if it can be discovered what Thomas means, i.e. if they can puzzle out what he meant to mean, but wasn't so good at saying with any absoluteness. When they decipher in that way Dylanists are at least speaking as themselves and giving some evidence (frequently cata-strophic evidence) about their estimation of poetry. One academic Dylanist (Professor Clark Emery in *The World of Dylan Thomas*) challenges me, on account of an essay written some twenty years ago, to have the nerve to find fault with the "altogether delightful 'Poem in October'". It wouldn't be difficult, it would be enough if I only pointed to a stale sentimentalism of language — "beckon", "set foot", "set forth", "pale rain", "tall tales", "marvel", "twice told", "summer noon", "heart's truth", always the inferior choice

(Mr Ackerman detects a special skill — but what skill, except a not uncommon ability to count up to 3, 5, 9 and 12? — in the fact that corresponding lines in each stanza of that poem have the same number of syllables).

Dylanists recognize and emphasize states but not qualities, I think. Religious, rhapsodical, lyrical, compassionate, archetypal — but what about the quality of such conditions? What about the literary stuffing, the echo of Keats, Francis Thompson, the Bible, Joyce, Hopkins, Owen, even Eliot? The properties — the worms, the mandrakes, the shrouds, the druids, the arks, the soul? The soft words canned (with canning's horrible power to soften still more), and then scrambled, with a show of being original, into premoulded rhythms — the words (so unlike the vocabulary of Hopkins, whose idiosyncrasy Dylan Thomas so often borrowed and pulped) never tested against reference and usage, against the living body of English, and against the totality and resistance of things? Who cares if this poet sozzled, or made a public dive at parties for the more appetizingly outlined, if still virginal breasts? (The answer to that rhetorical question, I am afraid, is that many Americans do care, in a *frisson* of excitement over the antics of genius.) Professor Tindall, in his exceptionally foolish guide to Dylan Thomas ("our Bunthorne", "our bourgeois idea of what a poet should be" — exactly, but he writes it) explains any English rejection of Thomas's poems as due to class: "the trouble with Thomas was that he came from the lower middle class", he wasn't Anthony Powell, he wasn't Betjeman; which frightful *bêtise* on Dylan Thomas's part united of course — but improbably — Eliot, Graves, Leavis, Amis and myself in a distaste for his poems. There is only one charge against him, against his poems. No Dylanist meets it.

No deaf but not dumb Dylanist seems to feel or know enough of English verse, that tough, self-renewing art practised by Englishmen and Americans, Irishmen and Welshmen, Scotsmen and Canadians and West Indians and others, to understand why the charge should ever be preferred or pressed — that legend, entrance, death and circumstances all discounted, and poems alone left, Thomas was a provincial of poetry, smoozing, if with the best hopes and intentions, a masticated old manner with a pop modernism: a Gaudi of South Wales, his poems, one must allow, exhibiting like Gaudi's Barcelona church, and his fake Bishop's Palace at Astorga, and his punning and his plasticine substance, a certain perversity of attraction.   1964

Dylan Thomas: Yet Another Last Word

Dylan Thomas does not need to be introduced, yet. But for the present day I shall have to introduce John Davenport, half writer of this pasquinade.[1] Davenport was a not very remarkable book-reviewer — or that is what he became, and how he ended. Mr Constantine Fitzgibbon, in his introduction, which is longer than mine, portrays him as "a generous, difficult, brilliant man with a very fine and profound knowledge of the arts", and a poet compared in his undergraduate days to Auden, Spender and Day Lewis.

Well, yes. Perhaps without too much offence I should add that in my memory this boxing figure of the literary underworld, this rather intimidating, deliberately intimidating, man, was almost the perfection of a type.

I am sure there are Davenports around today, full of infinitely unfulfilled promise, incapable of performance, and not very nice about it. The story used to be that only Jack Isaacs, a nicer but at least in avoirdupois a not dissimilar figure, in the different world of scholarship, had signed more contracts with publishers for books which were never written — or begun, I suspect.

You never knew where you were with Davenport; worse, you did not quite know where Davenport was, if anywhere, except that he belonged to a particular camp. The junior literary world then, in middle to late thirties, had two camps, distinguished by ex-Oxford and ex-Cambridge keepings. The Cambridge camp — Davenport's — didn't do very well. It had its able figures, but few of them matured. They looked across a decidedly intervening space at ex-Oxford, resentfully. They had no Auden, no MacNeice. This ex-Cambridge resentment — all right, sir, keep calm: in those days Oxford and Cambridge, through no fault of their own, *were* the English academies to which the clever needed to aspire — this resentment was slightly or strongly visible in, for example, *Scrutiny*'s ridiculous dismissal of Auden or Empson's poem "Just a Smack at Auden"; and it was visibly active in John Davenport.

That more than half explains why Davenport and Dylan

---

1 *The Death of the King's Canary* by Dylan Thomas and John Davenport (1976).

Thomas collaborated in their *Death of the King's Canary*, which fear of libel — and perhaps the good sense of publishers — kept out of print in the Forties. Both were outsiders, and they felt it. Davenport was a literary outsider. Whether innocėnts like to believe it or no, there always is, not in such a bad sense, a literary inside and a literary outside, over the tracks, dependent upon a line of inheritance. It was clear by the late Thirties that Auden and MacNeice were the inheritors, after Eliot (as Yeats, decades before, had inherited from Swinburne). Eliot and his meinie recognized them as such; and Davenport was not in any way their man.

Dylan, *per contra*, felt himself an outsider socially — and again I beg you not to protest: such feelings are real and powerful — socially and by indifferent education. In this, if in little else, he had his affinity with Keats, who "being a little too sensitive on the score of his origin, felt inclined to see in every man of birth his natural enemy" (Leigh Hunt's observation). Put these resentments together and you see how this couple could unite in a squib against the underworld of art and letters, of which they were portions, whether deservedly or no.

Mr Fitzgibbon contrives to compare Thomas/Davenport in this *Death of the King's Canary* with Wyndham Lewis earlier on in *The Apes of God*. The comparison is ludicrous, I'd say, if only in cause and intention. Lewis had the fiercest strongest views of what human consciousness and culture should avoid like the Black Death. Thomas/Davenport displays about as much intellectual passion about anything as would butter a cocktail canapé.

Between them, they invented a farce about the selection and murder of a new Day-Lewis-like Poet Laureate. They sneer and giggle at the sub-world which supported them. Chapter one, in which the Prime Minister reads boks of verse at Chequers at night over too much brandy, and picks the new Laureate, is enjoyable for poem-parodies nearly all, I am sure, by Davenport. At any rate, two of them, delightful take-offs of Edmund Blunden and Eliot ("West Aberlard", by John Lovell Atkins) are quite beyond Dylan Thomas's skill or sophistication.

Then the joke, the sub-satirical squib, drags on — parties, boredom, bohemianism, scraps of Dylanesque description, which sound like him talking once more, and of Davenport's knowingness. There are semi-demi-take-offs of persons by the dozen — of poor old Jack Squire (whom Larkin and Betjeman have now upgraded as a poet) getting boozed and borrowing dough and toadying; or Blunden again, at the new canary's manor house at Dymmock, where "upstairs a woman was chasing a man, a man was making his face up, a poet was screaming, a man was planning a crime, an anarchist was shaking petrol out of his boot", and downstairs "the pathics simpered, the anonymous female pickups ogled old artists and peers, a man in the library, out of sight, tore the pictures out of unpleasant books and put them in his pocket, women meditated upon disease and money, a temporary waiter was found asleep by the sloe gin". In this Suffolk *Walpurgisnacht,* Blunden works on a sonnet he will call "Tree Creepers in Dymmock Park".

Characters from a superior world, treated as if they were of the same stripe, are slightly brought in — Wyndham Snowden (Wystan Auden), for instance, or Harry Bartatt (Henry Moore). Their names, with the others, such as "Hamish Corbie" for Aleister Crowley, indicate the level of onomastic wit. An odd thing is that a character usually starts as a vaguely recognizable somebody and is then allowed, without conviction, to turn into nobody in particular.

In this little knockabout, I found two authors tediously biting their own backsides; and I reflect that publishing it (see the jacket) as "an extraordinary literary event" is about as low as English publishing, in its present low condition, can descend. Or is there still something to be fished, cynically or pertinaciously, out of the supplementary bottom of the barrel of Dylan Thomas?

1976

A Short Note on an Old Friend

In between three opening sections which I suppose MacNeice would have altered, and closing sections which he only sketched, this incomplete account of himself[1] is masterly, and the best thing Louis MacNeice ever wrote in prose (which was not his *métier*). He was a clear-minded man, but I think prose, or criticism, the kind he usually wrote, proceded on too straight a line, in a dimension too thin and single, to engage all of his ability. In poems he could walk around and around. Describing himself he could also walk — was compelled to walk — around and around.

He once astounded me when he was in his twenties (since he seemed, to those who didn't know him exceptionally well, to be aloof without chinks behind his black aquilinity) by saying that he liked nothing better than to talk about his personal difficulties; in this book he talks about himself freely, most intelligently, incisively, and without self-pity. And much or most in his Irish childhood must stir extreme pity or dismay, in the reader: the child losing his mother, from melancholia followed by tubercolosis, rather afraid of his then ill and unhappy clerical father, and companioned, if with a sister, also with a Mongolian imbecile for a brother.

Here, perfectly stated, one sees place and personality and personal circumstances interlocked, compelling this extremely intelligent child into fantasies. The urges to fantasy develop: he leaves Ireland, he goes to an English preparatory school (under one of the Powys brothers), to Marlborough, to Oxford; teaching classics in Birmingham and London, meeting life, marrying and then being deserted, as if back down the snake to square three.

I recall both a doubt and a tug when I started *New Verse* — being repelled by the semi-Sitwellian rococo in MacNeice, yet tugged into asking him for poems because, at his happiest (if that is quite the word), the rhythms felt right and the *matière* involving the rococo was so evidently authentic. MacNeice's evaluation of himself at Marlborough, Oxford, and Birmingham, and in the thirties, exhibits more luminously than any document so far published the effect of that time and its diversely pulling forces within one sensual and acute and

1 *The Strings are False: An Unfinished Autobiography* by Louis MacNeice (1965).

honest *makar* in the upper middle class: the pull of a culture pickled in decadence, the pull away from the decadence, the pull, nevertheless, of the enjoyment of things, the pull to the generous renunciation of privilege, and the pull away from the political surrender of the will.

Varieties of Parable[1] introduces MacNeice's poetry, naturally in a sidelong way, better than Mr Press's superficial (rather nose-in-the-air) pamphlet;[2] it may inform some of MacNeice's neo-academic detractors that his scholarship was superior to theirs, and his prose writing, too, whatever its shortcomings. Myself, I find these reprinted Clark Lectures (though exceptional in a series so often tiresomely mediocre) intriguing more than satisfying. He begins with Spenser and Bunyan, works through to Becket, Pinter, and Golding, explaining parable ("allegory" seemed too narrow and depreciatory a term) as a revived means of trying to express the inexpressible ultimate (" 'When am I going to get to the heart?' said Peer Gynt as he peeled the onion"). But parable is the nature of his own poems; and here one learns that he discovered "The Faerie Queene" when he was twelve, and that it was a poem (bonier and less sweet than its reputation allows) which he always read and admired. Distrusting any "truth" polythened like a battery chicken, in his best poems he enjoys, yet is not hedonistic: accepts pleasure, in their "quest", as pleasurable, but not as an end. Mr Press (can he have been almost at Downing?) spends nearly half his British Council pamphlet reproving MacNeice for imperfections, and then misses his centre, saying he belongs "to the select company" of those who communicate delight "in the minutiae of daily life, the sense of happiness and well-being that springs from good health, mental alertness and emotional vitality". But MacNeice knew that iridescence on the net is not the escaping Purple Emperor.

1   *Varieties of Parable* by Louis MacNeice (1965).
2   *Louis MacNeice* by John Press (1965).

The Silver Biro

Reading this third volume of his literary reminiscences,[1] I have to remember that Mr John Lehmann has been — but then he does tell us so — an editor and himself a writer associated with the Thirties, as they are now inescapably labelled. So I am going to treat his narrative, his literary substance, as a warning.

Association and substance, association and achievement, should in some way, in some degree, go together. Association described should be a light which helps us at any rate to see a "period" — for what that is worth; to distinguish between individual power and period influence in and upon the contemporaries, the valuable contemporaries, of a someone who sweeps together his reminiscences and shapes them into his autobiography.

How is it then that despite an anecdote or two, about Gide, for instance, or about Eliot (who told him how he came to write some of his later poems, and how a poet should perform in his old age, and revealed that his famous *Criterion* lost £500 a year, and never sold, per issue, as many as a thousand copies) — how is it that Mr Lehmann's manner, as I turned the pages, and his matter as well, so often reminded me of the writings and the thoughts of Jennifer?

I must explain. Jennifer is the diarist of the *Tatler* and of the *Queen*. A few weekends ago an interview with Jennifer appeared in a Sunday Supplement or Colour Magazine. "It is so nice," said Jennifer, "to look back on weddings and parties. . . . A lot of people look back on their old *Tatlers* and read about the happy days they had." "I just select the people I name in my Diary," she said, haphazardly. "One knows a lot of them personally." Writing in such a tone, this for the most part kindly Lehmann-Jennifer of yesterday's avant-garde recalls the birth or the course or the failure of several literary ventures which in their time seemed to me to be no more than tepid — *Penguin New Writing, Orpheus,* the *London Magazine* in its early run, and *New Soundings,* a radio magazine which coincided with the beginnings of the plunge of the Third Programme fifteen years ago into mediocrity.

It is extraordinary how names — names, not substance —

1 *The Ample Proposition. Autobiography III* by John Lehmann (1966).

slip in and slip out of these reminiscences. This writer, that writer, this book, that book, "interested" Mr Lehmann, was read by him "with mounting enthusiasm". This poem or that poem moved him, or was "strange and beautiful". But why? The sprite, pleased with the iridescence of his own wings, goes from flower to flower and gives no reasons. The little and large vanities, the spirts of self-reassurance — "my hosiers", "my library", "my housekeeper Ivy", "the extraordinary legend that *New Writing* appeared to have created", "my literary position", the American who came to tell him that he was the best publisher in England — all such I could bear if some vision obtruded. I could bear to accompany this sprite in ruminative walks by the Buckinghamshire Thames "with my mother's large white poodle Chico", I could endure his manner of writing — "All this was immense fun", "albeit with a heavy heart", "We found the poet awaiting us in genial mood", "whose work remains unique in the American scene", I could tolerate the divagations — "My interests were by no means confined to the literary world" — into travel impressions, gardening talk, or little puddles of flat verse ("the small voice of my own muse"), if more hard and simple information were given, incidentally or even by accident. I could overlook the abstract Shakespearian title, that *Ample Proposition,* aping American academics on Henry James, I could put up with the unsorted procession of the chiefly minimal — with the avifauna of Mr Lehmann's lost paradises of literature which mostly recall the listed birds which flutter between his country cottage and his hammer-pond — "The dawn chorus in early summer is deafening, and in winter crumbs thrown on the hard ground bring, beside the robins, hedge sparrows and house sparrows, cole-tits and blue-tits, thrushes, chaffinches (and even sometimes a bullfinch), wood-peckers, nuthatches, tree creepers and wrens, and swooping down for sudden forays, jays and magpies, rooks and jackdaws and pigeons" — if only *living,* just a little living and just a little thought, appeared under Mr Lehmann's touch.

Mr Lehmann would have been wiser not to have stripped like this for universal inspection, for here comes my warning, a double warning, first to such fellow-travellers of a "movement" as Mr Lehmann, on account of the tomahawk men who always succeed literary movements and try to discredit them by cutting down their weaker members; and then to the tomahawk men themselves, in their own counter-movement, their own inevitable counter-view of what should be what in modern writing.

I admit to them as they scream for scalps — "Yes," I say to them, "you are right: son of a Cambridge rowing blue and *Punch* versifier, your Etonian Mr Lehmann is another of those born with a silver biro into the moneyed upper-middle class who have looked around and decided that they as well would 'pursue a literary career'."

"Ever so slightly," I continue to the tomahawk men, "this Mr Lehmann you are after has slummed from a Bloomsbury fringe, from Lytton Strachey's sofa, leftwards, in a sense both political and literary. But let me tell you, sniggering or whooping redskins from Nottingham or Reading, you also will be embarrassed in time ahead by such autobiographies from your own generation, your own comrades, your own 'movement'; and lucky you will be if they are so innocent.

"From this more or less innocent confection," I add, "from this soft marsh, as it may be, with its few islets, no general condemnatory deductions are in order: though you may think so, its mediocrity does not 'condemn a generation'; and the state of letters is in all generations, on the whole, a swamp, suitably inhabited, few making, few discriminating, few fighting to an individual firmness."

This Mr Lehmann was at any rate, I believe, a kind editor and a kind publisher. If there are few words of sense, and none of distinction, in his autobiography (or in this volume of it — I have not read the others), there are few words of malice. He appears solicitous to please everyone, including himself.

The Black Goddess

Should Robert Graves tell us why Shelley's "Skylark" "ranks among the shoddiest poems ever wished on us as the product of genius"?

Yes, if he has time. Should we listen? Yes, because people at all times, especially expert people, and especially at this time, are donkeyish in their estimate of poetry, and every other art. Always there is a troupe of deaf and denatured donkeys telling us what new — or old — poems to read, what new — or old — poems to disregard. What they are writing now, in reviews (poetry is more reviewed than ever it was), may not have the melancholic humility of the bray. Lacking the old bewildered or plaintive note of asking why, their bray is simply asinine in promoting the worthless. To change animals or to mix them, the mode is a criticism which derives both from the ass and the weasel, appropriate to a time of expended impulse. Not to talk of poems, I would scrap most of the writing about poems I happen to have encountered in the last ten years, for the occasional sober piece which has crossed the dismal Humber from middle-aged Philip Larkin or the derisive instructional pieces which have come more frequently from old Robert Graves, faithful to the bitching Muse in his Balearic island.

With the improbability of dinosaurs, two long pieces lie across the entry into his new book.[1] One is Graves orating to the London School of Economics on Mammon, the other is Graves lecturing the scientists and advanced technologists of M.I.T. against the "cosmical nonsense-region of electronic computers" in favour of the "Paradisal region" of magical creativity. He remarked that he had searched among them for a mystique of modern science, but had found only a sense of fate. I think these pieces fail through over-stuffing, and a certain, almost journalistic accommodation of the author to his audience. Then he swings into poetic vulgarity, technique in poetry, and the poet in the valley of dry words: he is Graves again, unaccommodating, giving instruction in the nature of the product which matters to him.

His poems being the poet, why is Browning vulgar, or Swinburne, or Kipling (with a side kick at Eliot and Pound), or Byron? "I pair Byron and Nero as the two most dangerously talented bounders of all time." Knowing how to recognize

1 *Mammon and the Black Goddess* by Robert Graves (1965).

poetic vulgarity still doesn't solve the poet's great problem of how he is to maintain "the gift of certitude". But it marks the boundaries of poetic virtue. "It is easy to take up a pen at random and plead *I'm just keeping my hand in*. But nine-tenths of what passes as English poetry is the product of either careerism, or keeping one's hand in: a choice between vulgarity and banality." Have at Eliot as extoller of technique, extol craftmanship — making an antithesis between deductive intellectual fabrication and the good products of self-acquired skill, setting Eliot in subordination to Hardy.

Possibly unfair, possibly not in balance.

But see what this strikes from Robert Graves — that "true poetic ecstasy makes sense, and more than sense"; that "a poet lives with his own language, continually instructing himself in the origin, histories, pronunciation, and peculiar usages of words, together with their latent powers, and the exact shades of distinction between what Roget's *Thesaurus* calls synonyms — but are there such things?" (there are not); that "a poem always chooses its own metre; and any attempt to dress up an idea in a particular metre is, at best, an amusing parlour game; at worst, dreary literature"; that a poem "begins with the usual line-and-a-half that unexpectedly forces itself on the entranced mind and establishes not only the metre, but its rhythmic treatment". And "every dictionary is a valley of dry bones". And the bones, as in Ezekiel's vision, can be made to knit and put on sinew and flesh, and live, and stand up, in fighting companies, in poems, by the poet; all of which is again a metaphor of craftmanship, since technique "takes one no further than articulating the skeletons with wire, and plumping them up with plastic limbs and organs"; and, alas, but how necessary a statement, "all poems are failures in the Muse's eye."

On a long, hard, uncomfortable bench before these and other remarks, these truisms if you like, should sit many poets and all critics, with more humility than they usually display. Push up, Alvarez; and make room for Mr Lowell — for example. And stop shuffling. And where is Cyril, in his shorts? And older Yvor from across the ocean? And — but insert your own names.

At the end Robert Graves admits to intimations of a Black Goddess. I used to find it tiresome when he went on so about the White Goddess, anthropologically, mythologically, archaeologically, in an apparently literal way, beyond evidence, in prose. But fact can be metaphor. And whatever Robert

Graves might object, his readers, if it suits them, can take his
— or *the* — always desirable, treacherous, unpredictable
goddess as metaphor, or they can take her metaphorical being
as fact: the two in one, preferring a person (scarcely to be
regarded in M.I.T. as other than hooey) to an essence in -ion.

He now sees, not quite clearly yet, a Black Goddess of
certitude and wisdom, reached only through the White
Goddess of incertitude. I cannot be made to care by Robert
Graves if she is related to the Black Virgins of Provence or
Sicily or up the cliff of Rocamadour; or if "I am black, but
comely" indeed refers to wisdom. But here he is, and a poet in
his seventies, thinking about a "more-than-Muse", "a final
reality of love", a certitude, a unitive peace, a goddess I hope
he is going to detect, and then delineate for us, as we crowd
our behinds, on the bench, more clearly.

Edith Sitwell's Autobiography

How are we to explain or explain away (since it is going to need some explaining away for our posterity) the eminence or the acceptance or the at times reverential praise of the poems of the late Edith Sitwell? The poems will fall apart. They strike me, when I look at them again, as a tumble of imitation reliquaries. Of her early poems — the reliquaries are the later ones — some had the tinkliness of a broken music-box, some exhibited the arch simple-mindedness, not always pleasant-mindedness, of a neo-Victorian bouquet of wax and silk under the jags of a dome. Then the war, the bombs, the Great Bomb, and the reliquaries, inside of which there might — or might not — be the scraps of some body of holiness.

I was sceptical when these earnest poems began to appear and to be praised. The psalm sounded — O praise Miss Sitwell in the holiness of her pity and imaginative insight — and swelled; and even old sceptics were converted. But not this sceptic, who looked inside, and found precisely the nothing he expected to find, on past form. It was — I shall vary the exposition and call upon St Adelbert of Prague and the luminescent fish once caught in the Danube — a fishy to-do. When that saint had been dismembered, it happened that his little finger fell or was thrown into the river: the fish swallowed the finger, the finger shone through the fish. But out of these Sitwellian reliquaries there shone, at any rate to my critical sense, no interior light even of that coldest luminescent kind. Crosses were inscribed or carved on the lid, inside there was not even the top joint of the little finger of St Adelbert.

As before, as so often in the Middle Ages, the best thing about these reliquary poems — "golden" having been Miss Sitwell's key word — was their externality of gold leaf, or tinsel. All the light, all the sparkle came from outside, and reflected from the gilt, had its source in simpletons, sophisticated and unsophisticated, English and American, who were still in need of relics to worship; which is part of the explanation of Miss Sitwell. And another part, confirmed by this miserable autobiography;[1] is that Miss Sitwell was one of her own most servile adulators.

She relates, to begin with, that she had a most unhappy childhood; which is no doubt true. If she is to be believed, her

1 *Taken Care Of. The Autobiography of Edith Sitwell* (1965).

father and her mother alike were true scions of English aristocracy at its most vacuous, ignorant, insolent, and vulgar, which — such has been our aristocracy's frequent eminence in these faults — is not saying a little. England's aristocrats have scarcely been the makers or safekeepers of English civilization. "My parents were strangers to me from the moment of my birth." Just as well, from the way she describes them. She needed to be straightened in an iron frame. She was ugly. She was bullied, she was violent, and she was lonely. *"Au matin j'avais le regard,"* she quotes from Rimbaud's *Une Saison en Enfer, "si perdu et la contenance si morte, que ceux que j'ai rencontrés ne m'ont peut-être pas vu."*

I might sympathize rather more, if the consequent and compensating vanity, the unbelievable self-adulation was not reflected backwards on to the account. "Perhaps I, at four years old, knew the incipient anguish of the poet I was to become." Arthur Rimbaud "in some ways my closest spiritual relation". "Fields of yellow jonquils that, in my later life, were like the spirits of my early poetry." " 'What are you going to be when you are grown-up, little E?' . . . 'A genius,' I replied" — which is thrown to the adulating reader with the unexpressed because unnecessary assurance that a genius she became. Her first love was a peacock, her second an owl, she writes; and there are two ways of interpreting either bird.

I might sympathize rather more if the adult who grew into her "Plantagenet features" contrived to replace hatred with charity, if contumelious insults were not flung back as well into the past years, at her parents, at her relations, at the servants, at the doctors, at her teachers. "He looked like a statuette constructed of margarine" (orthopaedic surgeon). "An alleged beauty. . . . The upper part of her body consisted of an enormous pink ham which served her as face" (friend of her mama's). "Endowed with a treble ration of shining protuberant teeth . . . always bared ingratiatingly" (the *kindly* maiden lady who tried to teach her to paint).

I might respect her more if the frenetic insults were not, page after page, thrown around as well as backward, if a self-extrication or transformation were visible such as Coleridge detected in Wordsworth, who out of a black nature made himself a deservedly happy man because he had learnt "the intrinsic value of the different objects of human pursuit". Everything returns to the egoistic measure. As when she was young, as when she was middle-aged, so in old age every response was conditioned by the beginning. She met at one time D. H. Lawrence and Frieda Lawrence, who evidently presumed neither to like her nor to admire her. How appallingly coarse, insolent, and arrogant the deferred revenge! Lawrence looked "like a plaster gnome on a stone toadstool in some suburban garden". How dared he be so beastly to *Sir* Clifford Chatterley — himself (during the First World War) having remained "safely at home, fornicating and squealing, shrilly, about the oppression from which he had suffered"! How appallingly and savagely she replies, thinking it worth printing the reply, to a slightly cuckoo if unsolicited letter from a harmless unknown!

Nastiness combines with triviality as one characteristic of this book, unameliorated by "success". "Were I not too kind to laugh at the cruel disappointment and envy suffered by certain poor little unsuccessful writers" — poets forty years younger than herself who wrote of her poems without enthusiasm — "I might be amused by the fact that although I am now seventy-seven years of age, the unsuccessful are still thrown into what is practically an epileptic fit brought on by envy and malice at the mere mention of my name."

"Were I not too kind. . . ." In England it is now customary to say, Ah but Edith was so kind in private life. One's concern is with her public life, the writing she exhibits; and in this book this writer, exclaiming because some people had abused her friend the poet Roy Campbell for "his verbal savagery about the Spanish Reds", urges that they did not know what those Reds had threatened to do to his wife and children ("Roy did not appreciate these threats. Some people are most unreasonable!") only a very few sentences after she had in effect praised this same Roy Campbell — for what? For threatening a Cambridge don (I suppose F. R. Leavis) with assault: "I'll walk into your College and tear the clothes off your back, and by the time I've done with you your wife and children won't know you." The cause of this physical threat: critical disapprobation of Miss Sitwell's poems. Such was her taste for vicarious violence where she was offended.

Add to the charges which condemn this book, sneering, malice, megalomania, arrogance and the rest, a very considerable stupidity, already apparent in some of the scraps I have quoted; and to stupidity, what is, after all, the most obvious characteristic of this writer: she was in everything she wrote an amateur, a poseur of art. Frequently she has to break off (can this life have been so meagre?) to instruct her servile readers in the virtues, not of poetry, but of her poetry, servile once more to herself. A poem is quoted. A poem is explained, once more, as so often in her previous work, in the familiar jejune chatter of the texture of her vowels, consonants and vocables. That "the words ending in the letter D are placed so close together makes, in this particular case, a slight leap into the air".

> Though *head* is immediately linked up again in the next line with *egg*, yet because it had no previous related sound, there is no effect on rhythm.

Comparing her experience "during the first inception and creation of a poem . . . with all humility . . . to the experience of the saint", this amateur poet thought that she must break now and then into writing her account of herself poetically. Now Dame Blake, now Dame Traherne, and now Dame Rimbaud, she proffers a sneezing parody of their vision — "In these countrysides, the people know that Destiny is reported, and has features like a hen. There have I seen pig-snouted darkness grunting and rooting in the hovels. The very clouds are like creaking wooden chalets filled with emptiness", etcetera, in a general air of cheap and frigid untruth. The senses were weak and invented lies, like a child (simple ones, too — the hands of Wyndham Lewis were not "thick" and "meat coloured" but of a singular delicacy. Dylan Thomas had no "look of archangelic power", or of William Blake).

There are quotations in this book. Excluding quotations from herself, they are the best of it — though often used to indicate a parity between quoter and quoted. The aptest one, included for the differently megalomaniac purpose of ridiculing the idea that her genius, the genius of the tumbled reliquaries, could be ridiculed, she took unwisely from the poet D. J. Enright. "Writers who detach tragedy from the persons who suffer it," Mr Enright declared in the *New Statesman*, "are generally to be seen soon after wearing someone else's bleeding heart on their own safe sleeve — an odious transaction and an odious transaction is what Dame Edith Sitwell's atomic poetry seems to me to be." And to me. But that was a condemnation too subtle and complete for this (poetically and publicly) impossible person to have understood. Yet in the end the disgrace lies more upon her febrile and snobbish supporters than on herself.

The Ogre in the Black Hat

1

It may be too obvious to say so, but when you discuss Wyndham Lewis you must discuss the best of him. You must leave out the mass of journalism he was driven to; including the journalistic portrait drawing or portrait painting — most of it. Then, when you arrive at the actual Lewis, you find identical hard qualities in his writing and his painting and his ideas.

I have been thinking through many hours spent with Lewis and I recollect him talking much more about painting than writing. If in fact he wrote more than he painted that was because he was the only English artist of the last fifty or sixty years blessed, or cursed from the painter's view, with a first-rate intellect: you cannot deploy all of such an intellectual passion, such a passion for the interlock and interplay of ideas as Lewis had, with paint brushes. The ideas persisted, and writing took over, inevitably.

If you asked me how much effect Lewis's writing has had on other writing of our time, I should say it has had very little indeed — so far. But that of course is a criticism of other writers; and not a criticism of Lewis.

Think of Lewis's intellectual pride in being anti-subjective, anti-psychological, anti-realistic, but always, if he could manage it, actual: he said that "in art we are in a sense playing at being what we designate as matter": the art-game is going as near as we can, without its extinction or neutrality, to the structure of matter or machine. Which means composing; construction; which means art, not as flow, but as building and tension; and if you look round, you see that the rhetoric of tension and construction has not at all been the quality of English or English-American writing since the appearance of *Blast* or *Tarr*; or the quality demanded by critical approbation. If Lewis's concepts or practice had been influential, rather than concepts of writing derived from later Pound, or later Eliot or D. H. Lawrence, we should hardly slobber, as so many of us do, over the poems of Robert Lowell, for example, or the prose of Laurence Durrell or Henry Miller.

I recall some of the things Lewis was apt to approve of and revert to in conversation. The statues of Easter Island, which seemed to thrust from the ground and push earth and nature away: they were man-figures or god-figures on the verge of matter, yet still predominantly alert. He liked to talk about Goya. He liked — this rather surprised me — Burne-Jones (but then consider the likeness of the close verticals of Burne-Jones, Charles Rennie Macintosh in his Glasgow Art School, and Lewis), at least when Burne-Jones remained vertical and linear and managed to keep clear of sentimentality. He liked Chirico — Chirico's piazzas and skies of coloured stillness, his shadows from unseen statues, his sense of something momentous which was about to happen, all held in a startling immediately apprehensible structure. He liked Cézanne. (You may remember Lewis writing that Cézanne was a brother of Bach and Douanier Rousseau a cousin of Chardin.) He liked Conrad, and he liked folksong records — yes, but folksongs as sung by folk singers, with their modal and rhythmical character unaltered and unsmoothed.

I recall some things Lewis disliked. He disliked Eliot's sinuous equivocal manner after *The Waste Land* and *The Hollow Men*. He disliked woman-shapes inflated by Picasso into india-rubber giantesses prancing along a foreshore. He disliked woman-shapes by Henry Moore — whom he respected — with small knobs for heads which are neither hills nor women, but something of both: such figures were equivocal, it seemed to him, I think I am right in saying, that in a heavy way they lay cloddish and inert on the ground. Rubber giantesses or knob-headed stone giantesses, they were both affronts to the shaping hierarchical function of this human power of the arts of painting or sculpture.

A common element in most of Lewis's preferred things, a common absence in things he disliked, is the wonderful, which is in part the wonderfulness of the thing built and dared by imagination. You could say of Lewis, violent as he seemed, that he walked in the temples of the highest human order and calmness and believed in permanence. I remember a worried producer talking to Lewis before a television show at Alexandra Palace: natural speech, Mr Lewis, no reading please, just the ideas as they come to you, Mr Lewis. Lewis paid no attention at all — or only the apparent attention of politeness, he was a very polite man usually, if at times a sardonically polite man. The ideas had already come; were down on paper in his pocket; they would be heard exactly as he meant them to be heard, and printed afterwards in *The Listener* without the weaknesses of something improvised.

Or you could illustrate Lewis in the legend — perhaps you know it, I cannot say whether it is legend really or fact — of Lewis's last words: that when he was admitted, at last, to hospital, blind, dying, a wreck of the big man that he had been, the ward sister bent over him, after he had been made as comfortable as possible in bed, and permitted herself a liberty: "When did we last open our bowels, Mr Lewis?"

Lewis replied — less polite for once, but still averse to the philosophy of flux instead of structure, of horizontal instead of vertical — "Mind your own bloody business."

2

By upbringing and talent and performance and behaviour Wyndham Lewis is, for sure, self-condemned to much biographical probing; of which this book[1] by the American academic Jeffrey Meyers is a first major offering. Jeffrey Meyers has taken pains, and if that description usually implies worthiness and shortcomings I mean it differently. He has tackled what is to him (though Lewis's father was American) the life of a foreigner. He avoids prurience, condemnation and sensationalism. The few survivors who knew Lewis well or slightly in his London heyday will be frequently surprised, and will find mists — though often mists of superficiality — clearing around a rocky enigma.

Though no writer could be more English, more London, Lewis was born on his American father's yacht, when it was tied up at Amherst, Nova Scotia. So by birth he was Canadian, under the law and by topographical accident. His mother, a young English girl of great beauty, brought him up single-handed, having left her impossible husband. There is a contradiction and contrast between Lewis's love for his mother and the often outrageously untender way he treated most of the women in his own life.

Rugby, the Slade, Paris, Notting Hill — then, gradually, he becomes the Enemy, the combative ogre in the big black hat, confident in the rewards due to the sanities and verities of creative intellect. In essentials, as Professor Meyers makes us realize, the rewards came to him, after all. Or at least he was respected by contemporaries on his own high level (and by Yeats, among older writers, who admired his rare quality of intellectual passion).

1 The Enemy: A Biography of Wyndham Lewis by Jeffrey Meyers (1980).

This biographer states, and neither exculpates nor condemns (though he respects). I am glad of that, because much of the plain true statement about Lewis certainly does leave a nagging taste of the inhuman. But of course against that inhumanity must be set his grand humanity of mind, his vision of what can be, has been, and ought to continue to be achieved by its high consciousness, his unwavering location of what matters most — or of one thing which matters most — in human activity and duty. Certainly, Lewis was a fire in the general mist; the fire would seem to die to a cinder and then — ho — up it flared again, and burnt steadily. He brought attack and obloquy on himself, but was never defeated. Something of what he was can be learned quickly and profitably, as Jeffrey Meyers indicates, from "The Sea-Mists of the Winter", the extraordinary article he wrote on going blind.

A division of talent, or a doubling of talent, militated against Lewis. What was he to be, painter or writer? If painter, what about that critical probing of life and mind which so possessed him, the constant stream and whirl of ideas? If writer, what about those boundaries of mortal wire, and all they could enclose? Writers who write about Lewis — and they include this biographer — are seldom good on him as painter and draughtsman. They misunderstand the power of his early abstracts or semi-abstracts, they exaggerate the merit of his later portraiture (earlier portraits by him were of a masterly grandeur) in which line and colour lost their tensity of action and declined to the commonplace. Younger painters were often moved by the acuity and intensity of his colour. Ben Nicholson, for instance, has often spoken of the effect on him of a particular yellow in Lewis's work, a tone, in its place, which sang out and seemed individual and unique.

Maybe that yellow came to Lewis from Goya, whose paintings and etchings he admired with passion; he fed — and this isn't enough realized by his biographer — on the controlled richness of imagination; in the case of Goya less, I would almost say, on the subjects of Goya than his colour-blending and that wonderful touch activating the lights and shades of Goya's etchings (which is inevitably lost in the familiar reproductions). I miss, too, an appreciation of Lewis vis-à-vis the myths and cultural mystery of mankind — the Lewis who visited Brittany and longed to see those pitted tufa gods rising from their platforms on Easter Island.

If I miss clear guidance on Lewis as painter, I miss as well a clarity about Lewis's thought, about that centre of himself —

reasonable comment, I would say, because such thought must be felt at least underneath the plain sequence of events and paragraphs in a biography of this kind.

Professor Meyers has conveyed the English scene — the London scene — well. In frying his fish, it does not greatly matter if a name or two gets itself misspelt, Harold Munro instead of Harold Monro, of the Poetry Bookshop, for instance; and I suppose we need not bother if some of Lewis's specially abominated persons don't sizzle in this pan — for one, Cyril Connolly, who pursued him with sneering reviews and whom Lewis despised as a lackey of Bloomsbury and a social trivializer of art. He might have added, too, that a book Lewis delighted in was Whistler's *Gentle Art of Making Enemies*.

Professor Meyers is open and honest about Lewis's flirtation — that seems about the right strength of word — with the extreme Right, and about his recantation. I wish he had mentioned that Lewis became disenchanted with the strong arm poses of Roy Campbell and eventually found his stupidity too much for him. But then, *au fond* Lewis aged well where others went rotten.

1968

The Reformed Puritan: Day Lewis as Poet

In "A Letter from Rome", published seventeen years ago, the as yet unlaureated poet spoke of one "who 'flowered' in the Thirties"; and he went on to affirm, with the ironic condescension — or social acquiescence — of a writer in his fiftieth year, that poets flowering in that famous decade were "sceptical", "susceptible", "dour", "enthusiastic", "horizon-addicts", "future-fans",

> terribly apt to ask what
> Our all-very-fine sensations were in aid of.

One may be allowed to isolate this passage — now that Mr. Day Lewis's *Collected Poems 1954* have been republished in paperback — as a base of operations for looking backward to old work, and forward briefly to the Poet Laureate in new poems and in his relation to other poets, including his relation, as translator, to Virgil and Valéry.

A first and fair inference is that we are faced here with a poet who has changed from mask to mask, many kinds, some of them masks of a changing contemporaneity, others masks from the literary cupboard. To have been a "Poet of the Thirties" — that categorization springs from literary journalism: if it validly described a poet, or a long stage of a poet's affinities and achievement, he would have been *ipso facto* a bad or a very limited poet: something quite other than a self in freedom. That is a necessary conclusion; and it is curious to see a poet accepting this, as he must hope, extraneous mask, even if for the purpose of removing it once and for all and showing what he imagines to be his one reality.

But then the one reality seems only another mask; and this different mask of the poet who writes "A Letter from Rome" is surely the one which proclaims, I have come through, I have matured, I am civilized, I am acceptable now, on my way from Red Square One to Rome, and Florence and Settignano:

> We did not, you will remember, come to coo.
> Still, there is hope for us. Rome has absorbed
> Other barbarians: yes, and there's nobody quite so
> Sensuously rich and reckless as the reformed
> Puritan. . . .

All the time, as I read back into old familiar poems or collections, *Transitional Poem, From Feathers to Iron, The Magnetic Mountain* ("Look west, Wystan, lone flyer, birdman, my bully boy!"), and *A Time to Dance* —

> I sang as one
> Who on a tilting deck sings

— then forward in direction of the translator and the Laureate, it is the attitudes that I observe, along with the many stylistic consequences of not becoming a genuine poetic self, not developing in other than negative qualities. I am impressed that the poet has willed himself adeptly into situations, modes and nuances, often with enthusiasm and good intentions.

An image to notice comes soon after the lines referred to already in "A Letter from Rome". "As when, composing a poem", this poet reveals,

>   the tangle of images
> And jangle of words pressing hard on you, mobbing you, may
> Compel you to choose the right moment to disengage
> And find the one word, the word of command which makes them
> Meekly fall in to their ranks, and the march continues. . . .

This is odd. Most poems, one would think, originate, and proceed, in exactly the opposite way; not under pressure from a tangle of images, or a jangle of many words, but in the few rhythmically patterned words, the phrase, the possible line, which is the word-shape, the word-consequence, of a stimulus to the person, uncalled for, unwilled, coming gently and quietly (if causing excitement as well) into consciousness, and then strongly magnetic of other words, till the cluster, the poem, is complete.

This other talk of a mob of tangled images and jangling words (compare Blake, in South Molton Street, asking his muses to come down into his writing hand, down the nerves of his right arm, out of his brain) suggests the poem as a jigsaw puzzle fitted together by the will, the poem as the act of will entire and not in part; projected altogether into being, not injected, at least initally.

The characteristics of the Day Lewis poem hardly ever contradict this assertion of the overplay both of the masks and the will. Frigidities predominate. Seldom does anything in a poem (though I might except the "Sketches for a Self-Portrait"

or the "Married Dialogue" in *Poems 1943–1947*) seem a
paradigm of "reality" or "truth". Everything gets itself spoken
like speech in a public assembly, in which words or images do
no more than illustrate in the common manner. Everything
advanced serves for abstract implication; and is not, at the same
stroke, itself:

> The house, we perceive, is shabby,
> There's dry rot in the wood

— i.e., no house, no dry rot, no timber, no double perception.

> From husk of words unspoken
> I'll winnow a ripe seed

— again no words, no husk, no act of winnowing, no seed
which is conceivably, as well, round in the palm.

> The moon slides through a whey of cloud

— no realization that whey is a messy *liquid*.

Scarcely an image — this is a poet who talks much of, and
via, images — withstands scrutiny. Shelley, Leigh Hunt, Clare
and himself drink a birthday toast to Mr Edmund Blunden, or
to "that happy girl" his Muse, out of a loving cup fabricated
from the metal of verse, in the shape of a tulip (the liquid for
the toast isn't revealed). Or the Alitalia plane which transports
himself from London Airport and his Thirtyish past to Rome is
willed into another peculiar shape: "Air-treading bull, my
silver Alitalia" (changing, before many lines pass, into an
angel, and a "bull-headed moth").

It is a reasonable comment that the two-year-old child who
said to the pilot on the air ferry tarmac "I like your big wheelbarrow", had seen something, and had responded; whereas this
poet nearing fifty had seen nothing — had "seen" neither a bull
nor a moth nor an angel nor a plane; devising only an item of
cold nonsense. Other characteristics of the verse of this educated
man wearing his various masks include a kind of unwitty
verbalism ("The wind that had set our corn by the ears"); a
repeated use of very old clothing ("O light mellifluous";
willows in a swaying copse which "wave their magic wands";
wild flowers which "beflag the lane"); much weak employment
of the word "like" ("Image and real are joined like Siamese
twins"); no subtle affectivity of cadence; and now and again a
stunning vulgarity, as in a song which does not sing, written,
he tells us, to an Irish air:

Oh light was my head as the seed of a thistle
And light as the mistletoe mooning an oak,
I spoke with the triton, I skimmed with the nautilus,
Dawn was immortal as love awoke.
  But when a storm began to blow
  My thistle was dashed, my tree laid low,
  My folk of the wave went down to their deep, so I
Frown on a thistledown floating capriciously,
Scorn as mere fishes the folk of the sea,
Agree the renowned golden bough is a parasite,
Love but a gallous-eyed ghost for me.

Not the song for Buck Mulligan. A heavy indictment. But
one can read through these *Collected Poems* and then skip ahead
into *The Whispering Roots* of 1970 (as if — the typical frigidity
— roots whispered) never arrested or surprised by much except
the excess of the infelicitous; never elevated by that mood in
which, for example, Pasternak speaks of ourselves as being the
guests of existence, never touched and delighted deeply by a
knowledge, in words adapted from another grave writer,
George Seferis, that the poems are drawn at once from this
poet's body and this poet's world — our bodies, our world.

The faults and frigidities continue unabated and unabashed in
the new poems. "Roots are for holding on, and holding dear";
"Their dreams coming full circle"; "Their country's age-old
plight"; "Of him [Michael Collins] who once dynamic as a
powerhouse stood". Little has changed, except a slackening or
thickening of the old fluidity, the old on-and-on-ness, which
showed at least qualities of connection and persistence.

Coming to translation, the Poet Laureate makes not un-
sensible remarks. "The translator" — the rare poet translator,
he means — "must take his original as a series of experiences to
be interpreted in the light of his own language, his own times.
He has to melt down and then to refashion",[1] &c.

Yet in his own translations, in which he adopts, too, a
literary mask (for the time being Valéry, for the time being
Virgil, just as in his verse he is at various times masked in the
manners of Lawrence, Auden, Hardy, Whitman, Meredith,
Clough, Fitzgerald, Dylan Thomas), one discovers the same
distorting mechanism between the thing and the expressed
outcome; witness, in brief, the first stanza of Valéry's *Le*

1 C. Day Lewis, *On Translating Poetry: The Second Jackson Knight
    Memorial Lecture* (1969).

Cimetière marin and the first stanza of Day Lewis's translation:
Valéry at once establishes a calm particular brilliance, which in
English is straightaway softened and departicularized (if un-
necessarily "explained"). Valéry's calm roof on which doves
walk and which quivers between the pines and between the
tombstones of the cemetery, i.e. his Mediterranean on which the
white boats pass, below, becomes

This quiet roof, where dove-sails saunter by,
Between the pines, the tombs, throbs visibly

— and before the stanza is over the strength of *un long regard
sur le calme des dieux* dwindles to the weakness of the "the long
vistas of celestial calm'. (About the translations from Virgil, it
is kinder after all not to speak, stretching as they do to such a
contrival of the commonplace.)

In truth this Jackson Knight Memorial lecturer treated his
listeners at Exeter University to old ideas, again, in familiar
clothes they heard of "us rootless moderns", "creative
instinct", "negative virtue", and conjuring spirits and giving
them "a temporary habitation". Here again they were
presented, in old style, with news of Shelley, Eliot, Auden,
Dryden, Johnson, Wordsworth, Cowper and Arnold.

Gentlemanly, but tedious; and one recalls, having mentioned
Pasternak, how that poet of such opposite nature and
cultivation, that poet of the just surprise, writes in his *Letters to
Georgian Friends* of Vronsky, in *Anna Karenina,* who bought
everything to paint with — in Italy — "all the necessary art
accessories": though nothing came of these purchases, nothing
came right, the mood was always wrong, the weather was
always bad; there were no pictures.

In this case there are, in fact, poems; but they seem to display
that "gentlemanly, amatuerish, idle attitude" of every Vronsky
of this era, which so repelled Pasternak, that same "upper-class
idea of art, an art for young ladies"; which in this English life-
work has results, not excessively absurd as a rule, yet, as they
extend, so flat that you could cycle on them.

These are poems situated to some degree in a comfortable
taste for a decayed idealism of style, to some degree in a desire
for what may also seem — because of the properties involved
— to be conveyed in a vehicle of modernity. "Redecorated
throughout, all modern convenience", without felicity,
without emotive cadence, illumination, or independence,
without tension, offering no surprise of recognition, no turning
of corners, no uphill or downhill, how often such verse has

enjoyed an extensive, if doomed, honour! How many poets, affined thinly to the greater talents of a period, have written on and on like this, a Binyon, an Abercrombie, an (Amy) Lowell, a Stephen Phillips, an Aubrey de Vere; to appear perhaps, in small type, in the sad bibliographies of literature. That their nature should quickly be recognized is important for the health of literature, that is to say, as the thing which is to be read. No poet is likely to be taken in. There is no specific reality here to imitate or follow.

1970

Campion's Garden of Love

I have a friend, now eminent for quite other things, who when he was twenty-four or twenty-five would go to the piano for me and pick out the accompaniment to Campion's

> Never weather-beaten sail more willing bent to shore,
> Never tired pilgrim's limbs affected slumber more

— Campion's music for Campion's poem. I wonder if he remembers, or would so far forget himself, forty years later?

Here, anyway, is Campion complete,[1] more or less, with the music for thirty of his songs, and with the treatises he wrote on music and poetry. I had to skip much of rather an extraordinary introduction by a professor of English (which might as well have been written in runes or in a language which certainly was not used by the syrens) to come at about the most sweet-spoken set of poems ever contrived in English.

What rather startled me was the editor's claim that he was bringing Campion to light once more. It is true there has not been a full edition of Campion for sixty years. But has he been in the dark at all in that time? Possibly in America (this is an American edition), but never in his own country, I should have thought. I have heard Campion on the air, Campion in concerts to the lute (at times in the slightly rarefied, if otherwise delightful conditions of a concert in some National Trust country house). I can go out and buy Campion records, I can read him in anthologies; and I am sure my head is not the only one to have as permanent tenants such lines as the ones I have quoted, or such other openings as "The peaceful western wind", or "Shall I come, sweet love, to thee", or "Wherefore shall I refuge seek, if you refuse me", or — how marvellous — "What fair pomp have I spied of glittering ladies", or such a close as this, to another of my favourites, "She hath more beauty than becomes the chaste"; or this, "So would I love that neither should repent", or "Is this fair excusing? O no, all is abusing".

Back one spins to that tiresome problem of "modern art" versus old melody. Professor Davis (but I must really thank him for this new Campion, introduction or no) seems to think that his poet has been driven out of English and American top stories by T. S. Eliot and too much attention to John Donne. I

1 *The Works of Thomas Campion* edited by W. R. Davis (1969).

would say that the "modern movement" of our century has driven nothing worthwhile out of any sensible head or heart (we are still in possession of hearts). It has shown that our living — by the way of art — requires more than sweetness. And I should have thought as a consequence that good art of every kind, era and country, is far better appreciated now than it was in the decades when our roost appeared to be ruled, say, by *The Forsyte Saga* or *The Good Companions,* or the gypsy canvases of Augustus John.

A girl of eighteen is well aware that love can be anything but a quiet garden, so she may read Donne to herself with excitement and satisfaction, now that Donne is in the company we all know about; and girls of eighteen (or twenty-eight) will go on doing so, whatever professors may argue. Which does not mean they will never read Campion, for a more even or mild delicacy; or rather that their young men will never read Campion (who is perhaps a more a man's love poet? Certainly Donne is the poet for lovers two and two).

Walter de la Mare — there you do have an underrated poet, not half so exclusively sweet and old-melodious as many people suppose — contrived a poem about Campion, or about one of the few things known of his sixteenth- and seventeenth-century life, that he had one sister, and that her name was Rose.

Rose, roses — the danger lights are on. But the Campion territory is not the less genuine for resembling a garden. Tidier, it is more a man's concern for the girl he cannot have or can only imagine. With Donne everything is now, is him and her, or me and you, or us, in the room, in bed, at this moment; whereas Campion will write of those

> that have not yet fed
> On delights amorous.

Or he will end a poem:

> 'Tis now flowry May
> But ev'n in cold December
> When all these leaves are blown away
> This place shall I remember.

In Donne love is a drama active like Etna, yourself, as you read, one of the two mutual agonists or protagonists. In Campion — for men — love is a spell, a charm, a scent, a want; a concentrate of these things in perfected shape, perfected flow and pause, and words perfectly of the heart's hope or regret or longing. I recall reading always to myself (under the powerful lights of *The Waste Land,* and *Ulysses*, and Picasso, and Stravinsky — and Donne) poems by Campion, "Sweet, exclude me not", and "When thou must home, to shades of underground" and "Shall I come, sweet love to thee". I used to read them much as one will play over and over again a short lyrical gramophone record; and I see exactly why, coming back to Campion with special emphasis now after many years. He too corresponds to something permanent in the ways we feel. Our feelings actually play in his sounds, his repetitions, his pauses, his tones, his rhymes, his brief shapes.

It seems obvious to me that this exquisite performance has never been out of favour in our century, and is never going to be out of favour in centuries to come, whatever needs or fashions predominate.

Poems and Pleasure

Risking a pair of generalizations, I shall say, first, that in our national community we've always been a little suspicious of showing gladness, or enjoying things too obviously. Enjoyment has seemed dubiously in accord with morality or with our traditional pattern of behaviour. For the second generalization I would say that now, the Sixties, continues to be a period in which admitting to enjoyment is rather too commonly regarded as a new kind of treason.

There is trouble in Vietnam; there is trouble in American cities; there is Mr Enoch Powell; there is Ulster, and Czechoslovakia; there is anxiety. We must be loyal to our view that everything is wrong, we must commit no treason against our uneasy sense that we are all to blame, against our sense of shared guilt. The corn is orient and immortal wheat — yes, but not here or now. Possibly elsewhere, although even the purest notion of pie in the sky now fails, and I think fails rightly, to be acceptable except to persons of — in modern circumstances — a marked eccentricity, rusticity, or rustiness of mind. It is as if we were exceptionally overwhelmed — yet without religious belief — by that curious and to me horrifying concept of original sin; for which I hurry to say I would not substitute any sentimental doctrine of original goodness.

I grew up in the Twenties, which I think were years, in this way and that way, of extreme lassitude and hypocrisy. Years, let's say, in the arts, or the arts as then commonly accepted, of flaccid evasion of the real thing. Then came, for example, Eliot's *Waste Land,* full of the drama of the opposite of cultural optimism, or take it easy; full of rats, abortion, trams, dusty trees, the unreal city under the brown fog of a winter dawn. The house agent's clerk arrives:

> One of the low on whom assurance sits
> As a silk hat on a Bradford millionaire.

"Exploring hands", you will remember, "encounter no defence. His vanity requires no response." He goes, the girl looks in the glass, and "paces about her room, again alone", and

> . . . smooths her hair with automatic hand
> And puts a record on the gramophone.

Then, too, came Eliot's friend, Wyndham Lewis, seeing the smallness in our age, satirizing a retreat from pinnacles of the mind into the generally infantile, satirizing the way men seemed to be advancing back first, instead of head first, into the future.

After that, the Thirties, and a poetry shifting from Eliot's rather uncharitable disdain for the sadly living or for the mediocre life, shifting to an acknowledgement of participation and responsibility. In 1933 I published in the magazine *New Verse* a poem by the very young W. H. Auden, a poem he long ago suppressed for various reasons, which began:

> I have a handsome profile
> I've been to a great public school
> I've a little money invested
> Then why do I feel such a fool
> As if I owned a world that had had its day?

And in 1938, five years later, I published a poem now celebrated, I think, by Louis MacNeice which included the lines:

> It's no go the Yogi-man, it's no go Blavatsky,
> All we want is a bank balance and a bit of skirt in a taxi.

Also: "Sit on your arse for fifty years and hang your hat on a pension", a poem which ended:

> The glass is falling, hour by hour, the glass will fall for ever,
> But if you break the bloody glass you won't hold up the
>   weather.

Now after a war, after the release of previously unimaginable energies, employable always for more destruction and damnation and for extinction, after an uneasy stretch of years, it does seem that recognitions of the nasty or the humanly unpropitious have come to figure in the serious arts, in political comment and complaint, and in day-to-day journalism, to a pitch of morbidity and exaggeration, if not falsification, quite as extreme as that evasion or false bonhomie of the Twenties; for which people of my age may see an image in the dull and homely pipe-smoking rounded face of that shrewd manipulator, Stanley Baldwin.

I am not sure what face I should choose for today, for monthly trade figures which people hope will be glum, for Biafran news, for almost all the news, and for much art. Perhaps it would be the set jaw and the wild eye of Mr Enoch Powell prophesying doom. Or screaming through a distorted jaw it might be a face brought to no longer bearable tension in a televised play by Harold Pinter, our Edgar Allen Poe. But the difference is there, and I complain only of this state of mind's exclusive, inclusive ubiquity. At which point let me recall a curious, if minor example. Last winter, I think last spring as well, hardly a night's television news went by — on screens fed by the BBC — without the flames, somewhere, in some city in Great Britain, some store, some warehouse, of a large destructive fire. I wouldn't suppose there were in fact more fires at that time than there are usually, but I used to wait for the night's fire: it was as if all England were burning, it was a disproportionate offering several times a week (I don't think I exaggerate) of ordinary inevitable accident; it was as if no visual bulletin could be complete without alarm and fear. In a small way, yet reaching to millions, this nightly fire was rather like the parading of hell fire and damnation in earlier ages, or among particular religious communities; like paintings of the red mouth of Hell and the Last Judgment. A perverse enjoyment, perhaps; which is not the enjoyment I am asking for, and asking that no individual should be afraid of admitting to himself or to others.

I am myself — like most of our community in these islands — no religionist. But it happens that I was born in the best room of a vicarage (facing south, over dahlias) and brought up in a vicarage, so I shall go back for a moment to that medieval Christian image of the gaping red gullet of Hell, in the shape of Leviathan, with flames, and large teeth, and an insatiable greed for sinners. In a book which came out last year, on images of Heaven and Hell in western Art, I read of a German theologian of the sixteenth century, I suppose of the Counter Reformation, named Drexelius, who maintained that the deity found no difficulty at all in cramming one hundred thousand million souls of the burnt, the skinned and the gutted — the damned in brief — into one cubic German mile. Little cause for felicity or for enjoying things if that was your belief, and if yourself might be burned, skinned, gutted, by demons. But then I had only to go through that book to be reminded that the medieval artist and believer was also in the habit of balancing Hell with Heaven in the same picture, or the same painting on a church wall. There, like Osiris before him, St Michael the Archangel held up the scales, and weighed the souls of the dead. If devils, on one side of the picture, at once clawed into Leviathan's flaming mouth the souls of those whose evil outweighed their goodness, at least on the other side souls of the proper weight were received gently and happily into bliss. So a Last Judgment preserved more or less the open situation, devoid of an excluding fanaticism, or of a morbid preferred insistence on hell and torture and gloom; and I am asking for an open situation, a balance in our own life of the mind: perhaps not a balance, but at any rate an oscillation, corresponding to reality.

We are not each of us — I don't speak just as a writer — called upon by decency or kindness or moral imagination or necessity or the inescapable facts or the universal weight and posture of things, to suppose all the time that we are having to wade, companions of Thomas the Rhymer in the border ballad, through red blude to the knee, seeing neither sun nor moon but only the glare of the burning of napalm on innocent bodies. The evil is evil; in any case, unpalatable fact, we do each and all of us have to die sooner or later. Even then it is proper, surely, to criticize and correct ourselves either way: we need to see the detestable and the enjoyable with equal vision.

The trap here is obvious, and double, of course. If we enjoy, possibly we minimize or we refuse to admit, face, speak against, act against the unspeakable. Equally if we are absorbed by detestation of the detestable, if we let this part become the whole, then we never smile, we never dance, when there is cause. We forgo a pleasure which is, or can be, much more than selfish in its vitally social effects.

There is a case everlasting, I would claim, for Epicurus, at least for the epicurean. In England we have inclined — in particular, poets and other imaginative writers have inclined — to allow enjoyment only under restrictions and conditions. Certain writers have been endowed with, or have developed, what Colette in France called "a compelling, fierce and secret rapport — with the earth and everything that gushes from its breasts". They have recognized it — one thinks of Jeremy Taylor, Milton, Traherne, Vaughan, Wordsworth, Coleridge, Gerard Manley Hopkins, in his different way D. H. Lawrence. But looking in another direction they have observed in some epicureans a coldness, an inhumanity, treating pleasure, not at all as a state of tranquillity, not as a reduction or destruction of fear, but as involving indifference to everything except itself. They have been afraid of this, afraid of indulging their senses, and they have admitted that rapport, admitted or excused, that excellence of earth, only under the orders of religious interpretation, or limitation. There can be — should be — a meaningful enjoyment inviting us to enjoy a ripe pear tawny and still warm with sunlight.

Painters, more immediate in their response, less worried by ideas perhaps, if you like less educated, do more often present their enjoyment for what it is — or they did do so. I think of Constable looking all this time for the "calm sunshine of the soul", declaring that he'd never seen an ugly thing in his life; of Turner lost in his wheel of radiance; of Monet, Renoir, Pissarro, Sisley, or Cézanne involved in the world's facets of blue and green and ochre; of Bonnard and Matisse and Dufy and of Ben Nicholson. In the Tate there is a picture quivering with enjoyment in exactly the way I mean, in the simplest terms and by the subtlest devices — go and look at it — Sisley's *Path to the Old Ferry*. But if paintings grant us our escape into enjoyment (I say escape, not as having to do with escapism but as one would talk of an escape to freedom over or under the Berlin wall), we have been in the habit of pushing the painter's admonition, such as it is, rather to one side.

But aren't we still left, in the main, trudging, almost happily trotting, along our road to unhappiness, our road to secular hell, by preference, in this present phase of being miserable? And I am saying in brief to hell with more hell in our minds than is justified. I am saying we should do better, writer and reader, artist and those who look and those who hear, with rather more recognition, rather more celebration, of secular heaven on this earth when it does briefly, intermittently and on that account poignantly occur. If our engagement is to life, if it is against the beastly (which we have to recognize and reckon with, all the same) it is *ipso facto* for the enjoyable.

1969

In the Stables of Pegasus

I had the following experiences after reading till late these essays and aphoristical remarks by the poet George Barker.[1] I went out, saw an amber small halo round the moon, noticed shining leaves on top of a tree, and heard a breadth and loudness of wind, and said, My God, how wonderful; and reflected at once on how we use those words My God as an inherited ejaculation. After in a dream I encountered Novalis walking with two children along the pedestrian close, from the supermarket. He looked like a modest accountant from the Borough offices; I was surprised to see him, because he had been dead for so long. Considering this dream I thought, Well, he couldn't have been George Barker.

In his time rational and mystical, Novalis, who had looked to me as "normal" as someone from the Borough offices, had naturally to begin, continue, and conclude with "God"; around whom, in our time — but is George Barker in our time, or in any time? — one is wise to put those two inverted commas. It is true these muddled pieces achieve in tone a simulacrum of authority or arcane insight. I see in them, in their author, an Arnoldian Scholar Gypsy, pensive, and tongue-tied — decidedly tongue-tied, in hat of antique shape and cloak of grey. The Spark has fallen on him — well, he believes it has; he has caught it, it escapes (giggling a little), he catches it again. But he can't get it into his vasculum with the frail-leaf'd white anemones, etcetera. At any rate he is too tongue-tied — my God, how his sloppy often ungrammatical sentences intricate themselves! — to illuminate his illumination.

God, Love, the Dionysiac, Imagination, the Real, Poetry — the ineffable is always difficult to catch, even if you have (which Mr Barker hasn't) the philosophic or the educated abilities of a Coleridge or a Novalis. (The effable is rather more in the tin, I might add: the Spark is given a habitat in the mystic rose on two legs now and again.)

George Barker fears, on one page, that he is being obscure and pretentious. Certainly obscure. But not pretentious, I would say; fuddled, in his transcendental hunt, in his avoidance of the possibly awful joke of being. I wouldn't say that even the dedication, "To the memory of Thomas Stearns Eliot", is pretentious; it is only unfortunate and deluded.

1 *Essays* by George Barker (1970).

He gives pleasure now and then. "The unicorn does not exist because it has better things to do." "The most poetical magazine title: *Harper's Bazaar.*" "It has always seemed remarkable to me that no winged horse has ever stalked into a library knocking over the leather chairs, whinnying fit to crack the electric light bulbs and depositing its golden excrement inside the swing doors as it paced out."

But if I ask myself what I know better after this "groping in the dark backward and the abysm of the mind", I think I must say, only George Barker, his swoons, his preferences, his confusions, the bright stutter too, and disconnections, of his verse.

This is a book I would expect to be received well in the land of Mrs Eddy — if that land still exists?

Gentleman of Letters: Allen Tate

It has to be confessed — and should be confessed more often — that good literary criticism is less common than good writing of other kinds. It asks for more than responsive estimation, or recognition of characterizing elements, or a theory of cultural value, or proper behaviour. Like all other writing, the criticism which persuades or provokes the reader, which delights him and instructs him or makes him argue with the critic or with himself, has inescapably to convey and project an individuality: it requires a man himself in words which don't, when a momentary reputation or position is maintained no longer, reveal themselves as moulded by the style of a period.

Mr Allen Tate proffers, in such terms, the always difficult problem of the critic — the poet as well — whom we have to like, inasmuch as he always has been on the right side. When there has been a mob, Mr Tate hasn't been leading it with a loud mouth; when there has been a lynching among poets or other writers, Mr Tate hasn't been there to give a flick of contempt to the horny toes. He is a Southern Gentleman of Letters. Yet should we be on any side but our own? And what are we to say of the writer of a party (a party not being a mob), when we find it difficult not to be inattentive to his writing? When we find his writing too plain, too removed, with no main root in a layer of sensation?

We read through Mr Allen Tate's essays — forty years' length of criticism[1] — and we are seldom, or never, outraged. His sentences are never tumultuous; and they are seldom stretched to an effective tightness. Are we missing much, when our attention falters?

It falters so often because, as we read, we have frequently to translate into straight terms; we have to say "translate" when Mr Tate says "render", we have to find the genuine substitutes — but perhaps such phraseology is its own total, its own condemnation — when Mr Tate, once more, says "twofold", "framework", "cash nexus", "the modern world", "not quite pertinent", "here in its full import", "for a brief span", "fundamental failure", "totality of experience", "mode of perception", or "not susceptible of logical demonstration".

There is no use blinking these facts, as Mr Tate would — and does — write. They constitute Mr Tate's carefully un-

1 *Essays of Four Decades* by Allen Tate (1970).

careful criticism; they are the material built into essays under such matching, caricatural titles as "The Function of the Critical Quarterly", or "A Reading of Keats", or "A Note on Critical Autotelism", or "Three Types of Poetry", or "Crane: The Poet as Hero". Among them all we begin to ask, Where then is Mr Tate? Does, after all, Mr Tate exist?

This is a matter of levels. It is pleasant enough to encounter a critic and poet who finds himself bored and irritated by talk of "the political responsibility of poets". It is pleasant to find Mr Tate affirming that "the poet has a great responsibility of his own . . . to write poems". He doesn't like talking poets, of whom we have many. It is pleasant to find someone declaring of the critical quarterly (Mr Tate isn't, by total uniform, a man of the campus) that it "now increasingly serves the end of acquainting unpopular writers with one another's writing". But observations of that kind hardly elevate us to the high plateau or to the high tops of criticism.

> The best American poets have tried to discover new and precise languages by which poetry now as always must give us knowledge of the human condition — knowledge that seems to reach us partly in the delight that one gets from rhythm and insights that one has not already heard and known.

But of course, one replies — in a phrase likely to be lipped rather frequently by the reader who does persist; the reader who is glad to notice Mr Tate's feeling of indebted admiration for Coleridge — and who is sorry that in a critic of such decency he finds so few, or none, of those Coleridgean sentences at which we pause, a little stunned and then delighted because a truth up to now unrecognized and unencountered has been enunciated, all of a sudden.

Mr Tate on poets and poetry brings us into gingerly contact with the ninety poems[1] (out of 250, a small published total for a long career) by which he would be remembered. He has written of his method of isolating "the general ideas implicit in the poet's work"; and as if he recognized that it is a method too unbodily, he has strengthened it with an essay about "tension" in a poem, meaning "the full organized body of all the extension and intension we can find in it".

Extension is the act of extending, enlarging; intension is the act of intensifying what is extended, a unitary effect. Touch-

1 *The Swimmers and other Selected Poems* by Allen Tate (1970).

stones of this poetry of the centre, this poetry of tension, include, he tells us, "Cover her face: mine eyes dazzle; she died young", or Eliot's

> We have lingered in the chambers of the sea
> By sea girls wreathed with seaweed red and brown
> Till human voices wake us and we drown.

This idea of tension shifts at any rate towards the poem as an object born of objectifying. Mr Tate continues (in that tiredly respectable language in which he can also inform us that his friend the late Herbert Read was "one of the finest poets of our time") that poets of America have used "a certain mode of perception" which he has named "the aesthetic-historical". Is this intended as praise or blame? Using some remarks of the late Michael Roberts, he expounds it by saying that American poets are "less firmly rooted in a settled poetic tradition than the British", so they are able "to seize and digest traditions and influences from many languages and periods".

Whether Mr Tate is being neutral (as Michael Roberts was) or depreciatory, it is that ability to digest which one often doubts. Coming, for instance, to Mr Tate's selection of his poems, we find him speaking, from the blue grass of the (not unremote) Kentucky of his origins, about Greece, about France, about England; about gods, heroes, philosophers, poets. Here in his poems we encounter, by name, Venus, Narcissus, Pasiphaë, Europa, Tantalus, Pelops, Priam, Aeneas, Pericles, Zeno, Parmenides, Plato, Socrates, Callimachus, Horace, Propertius, Webster (skulls beneath the skin), Kyd, Ford, Donne, Marvell, Pope, Collins, Landor, Blake, Rimbaud, Yeats; this American poet at times attitudinizing, as if to say, "These are mine, as well", at times (slightly) despairing, like his friend and fellow-Fugitive and fellow-Southern-Gentleman Poet, John Crowe Ransom (to whom the essays are dedicated), in his delightful and strong *Philomela*.

The call to the classical Elsewhere is most tactful and acceptable in "The Swimmers", the name of which Mr Tate gives to this selection (not surprisingly, because it is about his strongest poem). Scene of "The Swimmers": Montgomery County, Kentucky, July 1911. Circumstances: five children, himself included, coming to bathe in clear summer springs. Impingement: a posse, a hanged Negro, his body, dragged off in a hearse which is only dust, a body which at the court-house is shrouded only in the sun. The call to Greece, in this sunlit horror, is no more than the quick velvety touch of mullein as these boys run towards Kentucky water — "mullein under the ear / Soft as Nausicaä's palm". No more, except, down the page, the word "odyssey" with a small o. A poem Allen Tate must think about with satisfaction.

Elsewhere, in Mr Tate's own more aesthetic-historical verse, indigestion may not dominate, but certainly interrupts; and as in the prose, we encounter in many of these neat, by no means untensed poems, respectable long-expired elements, alike in phrase and in movement. Poems will begin — each time we have been there before — "Didactic Laurel, loose your reasoning leaf", "Irritable spring, infuse", "Lady of Light, I would admit", or "Captain of Industry, your aimless power" — tributes to Mr Tate's education, not to his gift from the Muses. Isn't it Nashville, Tennessee (where Mr Tate attended Vanderbilt University), which flaunts a replica on a reduced scale of the Parthenon, in concrete (yes, somewhat, but only somewhat, recalling the not quite naturalized Palladian villas of England, the not quite naturalized grots and nymphs of the era of our own Parnells or Akensides)?

The "taste" is perfect (except when Allen Tate tries the jocular or the generally inconsequent), the material isn't concrete, the intention is serious, the extension ingenious, the intension worked for — and the tension deceptive. Few poems entice us to a second reading, possibly only "The Swimmers": that does demand reading again, and then again, with the peremptoriness which is inflicted on us by the real thing. Poems that may have given us a turn, a sense of novelty, years ago — such as "Mr Pope" — reveal their brittle derivation on re-acquaintance.

There is too much evidence of the contrived, the hoped for, beyond the gift of the poet — a poet, Mr Tate admits in his essay of 1968 on "Poetry Modern and Unmodern", who has never been quite able to do what he wanted to do, one reason for this perhaps being the difficulty of discovering what he wanted to do; which may be translated into the difficulty of discovering a Muse when all you have is the membership of a select club. He tells us courageously, yet revealingly, that he discovered modernism — "or perhaps I had better say, the shock to the twentieth century sensibility out of which modernism developed" — not through Yeats, Eliot or Pound, but in James Thomson (B.V.), adding that it remained only — yes, only — "to find the right language and to establish a centre from which it could be spoken". His selection is rounded off with — should we say? — the only literate English

version of the *Pervigilium Veneris* (though this reviewer does
not care for Mr Tate's ingenious refrain, "Tomorrow may
loveless, may lover tomorrow make love", either for euphony
or accuracy; and he does not see how Mr Tate so conven-
tionally knows that "few people today read the *Pervigilium
Veneris*"; any fewer, that is, than might be expected for poems
which haven't been written by Shakespeare or Mr Robert
Lowell).

1971

Craft Cheese; or How Poems are Treated

Professor Cleanth Brooks mentions disclaimingly, detergently almost, that he is labelled a New Critic; then he proclaims that whatever else the critic may criticize, "there may be a great deal to say for criticism that puts its heaviest stresses on the writing itself," and unsurprisingly he goes on, "The most important thing about Shakespeare, for example, is the fact that he was a great dramatist."[1]

There you are. And if you reach this page xiv of the prelims you may suspect that ahead of you there stretch 380 pages at least spotted with the banal. So it will prove, though not disagreeably. Cleanth Brooks does show himself again to be different from what may be called (I hope without offence transatlantically) our own native, resident or semi-resident Americans: he doesn't go on in a hard superior way about next to nothing. He is polite, modest, and wide. He actually quotes when he is discussing poems. He doesn't erect a small canon of the respectable, he doesn't parade his bad bogey authors, the ones, if you are crass enough to enjoy anything about them, who mark you as some crutch pheasant of Sunday or weekly journalism, some provocation for an even longer epistolical whine from Mrs Leavis.

He likes the prose which Yeats wrote about literature and being a poet, and wishes

> to show that Yeats had a very clear notion of what poetry was and specifically that he conceived of it as providing a special kind of truth and therefore distinguished it, on the one hand, from mere self-expression and, on the other hand, from propaganda for a cause

(which isn't much more than wishing to show that Yeats was a major poet, which was already obvious?). Auden pleases him as a virtuoso of poems and the critical asking of questions. He praises the short stories — or one of them — by that underpraised American Peter Taylor. He rather nicely insists on the classical decorum of John Crowe Ransom's delicious poems by showing how Ransom pushes himself away from the poems, keeping at an aesthetic distance, like Milton, he says, vis-à-vis

1 *A Shaping Joy: Studies in the Writer's Craft* by Cleanth Brooks (1971).

"Lycidas" and his other short pieces.

He comes to Frost and Housman, and sensibly remarks the existence, after all, of a modern "nature poetry" or poetry touched with delight in a nature which is in fact, and is now recognized, sometimes regretfully, as a mindless, alien, indifferent bundle of phenomena. He is shrewd on sentimentality (talking of Housman — he likes Housman) as "a failure of tone"; although just that failure is invisible to him in Frost's "Stopping by Woods on a Snowy Evening".

At times, like most critics of poetry, he betrays a casual ignorance of what a poem, at some point or another, is actually dealing with. A little piece of "close reading" which isn't close, of Housman's XL in *Last Poems,* comes to traveller's joy beguiling, in autumn, hearts which have lost their own joy: he says that in the autumn sunshine "the flower called traveller's joy" silently extends "to the joyless wayfarer its grace of self, the namesake of joy". If he had discovered that traveller's joy isn't a "flower", but a tough, woody, rather murderously beguiling creeper, grey if admirable in the autumn with bearded achenes — "Old Man's Beard" — he mightn't have been content with "Each of the vignettes suggests the secret life of nature revealed to a rapt and solitary observer", he might have come deeper into the significance of the poem. Which is only one more, if a different, example of the freqent superficiality of *A Shaping Joy.*

I don't think this broad if slightly simple-minded book, named after a phrase in an essay by Yeats, was really entitled to be subnamed "Studies in the Writer's Craft". At any rate a thing it doesn't show is much acquisition of such a craft — if that sentimental word has to be used — in its own writing. It is a bet that any banal phrase will turn up — crossing watersheds, the usual task of poetry, appropriate pigeonholes, Blake's dark satanic mills had arisen in England's green and pleasant land, embarrassment of riches, and my task is made somewhat easier, and the house of poetry has many mansions. Professor Brooks says most of his essays were lectures, but I don't think that explains — or if it explains, would justify — the simple-mindedness; and certainly it doesn't excuse the style. Still, if it is a vulgar style, it is loose and unconceited: you can understand what this academic literary man is up to (Professor Brooks, says the jacket — mischievously? — "keeps the methods of communication marveliously [*sic*] unblocked"), even if it is never exhilarating and seldom — except in paraphrase or précis of what his subjects write — very interesting.

Black Night for Poesy?

I believe these "observations on poetry and its enemies" amount on the whole to interesting nonsense, in a way which is also interesting.[1] The way is quotation. Between a third and a quarter of the book is quotation direct, to make no mention of quotation indirect, in paraphrase. A guerrilla leader for poetry (poesy, I incline to say), John Press deploys his rabble of extracts, both authoritative and without authority, to show how this art is now pushed to a "frontier of darkness", beyond which it may become extinct.

Plato — oh dear — is the name which has to come first: let poets be banished from the state. They are sensual liars, they are properly attacked by moralists, social perfectionists, political bosses, tidy administrators, and — serve them right as unreasoning indulgent useless perverters of truth — by the rationalists of science.

The quotations are enjoyable — Yeats, for instance, on Donne: "Donne could be as metaphysical as he pleased, and yet never seem inhuman and hysterical as Shelley often does, because he could be as physical as he pleased." Or Lady Violet Bonham-Carter recalling how (long before he used it in his war utterance) she had introduced Churchill to Clough's "Say not the struggle nought availeth", and how Churchill had remarked what a marvellous poem it would be to quote in a by-election (to which John Press might have added Churchill on Picasso and kicking his behind, at the Academy Banquet).

Being so numerous, all the same, the quotations don't leave their generalissimo much room for his own words (which very often are not really his own, but such as *the poet's task* or *striving for mastery*, or, with no sign of quotation marks, as if he had thought the words up for himself, *the still sad music of humanity*).

As a criticism I hesitate, after all, between interesting nonsense and interesting obviousness as a right description of this book. What is said has so often been said more keenly. With his sympathies rightly directed, John Press will just bring it up to date. He directs a right throw, for instance (but isn't the old clay pipe unside down in that ample mouth too easy to hit?), at C. P. Snow on Two Cultures, he recognizes that the common mind and the official mind everywhere have the same

---

1   *The Lengthening Shadows: Observations on Poetry and its Enemies* by John Press (1971).

desire to suppress or control.

I don't complain — very much — that his book reads like thesis notes around assorted cards from a card-index (which by the way does not happen to include anything about Goethe, when he reaches poetry and science, or anything about Taine's horrible foretelling of the contemptuous role democracy would assign to its writers). The real nonsense seems to me John Press's conviction that poetry or poets are now in unprecedented danger — or danger of extinction. Isn't this our kind of millenary conceit? I do not myself believe that everything now is worse, like sliced loaves (what would John Press make of the not uncomforting fact that the French nowadays install bread-slicing machines behind the *boulangerie* counter so that each customer can have his loaf sliced only if he should prefer it that way?) I don't myself believe that global vicissitudes or powerful common men with chambers in Albany or Ministers for Cultural Turnstiles, or commissars, or editors, or journalists of any kind, or advertising copywriters or advertising image-makers, or dry academics, are capable of extinguishing any art. We continue to be born, enjoy, suffer, die; in which condition the making of poems, etc., is inevitable and will be extinguished only if makers and all are extinguished; which is another matter.

Of course it is as well to know how to recognize the enemies of a good thing, but what John Press forgets is what Whistler screamed in perfect verity — that there never has been an artistic period, or country, or people, and never will be.

Breeches of Bright Velvet:
Two verdicts on Chatterton

We write about a poet and think that for ourselves at least we have him fixed. What if we try again, years later? With change of focus, change of exposure? Of these two pieces about Chatterton, not quite a Dylan Thomas of an earlier age, the first was written and broadcast in 1946. A quarter of a century later I tried again, when I had long forgotten that my first attempt existed. Others than myself may find it interesting and curious to compare the two.

I. CHATTERTON FIRST EXAMINED

The trouble with Chatterton is that there are two Chattertons. One is the poet, the Chatterton who exists in the poems. The other is the sensational Chatterton, the seventeen-year-old boy — who was a genius, as we say; who was misused by that in some ways nasty character Horace Walpole; who starved; who committed suicide in a London garret. It is, I agree, a wonderful, pathetic story. But the important Chatterton is the other one, the poet; and if Chatterton had been run over by a coach, or slipped on the stairs, or fallen into the river on a dark night, he would still be as important, he would still be worth reading, as a remarkable English poet.

All the same, I want to remind you of the scene of Chatterton's death, as it was imagined, very exquisitely, by the Pre-Raphaelite painter Henry Wallis. The picture is in the Tate Gallery. Chatterton lies dead under a small attic window, through which you can see St Paul's. He wears breeches of a vivid satin blue. Red hair curls round a handsome face — the model for the picture, by the way, was another poet, George Meredith, with whose wife the painter disappeared. Near his feet a plum-coloured coat hangs over a chair. It is a very rich painting, a painting of richly combined colour; imagined, but true, in spite of somewhat sententious details which have to be "read", because to my mind it symbolizes the richness and the colour of Chatterton's poetry.

> On Tiber's banks, where scarlet jasmines bloom,
> And purple aloes shed a rich perfume;
> Where, when the sun is melting in his heat,
> The reeking tigers find a cool retreat,

Bask in the sedges, lose the sultry beam,
And wanton with their shadows in the stream —

Chatterton is alert, like Keats, in more than one sense at the same time, vision and the senses of smell and touch. That is what I mean by Chatterton's colour and richness — scarlet jasmines mixed with scent and purple aloes, and tigers reeking in strong sunshine (in nature, by the way, there are no scarlet jasmines).

You will have seen a macaw at the zoo. Macaws can be scarlet and purple and green; they come from tropical South America; and macaws are a favourite bird in the tropics of Chatterton's poetry — as though he had seen macaws, as he well may have done, brought back on the quays of the Port of Bristol.

Here is one of Chatterton's macaw poems, which he called, not exactly knowing where macaws came from, "An African Song":

> Haste, ye purple gleams of light,
>   Haste and gild the spacious skies;
> Haste, ye eagles, take your flight,
>   Haste and bid the morning rise.
>
> Now the Eastern curtain draws;
>   Now the red'ning splendour gleams,
> Now the purple plum'd maccaws
>   Skim along the silver streams.
>
> Now the fragrant-scented thorn,
>   Trembles with the gummy dew;
> Now the pleasures of the morn,
>   Swell upon the eager view.
>
> Whither does my archer stray?
>   Whither is my Narva fled?
> What can keep his soul away
>   From the transports of Mored?

All these African poems by Chatterton were written by him in London, in the last seven or eight months of his life; and I think they show his real bent, his real nature and peculiarity as a poet rather more than his famous Rowley Poems, his imitations — or imagined re-creations — of Chaucerian English. The African poems are much less known, less read, and less admired, so I am going to take a longish piece from one of them, from "Heccar and Gaira"; Heccar and Gaira are two warriors, and Heccar reminds Gaira of his wife Cawna and of the depredations of the pallid children of the wave, the slave traders — remember that Chatterton was a Bristolian and Bristol a slave traders' port:

> Rouse not remembrance from her shadowy cell,

Gaira replies,

> Nor of those bloody sons of mischief tell.
> Cawna, O Cawna! decked in sable charms,
> What distant region holds thee from my arms?
> Cawna, the pride of Afric's sultry vales,
> Soft as the cooling murmur of the gales;
> Majestic as the many-coloured snake,
> Trailing his glories through the blossomed brake;
> Black as the glossy rocks, where Eascal roars,
> Foaming through sandy wastes to Jaghir's shores;
> Swift as the arrow, hasting to the breast,
> Was Cawna, the companion of my rest.
>
> The sun sat low'ring in the western sky,
> The swelling tempest spread around the eye;
> Upon my Cawna's bosom I reclined,
> Catching the breathing whispers of the wind.
> Swift from the wood a prowling tiger came,
> Dreadful his voice, his eyes a glowing flame;
> I bent the bow, the never-erring dart
> Pierced his rough armour, but escaped his heart;
> He fled, though wounded, to a distant waste,
> I urged the furious flight with fatal haste;
> He fell, he died — spent in the fiery toil,
> I stripped his carcase of the furry spoil,
> And, as the varied spangles met my eye,
> "On this", I cried, "shall my loved Cawna lie."
>
> The dusky midnight hung the skies in grey;
> Impelled by love, I winged the airy way;
> In the deep valley and the mossy plain,
> I sought my Cawna, but I sought in vain.
> The pallid shadows of the azure waves
> Had made my Cawna, and my children, slaves.
> Reflection maddens to recall the hour;
> The gods had giv'n me to the demon's power.
> The dusk slow vanished from the hated lawn,

I gained a mountain glaring with the dawn.
There the full sails, expanded to the wind,
Struck horror and distraction in my mind;
There Cawna, mingled with a worthless train,
In common slavery drags the hated chain.

Now judge, my Heccar, have I cause for rage?
Should aught the thunder of my arm assuage?
In ever-reeking blood this javelin dyed
With vengeance shall be never satisfied;
I'll strew the beaches with the mighty dead
And tinge the lily of their features red.

That last line — "And tinge the lily of their features red" — or
that earlier line "I gained a mountain glaring with the dawn"
exhibits the kind of grandeur, the kind of extravagance which
Chatterton could produce again and again. Sometimes one or
two lines like that come just when you think the poem is dull,
silly, and underdone.

Like snows that trickle down hot Ætna's steep.

Chatterton's poetry was not only drawn out of mediaevalism
and the tropics — out of two distant countries, one in time and
one in space which he had only imagined and never seen. The
brilliant eyes which all Chatterton's friends remembered — his
brilliant grey eyes, took in, gloomily and grandly, details of the
autumn landscape at Bristol:

The yellow Avon, creeping at my side,
In sullen billows rolls a muddy tide;
No sportive naiads on her streams are seen,
No cheerful pastimes deck the gloomy scene.

Yellow was a favourite colour, a favourite adjective in
Chatterton's mind. He writes in one of his Bristol poems, the
"Elegy to the Memory of Mr Thomas Phillips":

Here, stretched upon this heaven-ascending hill
    I'll wait the horrors of the coming night,
I'll imitate the gently-plaintive rill,
    And by the glare of lambent vapours write.

Then comes the yellow line:

Wet with the dew, the yellow Hawthornes bow;
    The loud winds whistle through the echoing dell;
Far o'er the lea the breathing cattle low
    And the shrill shrieking of the screech-owl swell.

With whistling sound the dusky foliage flies,
   And wantons with the wind in rapid whirls;
The gurgling rivulet to the valley hies,
   And, lost to sight, in dying murmurs curls . . .

Chatterton played about with that poem, wrote and rewrote it.
One can see how his mind was made up, and how his mind
worked, from the changes. The gurgling rivulet curling out of
sight in dying murmurs suggested to him a snake, so he
rewrote that last stanza like this:

With rustling sound the yellow foliage flies —

yellow instead of *dusky* —

And wantons with the wind in rapid whirls.
The gurgling riv'let to the valley hies
   Whilst on the bank the spangled serpent curls.

In other words, there is one of Chatterton's tropical snakes
luxuriating in the coloured autumn of some stream side in
Leigh Woods; and there you see the furniture of Chatterton's
mind. You would find in it, if you could open the lid, a pretty
strange mixture — brown owls and scarlet macaws, Gothic
ruins and African jungles, knights in armour and black naked
warriors with high-sounding names, striped tigers and hot sunshine, yellow leaves and autumn fogs, snakes and spices and
volcanoes with Bristol's muddy river rolling along to
Avonmouth, all mixed with mad nomenclature imitated from
the then best-selling epics of that other forger — if the word is
valid — James Macpherson.
   To that medley, though, you have to add the pride, vigour
and intelligence of Chatterton — the power to write strong
lines of suggestive exoticism as about scarlet jasmines and
purple aloes, or such lines as those which conclude his poem
"The Resignation":

The gloomy mantle of the night
   Which on my sinking spirit steals
Will vanish at the morning light
   Which God, my East, my Sun reveals —

which justified Wordsworth in coupling him with Burns and
calling Chatterton "the marvellous boy" — "the sleepless soul
that perished in his pride".

Thinking it all over, I should call pride — energetic pride — a chief mark of Chatterton's poetry. And pride is a mark of really high poetry, as Chatterton's might have become — of poetry in a phrase of William Blake's, who was one of Chatterton's admirers, which "exists and exults in immortal thoughts".

Think of some of the poets of pride — Shakespeare, Marlowe, Sir Walter Ralegh, Dryden, Pope, Landor, John Clare — it is their company Chatterton belongs to. Of course, Chatterton's poetry, Chatterton's pride, is incomplete — since he was eighteen when he killed himself. He only began:

> I thought of Chatterton, the marvellous boy,
> The sleepless soul that perished in his pride;
> Of him who walked in glory and in joy
> Following his plough along the mountain side:
> By our own spirits are we deified:
> We Poets in our youth begin in gladness;
> But thereof come in the end despondency and madness.

The end which comes to poets of pride, came much too quickly to Chatterton; we only have the beginning in gladness. But I do not think any other English poet — so far as we know — began with powers more remarkable: and that is why Chatterton, with his macaws and tigers and ruins and snakes, is there to be read; and not just remembered as a romantic boy who killed himself.

1946

2. CHATTERTON RE-EXAMINED

It was two hundred years ago last year — so this bicentenary edition comes a bit late[1] — since Chatterton killed himself by taking arsenic in a Holborn garret; after which we gave ourselves a new blessed martyr: poetry slain by orphanage, poverty, and that most civilized of men, Horace Walpole. He was — I think I may have to remind you, since the legend is less in circulation now — eighteen years old; and Walpole's

---

1　*The Complete Works of Thomas Chatterton* edited by Donald S. Taylor with Benjamin B. Hoover (1971).

fault was not to have returned some (prose) pieces on "the ryse of Peyneteynge, yn Englande" which he tried to pass off as "wroten bie" a Bristolian priest of the late fifteenth century, "T. Rowleie".

Letters and enclosures come to us out of the blue; we — for any one or several of a hundred reasons — do not always return the enclosures as promptly as we should, requests or no. But then legends require a villain, and Walpole was the kind of man, the apparent dilettante and no more, the aristocratic dabbler, whom strangers dislike (properly, as a rule). Everything, as in a saint's legend, was seen, *ex post facto*, from a knowledge of the martyr's situation; of which wicked Walpole was inescapably ignorant, after all, and for which he was in no way to blame.

Once arsenic and very real despair had disposed of Chatterton, the English public had before it (as well as the Walpole story) all of Chatterton's Rowley poems, published posthumously in a time avid of the medieval, uncritical about it, inclined to welcome the bogusly ancient; and then, as always, warming to the fascinations of controversy.

Were the poems read? One imagines they were, if in the distorting light of the era and of the new legend — "I thought of Chatterton, the marvellous boy", as Wordsworth said for everyone in that wonder poem "Resolution and Independence". Are they read now? Not much, surely. Should they be read now?

That is to be asked of this bicentenary edition of everything decipherable that Chatterton ever wrote, Rowleian poems, Ossianic prose poems, African eclogues, squibs, album verses, satires, letters, antiquarian cook-ups. His American editor takes him very seriously. He works over Chatterton's pseudo-medieval language, he glossarizes it with new care, he quotes Saintsbury on Chatterton's prosody, he attaches a commentary to each piece and poem, he includes Vivin-like drawings by Chatterton, yet never seems clear about his own activity. Is it poems he is dealing with? Is it problems of the verbal and antique inventiveness and the precocity of the marvellous boy?

He inclines to say "Note the alexandrine", or "The virtuosic prosody of the play deserves comment in some detail"; or "The interlude proceeds in ten-line iambic pentameter stanzas rhymed ababbcbcdd, except that the final couplet is dropped after 1.126 and an extra final couplet is added after 1.246" — which last example wouldn't help much were he commenting on a masterpiece, and not on one of the longer, more tiring bursts of Rowleyism.

In regard to poetic quality, of course there is no merit at all in Chatterton's overlay of invented English. It adds nothing, it often makes the ridiculous more ridiculous: "Whatte dynne ys thys? whatte menes yis leathalle knele" (which reminds me of the sign above a curiosity shop in Bradford, ANNE TEAKES); it ofen serves to conceal the goodness of the few good things. This baby medievalism makes it hard, for instance, to enjoy the "Mynstrelles Songe" in *Ælla;* which may be pastiche (so is the "Belle Dame" of Keats), but must still be considered the best poem he ever made. One sees (but I don't think the editor does) how Chatterton went to work: he wrote the song down in straight English;

> O! sing unto my roundelay,
> O! drop the briny tear with me,
> Dance no more at holiday,
> Like a running river be;
>   My love is dead,
>   Gone to his death-bed
>   All under the willow tree.

Then he tarted it with his doubled consonants, his altered and additional vowels, and so on, till he could lean back and approve, perhaps cynically:

> O! synge untoe mie roundelaie,
> O! droppe the brynie tear wythe mee,
> Daunce ne moe atte hallie daie,
> Lycke a reynynge ryver bee;
>   Mie love ys dedde,
>   Gon to hys death-bedde,
>   Al under the wyllowe tree.

Of course the only thing to do is call Chatterton's bluff and change this Mynstrelle's Songe resolutely back to his Minstrel's Song. Anxiously his new commentator quotes another commentator on a comment by Saintsbury about the "wonderful judgment with which the vowel values adjust themselves" — "But does this help us if we do not know what the vowel values are?" O innocence.

Chatterton was certainly precocious in energetic deter mination, he was like young Tennyson shouting and writing lines of epics which were fortunately lost on the winds of Lincolnshire or in the wastepaper baskets of his father's parsonage; he goes on and on; he senses form and movement, he can imitate or derive or adapt — derive from Spenser or what was to be found, genuine or spurious, in Percy's Reliques; he can, he does interminably, imitate plain eighteenth-centuryism in his satirical couplets. About as near as his editor comes in the direction of criticism is to remark that his models were his markets.

Reading him all through again, I reaffirm to myself that there isn't much in all his work, whether in movement or image, of which one can say, *This* is Chatterton, indisputably. I detect unique Chatterton in an image or two of rivers (he was fascinated — no joke intended — by the Severn Bore), in an occasional brightness of yellow, or yellow cowslips of April, yellow leaves of autumn — "Wet with the dew the yellow Hawthorns bow" — as if he felt the cowslip scenery of the Downs, above Bristol Gorge, which still exists in a tamed way:

> Whanne Autumpne blake and sonne-brente doe appere,
> With his goulde honde guylteynge the falleynge lefe,
> Bryngeyne oppe Wynterr to fulfylle the yere,
> Beerynge uponne hys backe the riped shefe;
> Whan al the hyls wythe woddie sede ys whyte —

Delightful, when spoken, and so stripped of the mock medievalism (the last line suggesting to me an awareness of trees on limestone hills hung with the autumn grey of Old Man's Beard); but it was too early for Chatterton to have sensed much of his world, for whatever ends, or to have individualized his rhythms within a more or less final range — in short to have become himself in his freedom. So *in extenso* he remains about the most tedious poet in the English canon — rather more so, by the way, if we accept the not very strong reasons advanced in this edition, for depriving him of his "Last Verses", the scorning lines which begin

> Farewell, Bristolia's dingy piles of brick,
> Lovers of Mammon, worshippers of Trick!
> Ye spurned the boy who gave you antique lays,
> And paid for learning with your empty praise.
> Farewell, ye guzzling, aldermanic fools,
> By nature fitted for Corruption's tools.

For me, he keeps those Last Verses. But in all his affair with posterity the laugh, I hurry to add, isn't at all on Chatterton, who could have matured into a great poet. The laugh is on the everlasting philistinism which does not care for poetry, but likes a poet to illustrate proverbial sentiments such as genius fulfilled, or poet even in rags, or vision in the dirt, or raffish yet wonderful: the licensed miracles of Bohemia. The condition (serve them right for having talent) is death, as early as possible, but at least before middle age; and as nasty as possible, Keats screaming above the Spanish Steps, Dylan Thomas in a drunken coma in a New York hospital, or Chatterton taking his forlorn, excruciating arsenic. Then the emotions roused can be reflected on to the poems, exaggerating their merit or distorting them, causing them at any rate to be read in a wrong way.

The perhaps ultimate laugh has to fall, when all else has dissipated, on such gross obesity of scholarship, such an over-weight of the solemn and irrelevant as informs and has created this edition of 1265 pages, after two hundred years. I do not quarrel with Wordsworth — Chatterton with his energy and his hawk's eye *was* the marvellous boy; and willing allowance does have to be made for the infections of a romantic, Gothic, and until lately Ossianic milieu. I do not quarrel with Keats, the major Chattertonian (Keats is in some ways what Chatterton might have become), saying over and over to himself the last stanza of what I shall insistently call the Minstrel's Song; I don't know that I quarrel with Wallis, the more or less Pre-Raphaelite painter, for giving us (it was in 1856, Rossetti wasn't over, Swinburne was yet to come) that delightfully improbable portrait of Chatterton — or George Meredith as Chatterton — lying dead in his bright breeches (after which Wallis went off with Mrs Meredith).

But now it really is two hundred years, two hundred years and one, since Chatterton killed himself; time enough — *O! noatte the Halexandryne* — for a final reassertion of good sense. At least matters can be tidied up now with the help of this rather monstrous, unnecessary, bicentenary excess of labour, paper and publishing.

                                                                    1971

Noaks is No Fool

I propose to say some unfriendly things about George Steiner's book[1] because (though it may command respect at this point and that) it's not a companion I should care to go strolling with, arm in arm, through mild October sunshine. It appears on the whole an ingenious piece of opportunism.

Certain other things it isn't, to begin with. Its writer being no fool, his book (though he is less cautious when writing letters on the subject) is not a plain assault on Eliot for the small *j* in jew. A continuum of four lectures in Eliot's memory, it regrets that Eliot wasn't so far-sighted into the future, so deep-sighted into modernity, so well-informed about the sciences, as George Steiner. But it genuflects (indeed it bows and bows in most directions — though more of that in a minute). Also this book — or booklet — is not a critique of literature, except in some unfortunate passages. It is *Some Notes* — "my sub-title is of course intended in memoration of Eliot's *Notes* of 1948" — *Towards the Re-definition of Culture*.

Literature is only a part of culture: in culture, let's say in "the cultural situation", a phrase rather closer to a Steinerism than I care to go, gas-ovens may be found; or the dream of socialism; or the jettisoning of the One God in whom the Utopian dream has its source. Or the problem of the élite and the mass; or the electronic musicalization of the young; or the assertions of McLuhan. Or the vanishing of confidence.

Considering culture, which remains so imperfectly defined when he has finished groaning through its purlieus, George Steiner is certain of one thing: we have lost it, pro tem; perhaps for ever. He does end by allying himself, in an unexpected, I thought slightly ingratiating way, with Nietzsche, with his *Ewiges Ja des Seins,* his Eternal Yes to Existence; we must go on, we are truth-addicts, we must open Bluebeard's last door, whatever is revealed. But he says emphatically, tolling his bell, that we live now in a "post-culture", not powered, not dignified any more by that humane confidence which drove us forward for so long.

He has something there; he is best on this dilemma of lost confidence:

1 *In Bluebeard's Castle* by George Steiner (1971).

Not to have known about the inhuman potentialities of cultured man what we now know was a formidable privilege. In the generations from Voltaire to Arnold, absence of such knowledge was not innocence, but rather an enabling programme for civilization.

But even that short paragraph appears shot with contradiction, assumption, or untruth. Cultured man, fully cultured man, if he could exist, wouldn't have inhuman potentialities. But he can't exist. Beating his bosom about modern imperfection, at times it is as if George Steiner had forgotten the Cain of the scriptures of his own people, arguing that human imperfection is now more imperfect than hitherto. The gas-ovens, the heaps of ash. Of course, we have found out about ourselves, our motivation, our "God" — at any rate his time-servers; we know it is nonsense to propound any more, for instance, the ineluctability of the rich man in his castle and the poor man at his gate (though were Voltaire and Arnold so deficient in that particular knowledge?). So acting "as if", from now on, will hardly do, hardly propel society — or maintain a culture.

When George Steiner moves to assertions about our "post-culture", I smell, all the same, a partiality for horror-stuff, for conceited self-immolation, which insensitizes him to the history of the previous enormities of all times and societies. He picks his evidence from a mass of horror which is, in fact, quantitatively, not relatively, more; owing to the increased numbers of man; owing to man's increased ability to count and classify. I don't know that there is much to choose — each employing what was open to him — between Hitler and a Fulke Nera of the Middle Ages; and if Eliot did spell Jew with a small *j* in his poems, isn't that an improvement, in our ever-lasting imperfectibility, on the record of the poets Spenser or Ralegh in Ireland, or on Ronsard vis-à-vis the Protestants in those filthy wars of religion which soared to the Massacre of St Bartholomew? And on *The Merchant of Venice*? And isn't there surely a perverse, conceited unhistorical pleasure in believing that no time ever was, or ever was felt to be, so rotten, precarious, and doomed as our own?

Of course, you don't — entirely — catch out George Steiner in any risky proposition. He is a very clever man (in which he reminds me of one very clever man in a Cornish town, whose story can wait for a paragraph or two). He is prodigiously informed (a fact his writing parades). If some colleague of his told me that, between anthropology, linguistics and

archaeology, he kept a triple diary in Tupi-Guarani, Old
Friesian, and Tocharian, I would believe it. He is adroit in these
essays; you think, "I've got him," and up he comes with your
own objection. Am I being motivated personally? "I've got
him," and up he comes with your Could I be
exaggerating? Or misinterpreting? But was it ever different? Of
course "there is a good deal of millenarian naîveté and recoil
from adult politics in the current passion for the environment.
Nevertheless". . . . Of course (you are just going to complain
about his line-by-line performance) "never have the meta-
languages of the custodians flourished more, or with more
arrogant jargon". Very deprecatory. But to come up with the
objections isn't to correct the earlier, or subsequent, con-
clusions and suggestions, which are not infrequently ridiculous.

I say ridiculous seriously, finding I have to apply to the
modes of this distinguished polymath, in this piece, my
Cornish story of Mr Noaks, who was also magisterial (a
magistrate, to be sure). Though clever, Noaks did odd things,
he dug a hole in the garden and buried the cat, and called it
"planting the cat". Curious thing for a magistrate to do, but
Noaks was a very clever man. He set two coach wheels
running down the street into a crockery shop. Curious thing
for a magistrate to do, but Noaks is no fool, Noaks is a very
clever man — even if Noaks does dress his servant up like a
Quaker and make him drunk and wheel him through the
streets in a wheelbarrow.

No, I am not impugning the cleverness of Noaks. I only find
it excessively curious — and ridiculous — when he explains
anti-Semitism and concentration camps by saying they are
Western Man's revenge for having had foisted upon him by
Jewry an impossibly hard, monotheistically ordained ideal;
very ridiculous when he writes that "in the pluralistic
simultaneities of a Sadian sexual assault, we have a brilliantly
exact figure of the division of labour on the factory floor";
ridiculous when he groans that "the African masks which
grimace out of post-Cubic art are borrowings of and for
despair". Etcetera.

Ingratiating, and opportunist. The charge embraces many
items, from the words in this book, so arthritically combined,
to all that they deliver. "There is a comprehensive decline in
traditional ideals of literate speech." There is; and in George
Steiner's exceptionally illiterate manipulation it begins in such
phrases as "plea for order", "the note of *Locksley Hall* can be
heard", "Intimations of a sense of distant catastrophe". Of

these are built extended clichés of illustration. He needs in his
argument to mention the French revolutionary time, the
increase and ordering of factory life, the conviction of progress,
the poet vis-à-vis such things. So we get — need you ask? —
bliss was it to be alive, the Satanic mills, the poet as un-
acknowledged legislator, Macaulay on progress, Yeats's
darkening flood on which the swan is now drifting. Such
enlarging units are combined with just the proper references for
now, a little genuflection to Sylvia Plath, a nod to Hugh Mac-
Diarmid, at his most vapid; or to Borges, or Nabokov, or
Canetti, or Ezra P.

True, with this ingratiation are mixed sentences, pages even,
of semi-opaque and barbarous abstraction; different properties,
it must be, of the same hand. Yet on the whole it is the
ingratiatory which prevails. Within a structure of diverse
name-dropping, I detect — no, I don't detect, it is too large to
be missed — an excursus designed to fit both the pro and con
of the talk about Two Cultures; designed to be Snow and
Leavis; designed as well to fit an at present *de rigueur* model of
the catastrophic. I see what sermons Friar Steiner would have
preached to anxious congregations in a packed church hall in
the fifteenth century, before ordering a two-tiered monument
for himself with the exemplary worms and toads of stone on
his underlying cadaver.

That wasn't — quite — the cadaverous image I have been
intending. As I read, it was the Piltdown Skull I thought about.
These four essays are not so elegant a construction as the Skull,
they won't last so well. But they are equally conjured to
respond to a situation, or situations; and to the catch-phrases of
vulgar shorthand by which situations are indicated. The
Piltdown Skull turning up in the Sussex gravel, responded to
the situation which demanded "The Missing Link". *In
Bluebeard's Castle,* turning up in Canterbury, in the University
of Kent, responds to our catch-phrases of the Two Cultures,
and Generations Divided, and Man's Destruction of the World.

As a P.S., if I cannot estimate George Steiner in his mash of
well-trodden Snow and Mathematics, I can fairly estimate him
in his mash of Leavis and Letters and Readers; about which
plenty (beyond his way, his tone, of writing) could be
advanced to show that Noaks, though no fool, is singularly
unattuned to the substances and contrivances of verbal art, in
poems especially. Witness the verbal slop which he makes of
translating his high piece from Nietzsche (no less than the kind
of thing he chose so often for his *Penguin Book of Modern Verse*

Translation a few years ago) or his proof, via *Lycidas,* that most Western literature of the past two thousand years or more "is now passing quickly out of reach". The latter I praise as one of our time's more risible offerings of academic buffoonery.

1971

A Kind of Blankness?

In Scott's *Journal*, republished lately, I came across this about Wordsworth: "Wordsworth has a system which disposes him to take the bull by the horns and offend public taste, which right or wrong will always be the taste of the public, yet he could be popular if he would." And this: "I was glad to see my old friend whose conversation has so much that is fresh and manly in it. I do not at all acquiesce in his system of poetry and I think he has injured his own fame by adhering to it."

In looking through a book of drawings I came on one by Rowlandson of a timid author with thin shanks standing by a supercilious publisher with a big belly on fat legs: his sales were evidently low. In a new book on Giovanni Verga, I find Verga writing in a letter that "we have to stay in this *via crucis* of ours beset with vexations and publishers"; and in another letter about the failure of *I Malavoglia* — "a total and complete fiasco" — that even his publishers said outright it was bad, that people avoided him as if he had committed a sin, and he would write his book all over again in exactly the same way, and that he needed all the strength of his convictions "to refrain from writing those silly niceties which please the public — and to laugh behind their backs afterwards".

So I ask myself, looking round, what is the nature of a public? For ourselves, as for successful Scott? And for more or less unsuccessful Wordsworth, and, elsewhere, more or less unsuccessful Giovanni Verga? I ask myself if that dead and good man Sir Walter Scott, who flashed a proper independence now and then inside his doggy dependence, didn't express in those few comments about Wordsworth an English situation which isn't constant, but does certainly repeat itself?

"He could be popular if he would." "He has injured his own fame." Wiggle your tail, Wordsworth, for the public biscuit. Worry about your fame. Alter yourself, my manly friend. It is as much as to say — it is always being said, it is, in 1972, as ever, the insistence of literary journalism — that the public to please is the immediate one.

This thoroughly amiable, voluminous scribbler from the Lowlands would like no one to avoid *him* as if his latest romance had been the commission of a sin. He isn't cynical, but a timeless public does not interest him. He conforms. And the kernel of the immediate public he conforms to is, more narrowly, that self-regarding club of those "in power". Scott is parroting and sharing a club reaction to contrary Wordsworth; he is saying to himself — himself the natural amateur and out-sider — that the professional should acquiesce (which, alas, Wordsworth, the grand professional, the grand insider, had already done in his Waterloo Odes and would do again when — let some present consciences be in ferment — he sealed his concluding self as Poet Laureate, and Lost Leader).

I read that F. R. Leavis talks of the literary present, in his new book, as a kind of "blankness": which mayn't be untrue. It seems a period like the "owl light" of the 1840s, of which Beddoes complained; the slack after-war dimness in which Mrs Hemans and L. E. L. were approved reading. But in this, as always, what we require isn't "leaders", unlost: or Leavises. In the wide society, also in the restricted society of letters, the lucky thing is to have enough mature or maturing authors whose loyalty, let these authors be various as they may, is evidently and always to the best; and whose reputation and influence are such as to compel that powerful club, which can't be eradicated, to something of an identical sense of worth.

It is that unhomogeneous body of principled writers, aware of the past as of the present, that we don't have. We had it for a while some forty years ago. A diversity of intellectual passion (the effective remembered discrimination of James; then Yeats, Joyce, Russell, Lewis, Eliot, Forster, Graves, Auden) afforded more referents than are now compellingly available.

Let me suggest a few consequences, some of them not important, though not unrepresentative.

If there were such writers the weak would be less soured and narrowed by the commination and pulpitry of Leavis.

If there were such writers, we should be in no doubt about the vital irrelevance of, e.g., the good Lord Snow.

If there were such writers (of course the ones I have mentioned still *are*; we still have their writings; two of them are still about; I am emphasizing what the active force would be of such a miscellaneous presence), then the amateur could less easily strut as the professional, the journalist would be less cocky about what he thinks is his own judgment.

If there were such writers, academics and art officials (the Arts Council, the BBC, etc.) also would, or could, be less bullying, less fly-witted, less obedient to vulgar notions of what is both earnest and energetic in new writing.

If there were such writers, it might be possible that a Royal Society of Literature would have for its president and chairman authors of somewhat more achievement than the good Lords

Butler and Birkenhead (that still egregious society, I see, was too much even for Sir Walter — "I do not belong to the Society . . . I don't like your Royal Academies of this kind; they almost all fall into jobs and the Members are seldom those who do credit to the literature of a country"); and it might be that a newspaper, *The Times*, wouldn't confuse the wider society, in its literary values, by allotting three close columns of obituary and fulsomeness to a Maurice Bowra where (but that was years ago) it disposed of the red beard and reputation and living works of awkward D. H. Lawrence in a quarter of a column.

If there were such writers, we might in England be at least checked in our Late Athenian vice of whoring after the new long before yesterday's new is old, cold, or absorbed; we might act more, or discern more, by a proper contemporaneity of the past in our literature; we might be able to depose criticism from its now absurd theological dominance.

In short, were there such writers — enough of them, loosely associated — then the proper writers might be acknowledged to be in charge of their own art.

That would be a change. We might also be released then, I forgot to say, from a plague of little magazines related only to the self-regard of their editors, and from a prodigious plague of idle incompetent poets, off our own muckheaps, and imported; of all sizes, in every milieu from St Ives to the Cotswolds or the Poetry Society, or the public poetry reading, or the English departments of the new universities.

That example of Scott, best of men in so many ways, but not of writers, may warn us, also, against a constant insidiousness. Intelligent, friendly, half-interested, yes: he even knew where his limits ran (as in his confession about Jane Austen and her talent for "the involvements and feelings and characters of ordinary life" — "The Big Bow Wow strain I can do myself like any now going but the exquisite touch which renders ordinary commonplace things and characters interesting from the truth of the description and the sentiment is denied to me"). Turn to him on Wordsworth — his friend, he insists, the poet who asks for the exercise of sensibility and intellect and just a little trouble; or turn to him on an evening with Coleridge: he fails in witness; even when alone, in his journal.

English literary association — all literary association? — is full of these genial fellows. They face every way. They don't undress in private (read, in Harold Nicolson's diary, the entries on a meal with Joyce, and a meal with André Gide). But you cannot abolish them. That is the Leavisite morality, and fallacy, and naïveté — that they wouldn't be here, if only our condition could be one of health.

You can inoculate yourself against them, that is all, by an unremitting committal to as many kinds and constituents as possible of the best. Publicly, too; in whatever writing ways your living has to be earned.

I conclude that in our recent decades, a bad moment for ourselves was when Auden left for the United States. It does seem from a distance that over there he has been the nucleus for an honesty, intelligence and subtlety which have enabled one not necessarily remarkable talent to help another. Whereas in England, in my writing time, unaffined talents have often hindered each other. They have been too easily shouldered out. They have fraternized with the genial fellows (this is sometimes called mellowing). The result — weakness, fragmentation, isolation, disagreement, confusion, lack of nerve and the whole insolence of a literary underworld.

★   ★   ★

The Mob: thank you, sane Alexander Pope, for that summarizing word, though now it isn't only gents who write with the intolerable fecundity of Ease. Our mob includes:

That Mob of University Persons who intrude into Writing.

That Mob of University Poets who write with Aridity.

That Mob of University Critics who judge with Superiority.

That Mob of University Editors who include with Folly; and exclude with Folly.

That Mob of Lowlanders who write in Lallans.

That Mob of Welshmen who write in Welsh so that (next to) no one in or out of Wales can estimate what they write.

That Mob of Scotch Editors who edit Scotch anthologies in which an English, Irish or Welsh poet becomes Scotch because of his Grandmother.

That Mob of Englishmen who vulgarly shorten their given names and read Themselves in public.

That Mob of Poets who teach Creative Writing.

That Mob of Writers-in-Residence.

Etcetera.

1972

Kuchuk's Bed-Bugs

How much of Flaubert, the fiction apart, is to be had in translation? I don't think the answer would be a credit to us, or to our publishing. Snippets, selections — well, we must be thankful for snippets, even if Flaubert's letters cannot work on us in full, and thankful for Francis Steegmuller — however long is it since he first published his *Flaubert and Madame Bovary?* — as devoted snippeteer-in-chief.

Flaubert in Egypt: A Sensibility on Tour.[1] Yes, in a way book-making, snippets sewn together from letters and travel notes of the twenty-eight-year-old Flaubert, with some embroidery snipped from the recollections and letters of his companion, Maxime du Camp. But listen: "Bird shit is nature's protest in Egypt: she decorates monuments with it instead of with lichen or moss." Flaubert, everywhere at home, is no tourist. Flaubert swims in the Red Sea: "It was one of the most voluptuous pleasures of my life; I lolled in its waters as though I were lying on a thousand liquid breasts that were caressing my entire body." Flaubert is Flaubert, not someone else afloat on accepted observations.

With a slight amazement, but no exclamation marks, with an eye ruthless or neutral, or at least steady, Flaubert contemplates peculiarity, perversion, corruption. "Tiger-striped hoopoes with long beaks peck at the worms in the various corpses," which are those of camels, horses and donkeys, not humans — whom Flaubert prefers alive. "An English family, ludicrous, the mother looks like a sick old parrot (because of the green eyeshade attached to her bonnet)." No one is likely to forget the bronze hardness of the whore Kuchuk Hanem — or her bed-bugs. "You tell me" — this from a letter to his former mistress Louise Colet — "that Kuchuk's bed-bugs degrade her in your eyes: for me they were the most enchanting touch of all. Their nauseating odour mingled with the scent of her skin, which was dripping with sandalwood oil. I want a touch of bitterness in everything — always a jeer in the midst of our triumphs, desolation even in the midst of enthusiasim." No one will forget the holy man who walked about "completely naked except for a cap on his head and another on his prick. To piss he would doff the prick-cap, and sterile women who wanted children would run up and put themselves under the parabola of his urine."

1 *Flaubert in Egypt* translated and edited by Francis Steegmuller (1972).

Several things emerge. One is Flaubert's boredom, which contrasts with the shallowness of the busy Maxime du Camp, for ever setting up his camera and photographing Abu Simbel or the Sphinx. Flaubert complains to his notebook: "This permanent lassitude that I drag about with me." But then boredom, at that age, can contradictorily be a kind of medium in which impressions are achieved, nourished and fixed. The embroidery bits out of Maxime du Camp are as unelectric as can be. As Flaubert said afterwards, when Du Camp began serializing his Egyptian recollections, the trouble was less a style "flat beyond words", than a total insignificance, "nothing in the way of meat, nothing really observed". Flaubert observed all dimensions of what attracted him with all senses; he was nearer to the truth of himself when he wrote to his mother: "I live like a plant, filling myself with sun and light, with colours and fresh air. I keep eating, so to speak; afterwards the digesting will have to be done, then the shitting, and the shit had better be good. That's the important thing."

No, an English author, in or after 1850, never did, never could, write like that. If the senses weren't closed (though perhaps they were for the appropriate seconds), the words were not able to come and could not be set down — even, as a rule, in private. English authors could manage the glowing Nile — Lear, for instance, in "The Pelican Chorus", as well as in purple watercolours:

Where the purple river rolls fast and dim
And the Ivory Ibis starlike skim.

So could Flaubert — "At six in the evening a sunset that made the sky look like melted vermilion and the sand of the desert like ink" — but those bed-bugs demanded an entry which in England they could have effected only in some sanitary report by Edwin Chadwick. For the English situation one remembers Henry James (for all his reticence, which isn't quite the same thing, or the same drawback) discussing in George Eliot's nature "the absence of free aesthetic life" and the extent by which the abstract preceded the perceived; and in Flaubert's art and nature the opposite, so that *Madame Bovary* was "adapted for the reverse of what is called family reading". If the members of the family hadn't changed, we should not have Mr Steegmuller's Flaubert in Cairo and along the Nile.

A Bottle of Brandy in Spitzbergen

How is Coleridge now received?[1] In a book about him or derived from him, of the kind which stifles me because it exalts Coleridge as the Christian exegete, and so reduces him as a poet, Basil Willey quotes him on the "truths" of religion — that they are (or were in his time) so impressed on people in childhood that they grew up taking them for granted. We grow up taking Coleridge for granted. We read *Kubla Khan* (which he published only with reluctance as a "psychological curiosity", but that is Coleridge's business, not ours), we read *The Ancient Mariner*, we embrace scraps and images; and then look round in him, dismayed, since we don't encounter it, for more of the same kind.

In the end we take to *Dejection*, we learn of Coleridge holding Sara Hutchinson's hand by the Buttermere waterfall (perhaps recalling that entry in his early notebook "Mem — not to adulterize my time by absenting myself from my wife" — that tedious querulous wife he had been so ill-advised as to marry); and we too regret his loss of the shaping spirit of imagination —

> O Lady! we receive but what we give
> And in our life alone does Nature live.

All the while — it can't and it shouldn't be evaded — we do accept him as half of the dichotomous poetical term *Coleridge-Wordsworth*, discovering the exact truth of all Coleridge wrote in exaltation of Wordsworth and his poems. Taking to Wordsworth, we may think of drudging through those abominable double columns of Coleridge's green-jacketed *Poetical Works*, mentally straightening all those turned-over lines, and never finding — on the outside of the familiar enclosure of the few splendid pieces — any lyrics which can match "Among all lovely things my love had been" or

> when against the wind she strains
> Oh! might I kiss the mountain rains
> That sparkle on her cheek.

— lyrics in which the love in Coleridge might have been able to detach itself (from thought?), and exclaim in such a free ecstasy.

1   *Samuel Taylor Coleridge* by Basil Willey (1972).

With regret, since our first excitement from poetry so much comes out of *Kubla Khan*, our first sense of the precariousness of the wonderful is also impressed on us by the person from Porlock; and it is the worse if we come on Wordsworth saying about Coleridge that if his

> energy and his originality had been more exerted in the channel of poetry, an instrument of which he had so perfect a mastery . . . he might have done more permanently to enrich literature, and to influence the thought of the nation, than any man of his age.

Might have done, might have been: they do remain epitaphs above the man's exceptional genius.

The last two volumes of Earl Grigg's great edition of his letters[1] are evidence of that — unless you accept all of the now fashionable justification for Coleridge which has produced Basil Willey's book. Here is Coleridge in the ultimate of his life cocooned in Highgate. His childen, and Sara Hutchinson, as they long had been, are elsewhere. Wordsworth and Dorothy — or what was left of them — are far away in the north. Only one of the 1,819 letters is to Wordsworth. Few are to poets, or concerned *in extenso* with poetry or the imaginative process. Few are to correspondents intellectually or emotionally up to him; ailments apart, he is obsessed with his metaphysics, one's response to which depends on whether one continues to see the Christian faith as "the perfection of human intelligence", and whether one continues to feel that the metaphysical is the one possible foundation of the imaginative act.

In 1800 — Basil Willey quotes this — Coleridge had written that while Wordsworth was "a great, or true poet", he was "only a kind of Metaphysician". He was constant. Analysing himself in one of the new letters, he claims that constancy, or continuity — "the Love, almost the Passion, for the Permanent: and the tranquil Complacency in Beauty, as distinguished from the Interesting, the Agreeable, the Delicious" — is the characteristic quality and property of his being (whereas his original sin is "Excess of *Power* with Deficiency of *Strength*"). Basil Willey again (he admits that the metaphysician rose as the poet diminished) quotes Coleridge at twenty-four in a P.S. to revolutionary Thelwall, "We have a hundred lovely scenes about Bristol, which would make you

1 *Collected Letters of Samuel Taylor Coleridge* edited by Earl Leslie Griggs, vols V and VI (1972).

exclaim O admirable *Nature*! and me, O Gracious God."

The Highgate Coleridge, anxious, yet without hope of doing so, to complete that "System of Truths respecting Nature, Man and Deity, evolved from one Principle", can say lightly that:

> in this bleak World of Mutabilities, and where what is not changed is chilled, and in this winter-time of my own Being, I resemble a Bottle of Brandy in Spitzbergen — a Dram of alcoholic Fire in the centre of a Cake of Ice.

But he admits to himself that in "life unendeared" he cannot write poems.

Is it fair to harp on his loss of shaping power, on what might have been, in one shape or another? In a way, no; Coleridge, as we can see now from the progressive, appallingly belated publication of all his works, having created, understood, and stated so much. A little sharply he reports an observation by his brother-in-law Southey; Southey claimed to hunt by eye; Southey saw his object, he dashed for it straight, whereas Coleridge hunted with his nose to the earth, tracked his hare or fox through every zigzag, catching only the scent, never the object. "It is a mistake," added Coleridge,

> to suppose, that the *end* is in all cases higher than the *means*: or that the *means* always derive their whole, or even their chief, value from the *end*.

By Coleridge we are given means in prodigious quantity and quality. As poet I suppose he must remain the properest poet of the young, in the few necessary poems. Perhaps Earl Griggs would admit that. I remember him beginning work on the letters, living in a single room in a smelly row opposite Carrera's Egyptian factory, himself young and penetrated by the *Kubla Khan* wonderfulness (it was the time of Livingstone Lowe's *Road to Xanadu*). Whatever else he has since recognized in the vast *terra incognita* (as it then was, considerably) of S.T.C., I imagine it is that wonderfulness which has driven him through forty years of editorial slogging.

As for "means", nose to the ground, so much combines to make Coleridge that exemplar of the species which he continues to be, after all, for the English or the Americans in their *Legenda Aurea* of verse — Coleridge remarking the concentric circles of light a rising trout causes on a river-bed, Coleridge affined to the Evening Star, Coleridge making life as "continuous as possible, by linking on the Present to the Past",

Coleridge exclaiming: "What a beautiful thing is Urine, in a pot, brown yellow, transpicuous, the image diamond shaped of the candle in it"; Coleridge the intelligent, psychologizing, criticizing ("I know myself so far a poet as to feel assured that I can understand and interpret a poem in the spirit of poetry and with the poet's spirit").

Meanwhile, out of these last of the six volumes of correspondence, two notes for ourselves, and for all who imagine a former (or a present) genuine gusto for poetry, and all who fancy they are in rapport with the contemporary best. The £50 offered him in his last decade for two poems was more profit, Coleridge says, than *all* of his publications had made him; and it was his conviction that good poetry is never popular, is never "honoured with the praise and favour of contemporaries", except in the sense of amusing "without requiring any effort of thought, and without exciting any deep emotion".

1972

A Hole Worlde of Thinges Very Memorable: The Writer and His Territory

I wouldn't be dogmatic on the advantages a writing man may or must derive, now, from a consciousness of his own territory, or a territory he adopts for a while. We have at least to be born somewhere, we become aware of the facts of a surrounding world, as we grow up, aware, in high degree, of some particular locality, the Puisaye for Colette, the Orenburg country for Aksakov, for Whitman the Long Island of herds, waves, gulls' eggs and men who fished for green-backed spotted mossbonkers, for Eliot his native city of St Louis, raw-edged by the dirty flow of the Missouri, for Auden the Long Mynd, for Langland the Malverns, and so on.

Place obviously matters to a writer as long as he does not stay there exclusively, I mean as long as in his writing he is there and elsewhere. Regionalism is something else: it is a vehicle of sentimentality in which the incompetents choose to travel, or a debasement thrust on writers by readers or promoters. In England it has always been fascinating to watch the pinning of Hardy into a region. "Wessex" was Hardy's own fault, he did draw the map. However he gets free, although sentimentalists peg it round him like a net. A "regional" novelist strictly, a "regional" poet, of "local interest", is a novelist or poet of no importance and no interest, fit only for subsidy by the Arts Council (who ever thought of a philosopher of "local interest"? As if Hobbes were of interest only to the people of North Wiltshire, or to August visitors to Malmesbury?).

The question is whether his special locality is inside or outside the writer; and even in that greater context it may be asked if a literature about place, literature of any real kind in which place predominates, is any more possible? I doubt if it is, except within limits which I shall indicate. But to restrict the problem in that way, to inquire, Can a book about place, other than some late issue out of Guidebook by Essay, be contrived any longer in such a way as to raise the individual, the local, the regional, towards the universal?, may illuminate modern writing.

One may think together of landscape and this literature of place (which may be verse, fiction or topography). The two

have risen together, not *pari passu*, and with the differences
proper to different arts, one the youngish parent — or god-
parent — of the other. Literature of place, prompted first of all
by the vision outwards of Northern, especially Flemish
painting, has expressed discovery. The first discovery was,
simply, that place or region existed. Once that was clear,
individual discovery of place was possible to each new
individual consciousness. From Leland, let's say, to a climax in
Henry James, place could be expressed, and with increasing
subtlety be made expressive. The English and Welsh journeys
of John Leland were undertaken for Henry VIII from about
1539 to 1543, resulting in *The Itinerary*, in a book, at any rate a
long scatter of notes and observations, which, ordinary and
bare as they may seem to us, stated the diversely existing
things of England and Wales:

> there is almoste nother cape, nor bay, haven, creke or peere,
> river or confluence of rivers, breches, waschis, lakes, meres,
> fenny waters, montagnes, valleis, mores, hethes, forestes,
> wooddes, cities, burges, castelles, principale manor placis,
> monasteries, and colleges, but I have seene them; and notid
> yn so doing a hole worlde of thinges very memorable.

"A hole worlde of thinges" — it is prototopography by a
first English topographer or topographical writer (for "topography" and "topographer" as naturalized words the first dates
in the *OED* are for the one 1549, for the other 1603. The date
in French for *topographie* is 1544; for *topographe* 1580, in
Montaigne, from whom Florio translated it as "topographer").
Poet in Latin, friend and encomiast of Sir Thomas Wyatt, and a
man of educated peculiarity, true it certainly is that Leland was
unable to command a prose adequate to the particulars of his
"hole worlde". Nobody has thought of his notes as literature,
ancestral to the books of place, to Thoreau's *Walden*, it may be,
or William Morris's Icelandic journals; but he responds, he
states a vision now and then. For a sample try Leland coming
to Bewdley, a place in 1972 miserable, pressurized and shabby
enough. Leland crosses over the bridge from the eastern bank
of the Severn, about sunrise. He observes a town "set on the
syd of an hill so coningly that a man cannot wishe to set a
towne better", and he goes on that Bewdley

> risethe from Severne banke by est upon the hill by west; so
> that a man standinge on the hill *trans pontem* by est may

descrive almost every howse in the towne, and at the rysynge of the sunne from este the hole towne gliterithe, being all of new buyldinge, as it wer of gold.

It is a beginning; and in the half century or century after Leland the shire surveyors exhibit the young consciousness of surroundings in something more of an expressive way. Richard Carew (another poet friendly, at least as an undergraduate, with better poets, and a man of subtle education and strong local affection) exhibits Richard Carew, if without intending to, in his *Survey of Cornwall*. The *Survey* — he was already working on it by 1584 — endures as more than of local interest by its fixation and creation of place in a baroque activity of style. We remember his delight in tidal water flowing into the country between hills and ebbing again into the sea, and in the union of the two streams, the salt and the fresh:

> The salt water leaving Padstow floweth up into the country that it may embrace the river Camel, and having performed this natural courtesy, ebbeth away again to yield him the freer passage, by which means they both undergo Wade bridge, the longest, strongest and fairest that the shire can muster.

Headlands "shoulder" out of the sea, a fishing hamlet "couches" between hills. In passing along Hall Walk, above Fowey harbour,

> your eyes shall be called away from guiding your feet, to descry by their farthest kenning the vast ocean sparkled with ships that continually this way trade forth and back to most quarters of the world. Nearer home, they take view of all sized cocks, barges, and fisherboats, hovering on the coast.

Between Carew and Henry James, the James of Dunwich — "almost all you can say of it is that it consists of the mere letters of its old name. The coast, up and down, for miles, has been, for more centuries than I presume to count, gnawed away by the sea. All the grossness of its positive life is now at the bottom of the German Ocean, which moves for ever, like a ruminating beast, an insatiable, indefatigable lip"; James of Newmarket — "Nature offers her gentle bosom as a gaming table; card-tables, billiard-tables are but a humble imitation of Newmarket Heath"; the James of Lavender Hill, Battersea, "so many rows of coal-scuttles", of all London in the sound that is "supremely dear to the consistent London-lover — the rumble of the tremendous human will"; — between the *Survey of Cornwall* and *English Hours, Portraits of Places, A Little Tour in*

France and *The American Scene,* milieu offered stylistic possibilities of stated contrast and actual discovery, whether far off or round the corner. The few quotations above show the Carew of the 1580s and 1590s and the James of the 1870s and 1880s as belonging — in regard to place at least — to one family of writers, with the difference that Carew's pictures are intermittent in his broad context of information and Henry James's, in his sketches of place, are extended, amounting to a developed verbal landscape, at a time when painted landscape was approaching its demise.

Contemporary with Monet, Sisley, Whistler, Renoir, Henry James spoke modestly and deprecatingly of his own impressionism: his pieces are "altogether governed by the pictorial spirit"; they are "impressions, immediate, easy, and consciously limited"; but still like Carew (or Leland even) he discovers, as a rule: his pages "represent a stage of observation on the writer's part which belongs to freshness of acquaintance".

For James, Europe was a perpetual discovery outside America; Stonehenge or Dunwich was a discovery outside London, engagingly alien to drawing-rooms or Chelsea or the Reform Club; for James himself we feel it was surprising to be in Monmouthshire climbing Skirrid Fach and commenting (like Donne not so far away at Montgomery Castle) on the size and quality of the primroses, just as for the reader of his *English Hours* it is surprising and engaging to discover the Master on the crawl, "very much in the attitude of Nebuchadnezzar", up a rough hill at the extreme of England, on the confines of Celtic barbarity.

But the conditions of a literature of place are exactly satisfied in his travel books. He discovers what he himself does not know, and what, he assumes, will come more or less fresh, or unobliterated by familiarity, to his reader. Outside society exists another society; outside the soiled exists the fresh; outside the complex the more or less simple; outside the existence of now, the seeming presence of then, or of the timeless. For Dorothy Wordsworth — to recall more writers of place — outside the small talk of sociability exists the Quantock copse of hollies, and hail pattering on the dry leaves, or the lakeland circumstances around a single foxglove; for Cobbett, in his *Rural Rides,* outside detested London exists the sudden hanger of the Selborne neighbourhood or the smoothness of an extent of down; for the happy egotism of Kilvert in his *Journal,* the other thing which matters may be the blue shoulder of Radnorshire mountain along with dog roses; for that sophisticated, neglected writer Cecil Torr human comedy and oddity coexist with the shapes and items of the setting around his small manor-house under Dartmoor.

Discovery must recur with each new consciousness. Even then the extended possibilities of place and contrast as a medium, actual or marginal (one need not assent to that deprecation of himself by Henry James, who is inescapably "in" his pictures or impressions, and who did say that the "perception of surface" was "a perception, when fine, perhaps none of the most frequent"), have narrowed greatly, if they are not by now exhausted. For many reasons. A mode is over-popularized and cheapened, and talent recoils from it. What was expressive of writer and milieu weakened long ago to a lax exercise of sensitivity. For instance years and years ago, volumes of such slackness at a low level made up the *Highways and Byeways* volumes of county exploration. I remember when young trying one after another of those books (which might have illustrations in line — superior to the prose — in a late landscape manner by F. L. Griggs or a more impressionist manner by Joseph Pennell, whose drawings were added also to James's *Little Tour in France* and his *English Hours*), and being unable to accept their flow of mild and vague response. No pause, no striking sentence, no phrases bringing fact into the open (such as James's observation up and down the now vanished quays of Nantes of "the bright greyness which is the tone of French landscape art"); also no exactitude of other than conventional and stale information, only a replaying of old cards from earlier books.

One could see the respectable, well-thought-of Macmillan men of letters snapshotting with their not very finely perceptive eyes, and turning up a Kelly's Directory or a Murry's Handbook, or picking and watering down engaging trifles from a county history in many volumes, or from Pepys — especially from Pepys.

To some degree the enlargement and popularization of other disciplines have weakened that kind of writing about place. More importantly a diminution of contrast, as between James's park-embowered world. You may recall a number of the *Architectural Review* which illustrated the same graceless renovation and change stretching, as I remember it, from Bournemouth to Carlisle. The kerbs and pavements of planning officers' suburbanization spread through the dominions of every rural district council, we live more and more without available contrast in a homogeneity either urban or suburban. Like stair carpets, paths in the Lake District *wear out*, as if they were on Hampstead Heath.

Should the litterateur of, or through, place extend his investigation and interpret more of the elsewhere? Give us Mexico or Ethiopian uplands via himself, and himself via the outlandish? He has tried: but even if the arts had not shifted towards abstraction, the place-book, or the place-touches of a novel, for example, would still impart best — except for imparting the writer — the unfamiliarities, not exactly of the familiar, but at least of the neighbouring — that which is not too much outside our keepings, that which we half know, or have seen or can see ourselves if we take the trouble.

James, it is true, liked to read of places he would never see. When an author — he was speaking of Pierre Loti, writing about the East and Morocco and writing his stories — provided him with "the happiest conceivable utterance of feelings about aspects", he never wanted to spoil those impressions by a visit. But we go everywhere, we exhaust the terrain, familiar or far. And already, in 1888, in another essay on his admired Pierre Loti than the one I have just referred to, James himself was asking "how long and how far accomplished and exclusive — practically exclusive — impressionism will yet go, with its vulture on its back and feeding on it".

Writer and painter are open to the same influences, but it is reasonable to suppose that written landscape will continue, however diminished, to outlast painted or drawn landscape. What the painter senses of his milieu is the material of an abstraction to the artist who uses words and language. So what I would expect is not the disappearance of a literature of place, but its more effective restriction to discontinuous forms. I expect more such writing of person and place as Henri Michaux's *Ecuador* (English translation 1970), the use, it is true, of the unfamiliar by someone who is both painter and poet, who changes in his brief book from prose to verse, and back again. Or I imagine something like notebook adaptations of the *nikki* of the Japanese poet, the travel-diary of linked poetry and prose (of which an example easily come by is Bashō's *Narrow Road to Oku,* translated in a Penguin of 1966 by Nobuyuki Yuasa, and by Donald Keene in 1956 in his *Anthology of Japanese Literature*).

1972

Poets who Kill Themselves:
The Extremists of Al Alvarez

I cannot find much in *The Savage God*[1] which makes it worth prolonged consideration. Mr Alvarez states that he has written a "study of suicide". His publishers state that he has tried to discover why people commit suicide. But I detect — and for this I do not require to be much of a Maigret — two authors in the same Alvarez, as here exhibited; and two books. They are not easily separable. One Alvarez ("who was educated at Oundle School, and Corpus Christi College, Oxford, where he obtained a first-class degree in English") has exploratory concerns or prime interests of a literary-sociological kind which centre upon a quartet of contemporary poets, and a postulated style he calls Extremism, shaped by the internal features of the present casting-mould, the present "situation". His poets, "the four leading English-language exponents of the style", are, as we know perhaps too well, the three Americans Robert Lowell, John Berryman and Sylvia Plath, and Sylvia Plath's husband and relict, Ted Hughes.

The other Alvarez is the bookman, the promoter and journalizer of his interests or concerns; and if a book is to be made — the journalist or journalizer taking over — it is likely that more readers will be attracted by the "situation" than by a close consideration of the favoured poets or their poems; and still more, if the "situation" can be subsumed and proffered in one of its morbidly fascinating elements.

The lead therefore is given to suicide. But conveniently one of the favoured poets can share the lead, since she obligingly wrote about suicide, and even more obligingly committed it; and since her story has become the object of a cult ("Anything by or about Sylvia Plath goes down well on these heights" — report from Hampstead in *The Bookseller*, 25 December 1971, on "Christmas in the Bookshops"). Mr Alvarez, who has so pushed and so over-valued the poems of Sylvia Plath, can say in his prologue that they are now classics, that he and none other introduced them to a Sunday paper, that he himself knew the poet, in life; and in death, on the kitchen floor — "The builders forced the lock and found Sylvia sprawled in the kitchen. She was still warm" — and in her coffin "She lay

1 *The Savage God. A Study of Suicide* by A. Alvarez (1971).

stiffly, a ludicrous ruff at her neck. Only her face showed. It was grey and slightly transparent, like wax" (all of which would have been in the Sunday paper as well, had the poet's husband not protested).

The book, accordingly, begins by mixing sensationalism and concern, which it continues to do in other respects, until the reader requires a separator to divide the two, or to divide Alvarez from Alvarez. He may remember, as he turns the handle, after adjusting the disparate buckets or the bowl and the bucket, that this critic has written of his indifference to the palpability around him; and if he should have looked ahead from the prologue to the epilogue, the reader may also be remembering that Mr Alvarez confesses himself to be "a failed suicide", a fact which gives him a special personal investment, we may suppose, in his notions of external and internal violence, and Extremism.

His notions? When the last fluid ounce has passed through the machine, much of the rather small bowl of resultant cream will be found to be tinned rather than fresh, after all; to be an altered and I would say debased borrowing from Camus on the Absurd and death and suicide, and man in revolt, and creating dangerously.

Here then is the scheme of the book. First, in that prologue, Sylvia Plath, who must be shown to have been less a pathological suicide than a bold explorer of the purlieus of death into which she was tempted, always in ultimate control, always taking an explorer's risk which at last (in that London house where Yeats had once lived) proved to be too great — Sylvia Plath sensationalized beyond the business either of his readers or Mr Alvarez. Then filling the greater part of *The Savage God*, a survey of conceptions and misconceptions of suicide and of the ways in which suicide has impressed itself on the thought and feeling and judgement of writers from Dante onwards (these are surveys of an averagely acute but secondary amateurism such as one might find in the lighter pages of *New Society*); finally, an exposition in more detail of the Extremism of Mr Alvarez, which is the controlled exploration, through art, of "the nihilism and destructiveness of the self", reflecting accurately "the nihilism of our own violent societies". The "best modern artists" survive, if they avoid killing themselves, as "suicides of the imagination: they are scapegoats on our behalf", each "finds himself in testing out his own death and vulnerability"; and the modern art "forces its audience to recognize and accept, in their nerve-ends, not the facts of life but the facts of death and violence; absurd, random, gratuitous, unjustified and inescapably part of the society we have created."

"Not the facts of life": Mr Alvarez signs off (though still to come is his little ingratiating epilogue on how he failed to manage his own suicide) by quoting Camus in his remark "There is only one liberty, to come to terms with death. After which, everything is possible." This is neat. It will be remembered, however, that Camus, who rejected suicide (and murder), declared, "But the point is to live", in our situation of the Absurd. Camus didn't stop with the nihilism or with the liberty, he went on to what the liberty makes possible and essential. For example, "Happiness and the absurd are the two sons of the same earth. They are inseparable." Or, "We must simultaneously serve suffering and beauty."

In the heartening light of Camus, of *L'Homme Revolté* and *Le Mythe de Sisyphe,* this journalizing author of *The Savage God* seems to me to be indulging in the violence and the chaos: he offers a bucket mainly of skim-milk which is black and poisonous — and no wonder, with the obscene carrion-crow of the fancy of Ted Hughes perched on the rim. From the first page the writing accords; it is vulgar and execrable, half assertive, half ingratiating, if fluent. "We sat out in the big wild garden while little Frieda, now aged two, teetered among the flowers". The writing proceeds by flaccid cliché, by the language of the blind and deaf who cannot be affected by our surrounding reality; an assortment of "worlds apart", "genius", "sheer ability", "success story", "genuine article", etcetera, which makes one call Camus back once more, asking "If we are not artists in our language first of all, what kind of artists are we?", and which deprives such estimations as it may deliver of authority or plausibility. In any case I distrust a critic who analyses a *zeitgeist* more eagerly than he attends to a line or a cadence; whose statements are too often careless (for example, Modigliani did not kill himself, Cowper did not die in an asylum); who is so uninventive that he cannot invent his own titles (the title of this book is purloined from Yeats, the title of the last book by Mr Alvarez was purloined from Marianne Moore, the title of his first book from Coleridge); and who is led by the carrot of his own theory to enthuse over art where art does not noticeably exist.

1971

Glances Eastward

I. THE CHINESE SHAKESPEARE

Who is Tu Fu? You have five seconds to answer . . . and if you
say "I don't know," you have the entirely reasonable excuse
that we have never been given all that chance to learn about Tu
Fu. Try an encyclopaedia. Probably it will say that he was the
greatest of China's poets, the great master — but this will not
be so very illuminating — of the eighth century AD of
splendour and death, of empire and disaster and the rebellion of
An Lu-shan. Then it will mention Li Po, his friend; and we
shall be in the picture.

We know about Li Po, we know his mother called him
Evening Star because she had dreamt, while she was carrying
him, that the Evening Star had fallen into her lap. We know
how Li Po was drowned — he was drunk in a boat and the
beauty of the moon's image on the water overcame him so
much that he tried to embrace it and fell in. We know poems
by Li Po in translation. But when we look for China's
Shakespeare, China's Dante or Victor Hugo or Goethe in our
rather haphazard, lopsided anthologies of Chinese verse, he is
not there as a rule; and we are usually told he does not
translate.

David Hawkes, Oxford's professor of Chinese, says the
same at the beginning of his *Little Primer of Tu Fu:*[1] "His poems
do not as a rule come through very well in translation". I
wonder. Knowing no Chinese, classical or modern Mandarin, I
have the nerve to wonder for one very good reason: whenever
I do come across a translation from Tu Fu, I get the strongest
feeling of his grand mastery and his individuality, of poetry in
which life — life, not Chinese life twelve hundred years ago —
is realized, through landscape or nature or situation, in an
ageless way which seems particularly in tune with our English
or European feelings; and didn't someone claim that genius is
what, in fact, comes through in translation?

Delicate grasses along the bank
Move in a slight wind.
My boat's high mast pierces
The night's loneliness. Stars

1 *A Little Primer of Tu Fu* by David Hawkes (1967).

Hang to these most
Wide levels, a moon bobs
On the great river's rippling.
Writing gets me nowhere,
Illness, age, bar my advance.
What am I like, drifting,
Drifting here? A single
Tern of the sandbanks
In between earth and heaven.

— which is Tu Fu thinking about life and himself on a night
journey down the Yangtze.

In a way the great solemn Tu Fu is the excuse and not the
subject of this delightful book. For years we have been used to
a particular kind of English-Chinese poem — the late Arthur
Waley's kind — every poem, or every poet, made rather the
same in a gentle, liberal, loose, tasteful English. We were given
the mood, and denied the poems. This time we get the poems.
I do not mean that we get perfect translations. We get one by
one thirty-five actual poems by Tu Fu, in Chinese characters
(don't be put off by that), standing up like columns on the
page. The characters are transliterated, and then each poem is
construed word by word, and explained. We discover about
Chinese rhyme and metre, Chinese idioms and conventions
and symbols —

Yuan-yang bu du su
Mandarin ducks not alone sleep
. . . Mandarin ducks are a well-known symbol of conjugal
fidelity.

Last of all comes a straightforward crib, in prose, so the
book adds up to a series of the pleasantest evening classes, or to
a do-it-yourself kit. My only grouse is that Professor Hawkes
(who is not in the least pompous or professorial) did not
choose the poems by Tu Fu that he liked best. For various
reasons he picked the thirty-five poems which appear in a kind
of Chinese *Golden Treasury*. Some of them are obscure, some
of them are poems (illustrating a general difficulty of
translation) which cannot really exist outside the original,
outside a context of classical China.

Still, the reader discovers where he can go for more of Tu
Fu: and wonders abound. Using the kit and the cribs so kindly
provided, I found myself trying translations or versions (as
above), whole or in part; I found myself writing out images
and lines of particular power and particular beauty — the

clouds floating above the mountain, whose changing shapes seem to add up to all time past and present, the bugles in the long autumn night mournfully talking to each other around a governor's headquarters, the green barrow of a princess (who lived seven centuries before Tu Fu), all by itself against the twilight, or the beauty neglected or abandoned by her husband in her garden in the evening —

It is cold, her blue sleeves are thin. In the failing
Light she leans against the tall bamboos.

2. THE TALE OF GENJI

It takes forty chapters or so of one of the most admirable of novels to reach the death of Genji — "The shining Genji was dead", dead but deathless, the shining price who can never sink into oblivion.

He has been alive now for more than a thousand years, and here he is in a new translation,[1] the considerate, impeccable lover, roving yet faithful; the Japanese prince of perfect beauty, perfect sensibility, perfect sensuality. He is impossible, yet in his unflawed perfection, in his adventures, his thoughts and feelings, he does exist. He is actual, he is real, he is human, he is credible.

That credibility I would say is the first extraordinary fact about this master novel of world writing. It is all artifice, which means all art. And tied to this art and artificial reality is the second extraordinary fact — that this vast novel is more than a thousand years young. It does not date. Written before our Norman Conquest, it never seems archaic. Everything about *The Tale of Genji* is remote, in space and in time and in culture, yet everything about it is here and now. If in this long dead world of the Heian Court in Japan there are set pieces, these public tableaux give way to private lives. In court company there are moon viewings, in private company there are sad settings of the tilted moon in the western sky at dawn, when Genji and a girl separate.

There was never a more poetic novel which at the same time is more filled with the here and now of action — of poetic action. How many delicate poems are exchanged attached to this or that symbolic blossom, how many gardens, rocks and pines are described, in this novel which is never bogged down

1 *The Tale of Genji* by Murasaki Skikibu, translated by Edward Seidensticker (1976).

in description. How many dresses and fabrics are described, just a touch to make the scene. How many wreathings of mist there are, and wild skies, and whitenings of the sea across a bay.

And the last extraordinary fact is how all this poetic here and now, all this marvellous immediacy walls the reader; he is in, he is immersed, he is held. The pace, the tone, the texture — they are all so good that of 1,100 pages not one, I think, is tedious.

From another new book,[1] Donald Keene's sketch of Japanese writing from 1600 or thereabouts to 1867, to the beginning of the modern era in Japanese life and literature, we may learn something of what the Japanese themselves have thought of *Genji*. One Japanese poet of Shakespeare's time said that nothing gave him as much pleasure as Genji: "I have been reading it for over sixty years, and I never tire of it." When he read it, he felt he was living in Genji's time.

In the eighteenth century one of the greatest of Japanese critics and scholars, Motoori Norinaga, called Genji "a tale of human life which leaves aside and does not profess to take up at all the question of good and bad, and which dwells only upon the goodness of those who are aware of the sorrow of human existence". It is about illicit love affairs, yes — but this "impure mud" in *The Tale of Genji* "is there not for the purpose of being admired but", he says again, "for the purpose of nurturing the flower of the awareness of the sorrow of human existence".

To be blunt Edmund Seidensticker's new translation of *Genji* breaks a myth: it is incomparably sharper, more poetic in the right way, more lyrical, and more successful than the translation we have all been used to by Arthur Waley. I have never greatly admired Waley's famous translations. When he translated Chinese poems he made all Chinese poets sound alike. When he translated *Genji*, he cut, squashed, invented and expurgated and expanded in a cavalier way, and treated us to drenchings of pseudo-romantic reach-me-down English.

Here is a very small yet I think sufficient pair of samples:

Waley: "At Akashi, as frequently happens in autumn, heavy winds were blowing in the bay. Genji began to find the long evenings very monotonous and depressing."

1 *World within Walls* by Donald Keene (1976).

Seidensticker: "At Akashi it was the season when cold winds blow from the sea to make a lonely bed even lonelier."

Arthur Waley earned our gratitude by introducing us to *Genji*, the strength of which struggled through his saccharine English. But the bluff has been called; and a grand masterpiece at last appears in its laconic strength and delightfulness, so that reading Seidensticker's *Genji* is now a new experience.

Donald Keene's book caps an anthology of Japanese literature which he made years ago. Many readers will value its short clear chapters for the account they give of the greater *haiku* poets — poets beginning with Bashō in the seventeenth century, who turned a few-syllabled form of comic verse into poems which contain the world, poems which give profound experiences "in their purest, most evocative essentials". It was a very strange proceeding, rather as if masterly poets had taken hold of limericks and packed into them all that makes a sonnet.

Translations abound, but it is good to see the poets in relation to each other, good to learn of their pronouncements, which are as apt to western as to eastern writing. "Do not seek to follow in the footsteps of the men of old," says Bashō, "but seek what they sought." Or — Bashō again — "Learn about pines from the pines; study bamboos with the bamboos." Or — from a lesser poet Hayano Hajin, in the eighteenth century, "A poem should be written suddenly without consideration of before or after, changing and developing with the moment."

Readers will find *haiku* they may not have met before — by Issa, for instance, written of a breakfast time near Mount Asama, when he was travelling:

At break of dawn
The fog from Asama
Creeps over my breakfast tray.

Or by Bashō, greatest of all *haiku* writers:

The whitebait —
At dawn an inch
Of whiteness.

The most wonderful piece quoted in translation comes, not from a *haiku* poet, but from Chikamatsu Monzaemon, the Japanese Shakespeare, as he is called, from one of his puppet plays, "The Love Suicides at Sonezaki". The lovers are walking to their death and the man says

Farewell to this world, and to the night farewell.

We who walk the road to death, to what shall we be likened?
To the frost by the road that leads to the graveyard,
Vanishing with each step we take ahead:
How sad is this dream of a dream.

It was Chikamatsu who miraculously defined art as that "which lies in the slender margin between the real and the unreal".

3. WEN I-TO

Wen I-to, assassinated in 1946 for opposing the Kuomintang, published only two books of verse, in 1923 *Red Candle* (the title of which is used for this selection),[1] in 1928 *Dead Water*, named from the celebrated poem about China as a ditch of water green with copper waste and cloudy with bacteria — out of which something might grow. A few pieces in translation (the best, revised by Wen himself, were in Robert Payne's *Contemporary Chinese Poetry, 1947*) suggested that he must be one of the great poets of our century. So he seems in this larger selection.

Of course in another language he cannot be listened to. But he can be seen. Once an art student in Chicago, Wen was a colour poet. He writes of pampering his life because he loved its colours. But if he saw colour with the lucidity of Tennyson or Leconte de Lisle or Rimbaud or Louis MacNeice, colour also revealed to him the human condition — specifically of his own China. "Quiet night, I cannot, I cannot accept your bribery."

Distress, anger, love purified his colours; colour and image are a way into his poems, in translation at any rate. "I first played a flock of white doves in a frosty wood, their coral claws treading on a heap of yellow leaves." Or (the ice melting) "white teeth midway in the stream are lightly rinsed by ripples". Or snow has buried houses, but "couldn't bury the thread of blue smoke" rising from them. Or Wen is a rotten fruit asleep "on the cold stinging green moss". Or "Life is the meeting of floating duckweed", or "When the mountain spring has arrived at the bottom of the well, where else can it flow?"

Two translations in particular suggest a great formal artistry in Wen. These are from poems about the death of his child (when he was in America). In one of them each of seven stanzas begins and ends: "Forget her like a forgotten flower." The other one starts off:

[1] *Red Candle: Selected Poems* by Wen I-to, translated from the Chinese by Tao Tao Sanders (1972).

I wanted to come back
Whilst your clenched hand was like an iris in bud

and finishes

I have come back
When the glowworm holds its lantern to shine on you,
When the cricket chirps beside your ears,
When you are sleeping with earth in your mouth.
I have come back.

Too much poetry now seems to have been translation to begin with. So it is something to have a book of translations all the time suggestive of the effects of powerful poetry. Tao Tao Sanders, Wen I-to's new translator, quotes a letter by him: "I only feel that I am an unerupted volcano, the fire burning me with pain, but I never had the means (that is the skill) to erupt away the earth that holds me in and release the light and heat."

Rather than contradict Wen I-to, I would suppose he knew what he might have done, while we have reason to be amazed by the light and heat which did emerge; and which are reflected in these English versions, adding up to the best new book to do with poetry I have encountered for some while.

Entering the Country of Verse

Having need to check something about Peter Grimes and his seascape I noticed that my three volumes of collected Crabbe, Cambridge Classics, 1905, still in their grey jackets, were priced by the publisher at 10s 6d a volume. Not bad — 10s 6d a volume, 31s 6d for 1,617 pages. I bought them new, twenty-one years after publication, from Harold Monro's Poetry Bookshop. I was twenty-six then, earning about £600 a year. Now, next to Crabbe, on the same shelf, stands Thomas Chatterton, complete, two volumes, Oxford 1971; published price — for 1,260 pages — £12.50.

I am not — or not exactly — complaining (Chatterton came for review, so he did not cost me £12.50). I am not exclaiming, in a now ritual way, about the excessive, inflated cost of books. I am not recalling — with shame — that culture has always stumbled and swanked around on the back of slavery or low wages. Culture is something which may disappear (except in communist countries, after all? That will be a laugh) unless increased, fair wages are paid for by the lowering of profits and not all the time by adding to the prices. No, I am saying that if complete Crabbe had cost as much as £12.50, when I was twenty-six and earning £600 a year, it might have been, and probably would have been, a long time before this reader become a devotee of Crabbe and made deep expeditions into Crabbe, past Peter Grimes to the bean-sheaf which "slowly blackened in the sickly sun", and on to that delineation, in a late disregarded tale, of the dying English year, when all is

> silent in the scene around—
> All, save the distant sea's uncertain sound,
> Or here and there the gun, whose loud report,
> Proclaims to man that Death is but his sport.

We are always hearing complaints about the modern illiteracy of poets (and critics, and reviewers). Fifty years ago it was easier, and cheaper, for a young poet to read his way into more or less the whole of English poetry. It hadn't become a library job. The poets of the centuries have now been dusted, edited, annotated, finalized: but at anything from £4.50 to £12.50 per collection they have retreated from private on to public shelves, and libraries are not the place to work oneself into poetry and poetics.[1]

Penguins can be bought, I agree, but in the bad, despised —

properly despised — Georgian days, in Edwardian and Victorian days, cheap editions were galore; not only of expected poets, such as Marvell or Donne or Cowper. Half a century ago someone who hadn't begun to earn could go into a second-hand bookshop (of which there were many more than there exist today) and pick up marginal as well as major poets at 6*d* or 1*s* or 2*s* a time.

Textually and in completeness he might not be getting Christopher Ricks's *Tennyson* or Kenneth Allott's *Matthew Arnold* or Ringler's *Philip Sidney*. The Selection (if he was buying someone's Select Poems) might be infected by a decadent, idealizing sentimentality. But there they were, most of the poems, most of the poets; handy in Macmillan's "Golden Treasury" editions, in Dent's "Lyric Poets", in Routledge's "Universal Library" (once a shilling each, new), in the "Muses Library" which Routledge took over from Bullen, in cheap reprints by Edward Arber, and so on, back to Bell and Daldy's "Aldine Poets" of the 1880s and 1890s in their dull green binding. They have vanished from the second-hand shops (in which the poetry shelves are thinly and repetitively occupied by *Barrack Room Ballads*, and Robert W. Service). Their like, broadly, has vanished from current publishing. There were anthologies. More of them, as well; and they contained more of the verse of poets who were still alive, around, and in copyright. I could rehearse a rigmarole of complaints against anthologies, going back to the case argued sharply and contemptuously against them, when I was young, by Laura Riding and Robert Graves. But let's accept (however much they hang up poets on a particular poem, whether Yeats on "Innisfree", or Drayton on "Since there's no help", or Gavin Ewart on "Miss Twye", or Auden on "Lay your sleeping head, my love") — let's accept that for those who will write poems (and for those who will read them) anthologies are a first way into particular affinities and preferences.

I have re-examined two anthologies I owned between school and university. One, attractive to me still at least for its pink covers, is *Shorter Lyrics of the Twentieth Century*, selected by W. H. Davies (in fact nearly all the selection was done by Harold Monro, who published it). The other, stuffy in dull blue, chosen by Sir Algernon Methuen, published by Methuen, and introduced by Robert Lynd ("Poetry was born, like Beatrice, under a laughing star", etc), is *An Anthology of*

1 This was written before inflation (plus greed?) pushed the price for Collected
   Poems up to £20 or more.

Modern Verse, 12th edition, 1923.

I suppose I must call both of them poor jobs, especially after the weed-killing operations of the past half-century. But between them it was these two anthologies — and I can't deny it — which gave me a first sense of Yeats, Eliot ("La Figlia che piange"), Hardy ("Afterwards"), Lawrence ("Giorno dei Morti", "Gloire de Dijon"), James Joyce, Edward Thomas, Wilfred Owen, and Walter de la Mare ("The Stranger", "Farewell"). Both were appetizers, initiators, even if every good choice was doubly or trebly accompanied by the inert.

Anthologies help poets — poets who are beginning — to feel towards the contemporary innerness of the real thing, towards the constantly renewed "modernity" of verse. Anthologies help a poet to his nerve.

Now, in 1973, start planning such a modern anthology, the right poems, right poets, right length, everything. Add up the bill for copyright (the *minimum* fee recommended by the Society of Authors and recognized by the Publishers' Association is at present £3.50 for a poem of up to ten lines, plus £1 for each succeeding ten lines), and see how far you get. See how many desired poems you will have to discard. The adequately right choice has become impossible, except now and again when a publisher has a sitting phoenix in front of him, such as a new modern Oxford Book, which is going to sell, whether its phoenix feathers are polychromatic or drab.

Would I go as far as urging (reluctantly, since I like my cheques, and poets, like other writers, don't get too many of them) that poems shouldn't be charged for? That in the interest of the educated liveliness of the art, poets and publishers should forgo the copyright fees they now divide? Almost — within limits and safeguards. Few poets would lose much. In the end they might gain, economically and in reputation; more of their verse in more anthologies would increase the sales and the circulation of their own books.

Of course there is another way. Why shouldn't the contributing poets and the selector, and the firm which publishes the anthology, all three, share whatever the anthology earns?

The obviously just thing. But to *that* question the probable answer is that publishers, even now, would be too scared by the difficulty of a little applied mathematics (let alone — who is to suppose that publishers differ all that much from librarians faced with Public Lending Right? — by a little extra work). But I remember the Author's Guild, in America, laying it down that each contributor to some anthology, prose or verse, "should receive an advance (a substantial and unrecoverable one) against his pro-rata share of one-half the royalties (the remaining 50 per cent to the editor)".

That is more or less how I would like to see it with anthologies, in this country, for the benefit of the poets, as well as for the brighter health of poetry — if poetry can be said to have a health.

Then, allowing it is better to have anthologies than not to have them, how should the anthologist do his work? I know how he shouldn't. Faced at any rate with anthologizing his contemporaries and his immediate forerunners, he shouldn't try to "represent" — no larking round in that way. It is no good — or not very much good — grovelling through the library stacks, in hopes of finding the good poems everyone has missed. There won't be many of them, and moles don't discover gold. The anthologizer must accept his arrogance and put up with choosing as if he was God (or Apollo). Since a poem isn't a Member of Parliament and can "represent" only itself, the anthologizer must say, "I consider *these* are the good poems of these modern decades by *these* few poets."

He must make something public, in the strictest way, out of the privacy and discipline of his own judgment; excited, when he regards it, in or out of his anthology, by everything he has included. He will often be wrong, sooner or later he will discover, and will have to admit to himself, that he was conned by some of the poems. It does not matter. Also, if he acts like God or Apollo in the first place, he will be less conned than those anthologizers, those functionaries, who have no confidence in themselves or in their own vision (if they have one) of the primary world or the secondary world of literature.

Poets, who make the poems, make the better anthologies. That is another thing; which I say with the thought of various anthologies — since the habit caught us — by Tennyson (inside the questionable Palgrave), Allingham, Patmore, Archbishop Trench (Wordsworth's friend, who invented the *Oxford English Dictionary*), Bridges, Yeats, Edward Thomas, de la Mare, Eluard, Allen Tate, Auden; and with regrets that we have no anthology chosen by Coleridge or by the anti-anthologizer, Robert Graves (though we could construct anthologies out of their pronouncements).

Anyhow, greater, minor, mediocre, it is poets who are the undeniable initiates of the poem. They are not bothered about being fair, or about the history of literature. They cannot be trusted about texts, or attributions, or dates, or explanations, or who influenced whom. Leave that to the functionaries. But they can be trusted, as a rule, to put poems, not poets, into anthologies.

They too can't escape being conned. Of course. But they are more open — well, some of them, I mustn't claim too much, are more open — to the poems which are genuine in the mode, equally, which is out of fashion, the mode which is current and familiar, and the mode which is novel and aggressive; whereas the functionary in the modern situation often toadies both to the "revolutionary" and the conventional, while rejecting immediately everything outwardly old-fashioned. I am perhaps saying — but that is really another larger, worse affair — that writing now is far too subjected to the dictate of the functionaries, and is far too little under the sovereignty of the writers.

1973

Ezra Pound

1. FRIENDS AND ENEMIES

It is like a novel, Eric Homberger's book[1] about Ezra Pound, who died last year. Was Ezra Pound the greatest of modern poets? Or a good poet? Or a good scholar? Or exactly sensible in his relations with other people? Other critics? Other poets? Or was he the most loyal citizen of his country? Or the most attractive of men? Was he genius, or charlatan? Or both? Or how much of either?

Every such question you will find propounded — I shall stick to that accidental pun, and shall say you will find propounded and anti-pounded in this book of collected responses to Ezra Pound, responses to himself and to things that he did, and to all that he wrote.

It begins with some first encounters. His young countryman, William Carlos Williams, encounters him, when they are both students at Pennsylvania, in 1904. Pound is nineteen, and Williams tells his mother, in effect, that Ezra is a misfit: "Not one person in a thousand likes him, and a great many people detest him and why? Because he is so darned full of conceits and affectation".

The note is sounded for an existence. Edward Thomas reviews him, and meets him in 1909, in London: "Ezra Pound's second book was a miserable thing and I was guilty of a savage recantation" — Thomas had praised his first book — "after meeting the man at dinner". Then comes D. H. Lawrence, also young, the same age, up from the Midlands: "He is twenty-four, like me, but his god is beauty, mine life. He is jolly nice" — was this the outsider talking of the outsider? — "He lives in an attic, like a traditional poet — but the attic is a comfortable well furnished one . . . . He knows W. B. Yeats and all the Swells". Yeats, as a Swell: "This queer creature Ezra Pound" (though Yeats came to respect him, in a puzzled way). And Rupert Brooke, on his poems, not on the man: "He is blatant, full of foolish archaisms, obscure through awkward language, not subtle thought, and formless". And — rather a prize exhibit — a publisher's reader's report, in 1916, on Pound's eighth book of poems: "Pages 9 and 10, sorry stuff to begin with. Page 15, an impudent piece . . . . Page 28, silly

1 *Ezra Pound: The Critical Heritage* edited by Eric Homberger (1973).

nonsense. Page 29, better keep his baser passions to himself. No one else wants them", moving to a conclusion that most of the poems "are more fitted for the Waste Paper Basket than the literary public".

In 1917 Yeats's brother, Jack Yeats the painter, writes (and one remembers that Pennsylvanian judgment of Pound at nineteen); "It is wonderful how people hate him. But hatred is the harvest he wants to gather — great sheaves of it, beneath a sky of disastrous moonlight". In 1920 the American critic Van Wyck Brooks asked: "In the name of literature what can be done to prevent Ezra Pound from becoming a bore?". In 1934 here is today's Warden of All Souls, Mr John Sparrow, commenting on a favourable and decidedly influential criticism of Pound: "it sounds", he says, "much as if an imposter had duped a clever fool, into writing high-sounding nonsense".

It goes on, this wagging, this jerking of the graph, decade after decade. If something ghastly comes about sooner or later — and it does — it will be no surprise. Meanwhile, respect and disrespect alternating in the same commentator in the same article, the same review, the same paragraph, no one of really unassailable distinction comes down — in this collection, I mean — whole-headedly for Pound. Or wholeheartedly, since there is not much heart, much affection, in the matter. No one — until Pound is very old and until his Cantos are becoming very numerous — treats him, in this book, as the Grand Master, doubts swept aside.

When the flag does go up, it is usually after the ghastly happening; which does seem an outcome of his character, not of his abilities. He stays in Italy during the war, he broadcasts for Mussolini (the broadcasts are incoherent and tedious, but certainly treasonable as I remember them, reading their barmy paragraphs at the time in the daily monitoring report of enemy radio). He is arrested when the war ends, and he finds himself, not on trial, but in that asylum at Washington.

He is in the asylum still when the Fellows of the Library of Congress award him a major prize, in his sixty-fifth year. For the rumpus — well set out in one contribution to Eric Homberger's book — imagine what would have happened had Pound been an English poet, had the Fellows of a British state library, which was also the Library of Parliament, given him such a prize, voting eleven to two abstentions and one against.

The award seemed to say, loudly, that something written is not the writer, or that yesterday's treason does not invalidate today's act of creativity. Or that a life of devotion to an art

counts more than one startling error. From then on, not quite
so paradoxically, the dispraise lessened, if it did not cease, and
when I say that this life-spanning assemblage of pro- and anti-
Pound reads like a novel, it is because it is so full of characters
in conflict with each other and with themselves; and because it
is a man's life, an author's life, and a queer one.

The characters react sometimes ridiculously, sometimes
brutally. They are rash, they are cautious, they are generous,
they are mean. Some are trimmers, according to current stock-
market quotations for Pound. Some in praising him, in dis-
missing him, seem to be dreeing their own weird, spinning out
their own doubts and difficulties, their own neuroses, with
Pound as an excuse. They cannot always separate the writings
from the in many ways "impossible" writer. That is Pound's
fault, as well as theirs: and central character in the novel, Pound
himself gesticulates; there he is jeering, sneering, jabbing,
delivering himself all the while (because no one had ever liked
him, from childhood?) to the common Furies, and the
common wits.

There he is calling all the critics who don't like him
"vermin", "spirochetes", and "pimps who do not want to look
either facts or ideas in the face". And wit reflected in turn, to
quote one riposte which comes back to mind, on the fact that
Pound had named his son — "mark the crescendo" — Homer
Shakespeare Pound — though wasn't it Omar really?

A tragic novel. I suppose — but it is easy to say this — that
combative Pound should have taken a tip from combative, but
more genial, Byron. Byron's heart wasn't so much jeering or
sneering as laughing.

> He first sank to the bottom — like his works,
> But soon rose to the surface — like himself.

That is how Byron laughed when he thought of St Peter
knocking Poet Laureate Southey out of heaven into Grasmere.
Ezra Pound was less sensible, less generous. He could not tell
his contemporaries that they were

> shabby fellows — true — but poets still
> And duly seated on the immortal hill.

He could not, and he did not, heed Byron's very sensible
warning that "complaint of present days/Is not the certain path
to future praise." So I finished this absorbing life story
wondering how much future praise Ezra Pound is going to
have, or — say in half a century's time — if he will have as

much of it as his poems deserve.

Twenty-four-year-old Lawrence perhaps was not far wrong when he wrote of twenty-four-year-old Pound having beauty and not life for his god (though it wasn't what Pound believed of himself). Pursuit of beauty except through the thickets of life can come up with decidedly unbeautiful shapes or consequences.

I can add a slight P.S. to this tale of reactions to Pound. Not long before Nabokov died in Switzerland he allowed himself to be interviewed by the BBC. I heard the interview, I heard Nabokov's reply to a question about Ezra Pound — which was: "Oh, that charlatan." The interview was printed after- wards in *The Listener* — without that reply or interjection about Pound. And *The Listener* would not explain the omission, or publish a letter about it. Such is canonization.

2. SUPPORT FOR THE POUND

For poets of my generation who inherited Hardy and Hopkins, not Browning and Swinburne, one of the exceptionally nagging puzzles has, for sure, been Ezra Pound, or rather the contradiction between his poems, most of which it is impossible to read without boredom, and the respect accorded him by Eliot, also by Yeats. Introducing the selection he made from Pound years ago Eliot gave orders, in rather unfortunate terminology, that Pound's verse must be admired. How could one disobey the great man without uneasiness; and how con- ceivably could one obey him, could one make those mostly anaemic evocations a part of one's imaginative living?

From Patricia Hutchins's book,[1] putting an idolatry aside, I think one sees the way things went with Pound and London and England and English (or American) verse, and Eliot, and Yeats. Young and with little money, dynamic and outspoken, Pound hit London in 1908, moved about a bit, and then nested himself in a bed-sitting room at 10 Church Walk, Kensington, off Holland Street. This was his HQ for discovering how poetry worked.

It did not work by Beauty, "the central word about which two generations were to warm their well-kept hands". Pound forayed among the adepts of Beauty and those who had intimations of twentieth-century change, helping to separate them, helping — which is the strong verb in the Pound affair — to dust off the genuine talents.

Robert Ross sniggered once of Sturge Moore, as he came

1 *Ezra Pound's Kensington* by Patricia Hutchins (1965).

white-robed and white-wigged on stage, in a barn, a character in one of his own stillborn classical plays, "Here comes the sheep in sheep's clothing." Pound recognized that the sheep's clothing of the time was being worn by some who were not sheepish at heart or centre, and he helped them to discard their wool; in which he consorted with an elder defleecer, Ford Madox Ford, then running his *English Review* from Holland Park Avenue. Ford in his brilliant magazine hoped to discover if there existed a "sober, sincere, conscientious body of artists, which would try to crystallize modern life in its several aspects". And from this book which explores Pound's London mind and London actions, I am struck by the parallelism of the two men. Ford's novels, however hard the resuscitators try, don't really resuscitate. Pound's poems don't really work. But both these men of remarkable sight knew about the workings of a true literature they couldn't themselves produce. Both helped others to produce it.

From his Kensington bed-sitter in 1912 (prefacing a book of versions of Cavalcanti) Pound declares that "the perception of the intellect is given in the word and that of the emotions in the cadence". Perfect rhythm needed joining to perfect word — "It is only when the emotions illume the perceptive powers that we see the reality," which is so little to be seen in Pound's own extended exercises.

It seems to me that Eliot generously, but uncritically for once, interpreted Pound's private services on his own behalf as evidence that Pound, dedicatee of *The Waste Land*, was the better poet. Pound also gave help to Yeats. But Yeats's respect for him was of a different kind. He wrote that Ezra, a hard-working, learned, pleasant companion, helped him "to get back to the more definite and concrete", that talking over a poem with him made everything "clear and natural", yet that in his own work Pound was "very uncertain, often very bad though very interesting sometimes", spoiling himself by "too many experiments", and having "more sound principles than taste".

That is the judgement which will stand, I believe.

Just a Thought about William Blake

A new publication about William Blake made me think of Blake's funeral. The publication is *Blake's Books*, by G. E. Bentley, a professor in Toronto. It costs £40, it lists in more than a thousand pages his books, his poems, his engravings, and everything written about him.

The funeral — that was in Bunhill Fields, at 12 a.m. on Friday, 17 August 1827. The King, the Royal Society of Literature, the Poetry Society, the National Book League and the Institute of Contemporary Art were not represented. Sir John Betjeman, Tom Moore, William Wordsworth, Dame Rebecca West, Lord Goodman, and the Literature Director of the Arts Council were not present; only a handful of obscure young men in their twenties — in the rain, I expect.

Posterity has been making amends ever since. Blake's meagre exit was not altogether the fault of society. Society has no sure way of recognizing all its great men when they are alive and at work or when they die. But it could always try a little harder, and at present few things are more sickening to me than its lack of respect for distinction of all the valuable kinds.

I turn on and wait. At last there's a word on the death of Benjamin Britten or Bertrand Russell, or Malraux — after several illustrated words on the exploits of the footballer George Best.

Maybe it could have happened in Rome, if they had had T.V. Martial, the Spanish-Roman poet, complained, about 70 AD, of being without proper acknowledgement or reward. Byron translated Martial's epigram — "Post obits rarely reach a poet." De Tocqueville, in 1840, analysed democracy's effect on literature: the public treated authors as kings treat courtiers — enriching them (sometimes) and despising them. "Democratic literature is always infested with a tribe of writers who look upon letters as a mere trade."

I am not talking of society's contempt only for the various kinds of artist. In general it is distinction of any kind, any of the kinds traditionally valued, to which we are more and more, and more, and more, indifferent.

For some of this excess I blame television — television mishandled, as in the vicious triviality of much of its news and as it seems to me of many of its book reviews. No one — certainly not public pontificators on broadcasting or those who serve on committees about its future — readily admits that as a medium television is broadly a super *Titbits* or *Answers* translated into vision, a super medium of snippet and feature.

We shouldn't have expected those mass publications of our century to have summarized for us adequately all that every distinguished scientist, writer or thinker contributed in his life. But we might expect television to do just a little better — to give rather less screen to dead throats, dead pairs of hands, dead pairs of feet; to T.V. personalities, pop singers, wicket-keepers, centre-forwards.

To go on attending to footballers, comedians or some charming tart who has taken up writing or singing, more than to a grand physicist or biochemist is infectious. It infects editors and reporters, and literary editors, it infects educators, it infects the Patronage Secretary and the Prime Minister (it certainly infected Harold Wilson and Edward Heath). Heroes of the past were Matthew Arnold, or Mill or Yeats; heroes of now include the backless front-men of television shows. And we acquiesce in this debasement of ourselves.

I am not expecting virtue to oust vice — or whatever else we may call it, such as genial or cynical mediocrity. I don't expect virtue to take charge of everything that may affect our values. I am only thinking, though, that ineluctable vice must be encouraged, cajoled, kicked, somehow, into paying at least its traditional respect to virtue.

Past distinction has to be respected, as well as present distinction. One of Blake's proverbs of energy was: "Drive your cart and plow over the bones of the dead." We should be with him. Bones fertilize, ploughs drive to harvests, and energy. There is nowhere else to plough.

In Beckington church, in Somerset, a memorial high up in the nave, nearly illegible, not particularly honoured, to which there are no pligrimages, commemorates the poet Samuel Daniel, who was a friend of Shakespeare, Daniel wrote a splendid poem, "Musophilus" — the only modern reprint of it is American, so lacking in piety have we become, in our generation — insisting that literature combines in one age all ages past; that by literature we confer with the dead and call them living into council; and that by literature "th'unborne shall have communion/Of what we feele, and what doth us befall". Coleridge knew those lines by Daniel, Auden knew them too.

Can you see good writing — for example — going on, at least as energetically as it should, without the encouragement of recognition? The encouragement of respect? Also the steady discouragement — that is necessary as well — of the ridiculous?

1977

A Modernist Incomplete:
Ivor Gurney

1

A revolutionary acknowledgement of life, followed by a revolution in substance and treatment — that has been the "modern" thing about the literatures of our century. How many writers realized, and pronounced, that "beauty", or nature as a beauty, was played out (Thomas Hardy's phrase); and renewed themselves, after beginning as beautifiers or beauticians. They were followed by other writers who picked up the new or revolutionary only as a manner, opportunists of an unmodern modernism which every acute, serious reader needs to clear out of his way. More interesting, more often neglected, are the might-have-beens, the writers in the act of discarding the outworn who died or were silenced by one destiny or another.

These in-betweeners, I would say, included Ivor Gurney, a poet of one of the generations of renewal. He was born in 1890, under the Cotswolds; he left Gloucester in 1911 as a scholar of the Royal College of Music. He endured trench warfare, was wounded, then gassed; and was for a while mentally sick, though in 1917 he published a book of forty-six poems, called *Severn and Somme*. After the war he returned to music, under Vaughan Williams. He composed; he wrote more poems, publishing fifty-eight of them in another book, *War's Embers*, in 1919; then in 1922, when a new gravity and a correspondingly strengthened style were claiming him, in his devotion to Hopkins, Edward Thomas and Tudor and Jacobean dramatists, his mind broke again, seriously, and irremediably. Never free, often in torture (though he was still writing), he died after fifteen asylum years, in 1937, in his forty-eighth year.

Gerald Finzi, who liked his verse and his music, proposed to Edmund Blunden that he should select and introduce a new book of them from his manuscripts. This came out — to no great acclaim, I recollect — in 1954 as *Poems by Ivor Gurney*. Leonard Clark has now worked through the manuscripts again and chosen between seventy and eighty new poems, adding some from magazines, some from Gurney's two early books, and just over half of the seventy-eight picked out by Edmund

Blunden — in all, 139 poems to discover him by.[1]

He has also printed again, slightly, though unimportantly revised, Edmund Blunden's introduction to Gurney and his poems. Blunden says two things. From early on Gurney had developed an unconventionality in which he was energized, animated and reassured by those early masters of his choice, especially Hopkins. That is true. Then he affirms that "whatever was attractive and poetically moving to the generation of writers called Georgian was so to him also, and he was content to be of that generation". That, I consider, is sentimentally untrue, exactly contradicting the earlier affirmation.

What distinguishes the type of Georgian utterance — if those novel raisers of the dead, Philip Larkin and Sir John Betjeman, will allow me to say so — is a time-serving timidity and thinness of diction of the kind Ivor Gurney was rejecting, the kind appropriate to an unexacting superficial view of nature and of individual and social man.

From a poem of 1919 the following isn't Georgian utterance:

> Autumn will be here soon, but the road of coloured leaves
>   Is not for us, the up and down highway where go
> Earth's pilgrims to wonder where Malvern upheaves
>   That blue-emerald splendour under great clouds of snow.

Nor is:

> Peace had the grey West, fleece clouds sure in its power,
> Out on much-Severn, I thought waves readied for laughter,

or

> . . . the toad under the harrow toadiness
> Is known to forget, and even the butterfly
> Has doubts of widsom when that clanking thing goes by,

these two latter quotations coming from poems of his sickness in 1922. If to begin with Gurney's attachment to Cotswold and Severn might be construed as Georgian, he very soon raises descriptin and presentation to exulting: Cotswold edges and ascents become as grand to him, exemplars and portions of the total earth, as the foreheads of Wales were to Hopkins, the Neckar and imagined Greece to Hölderlin, the beaches of an uncontaminated Long Island to Whitman (whom Gurney

---

1 *Poems of Ivor Gurney 1890–1937* chosen by Leonard Clark with an Introduction by Edmund Blunden (1973).

admired). He had that vision of reality which Auden, and at least some of us, believe to have been "the initial cause of all genuine works of art". He spoke of his vision of Gloucestershire edges and ledges as he spoke of his vision of composers, of William Byrd, of Bach —

> O Bach! O Father of all makers, look from your hidden
> Hold where you are now and help me.

Only — the tragedy of his life, and loss to everyone — illness came, illness broke his connective mind, before his full emergence. The carol is often missing as though it had been picked out by madness or never achieved, leaving a poem to be no more than a heap of words. Even then he did achieve his poems of black torture. Edmund Blunden included several of these. A complete one is *The High Hills Have a Bitterness*:

> The high hills have a bitterness
> Now they are not known
> And memory is poor enough consolation
> For the soul hopeless gone.
> Up in the air there beech tangles wildly in the wind —
> That I can imagine.
> But the speed, the swiftness, walking into clarity,
> Like last year's bryony, are gone.

Another very moving one begins

> There is nothing for my Poetry, who was the child of joy,
> But to work out in verse crazes of my untold pain;
> In verse which shall recall the rightness of a former day.

Others are added by Leonard Clark, one which says

> Forced meals there have been and electricity
> And weakening of sanity by influence
> That's dreadful to endure. And there are orders
> And I am praying for death, death, death,
> And dreadful is the indrawing or out-breathing of breath.

another which ends

> In Death his rose-leaves never is a crease.
> Rest squares reckonings Love set awry.

Gratitude does not prevent me from being nagged by one statement of Ivor Gurney's new editor. In the four collections there have now been printed 182 poems out of 880 which are known to exist. No fewer than — how many do you think? —

698 remain unpublished. Do we have all the best, all the ones that deserve publishing?

Well, Gurney's old editor explained the difficulties. The manuscripts (all or most in the public library at Gloucester) amount to "a profusion of poetry", in which everything "is slowed down by an afflicting incoherence". Some of the poems repeat themselves, some of them wind into each other. Many "are in a sense variants of the same foundational poem", and it is puzzling to decide which "are the prototypes or at any rate the strongest and most communicative of the essentials in his outlook".

Perhaps we have the best. I am not convinced of it. For one thing Mr Clark's editing is so unclear and perfunctory, he seems to little to understand the kind of poet he is serving that I think excellence, among all those 698 unpublished poems, might, just might, have been excluded as nothing but eccentricity or incoherence. Many poems now presented to us are welcome; several, in a sad way, do consist of words heaped together. Several which Edmund Blunden chose have been omitted with a lack of discernment. One is the rather disconnected, enjoyable poem about the brick kilns along the Severn. Another is the poem about larches, which begins:

Larches are most fitting to small red hills
That rise like swollen ant-heaps likeably
And modest before big things like near Malvern
Or Cotswold's farther early Italian
Blue arrangement. . . .

(In fairness I should also say that Mr Clark has left out a good many null or dull poems which Blunden had included.) Then nothing is quoted from Gurney's letters — of which there are many. We are told little about the character and quality of Gurney's music. There is nothing to explain the choice of texts which differ from Edmund Blunden's texts. Evident misspellings or misreadings occur. Twisted borrowings are rife ("The poetry is in the agony rather than in the pity", "singing songs of the heart's pain and the world's loveliness"). One image is about the most bizarre I have ever seen applied to a man's poems: "Poem after poem show *(sic)* how the words gushed out of him, as if he were some St Sebastian stricken in many places". Sometimes we are told, sometimes we are not told that a poem has been published earlier; and at the end there is an index of first lines which isn't alphabetical, and so isn't an index. A rare old mess, for a poet who wrote — truly —

The songs I had are withered
  Or vanished clean,
Yet there are bright tracks
  Where I have been.

Whether other poems by him ought to be printed or no, some
day obviously more must be discovered or uncovered in the
way of introducing Gurney, and in terms at last of his peculiar
uncompleted modernism, instead of the well-meaning,
muddled terms of reaction.

2

Now we have a life of Gurney[1] written by another native of the
city which he called in one of his poems the "mistress of the
widening river". We learn of Gurney's father, a quiet
unfulfilled character, who had his own one-man tailoring
business, and of his mother, a woman unable to show affection
or to be affectionate. It is from his mother that Gurney seems
to have inherited his psychotic gene.

His biographer shows how Gurney had the confidence of his
high feelings, at the foot of his Cotswold Olympus. But we see
him in the years of his return from war and hospital and
musical traning more eccentric, more disordered, his illness
hardening into the madness which brought him into his asylum
at Dartford in Kent, when he was only thirty-two, his mind
thereafter breaking slowly into pieces on the way to that, after
all, early death when he was only forty-seven.

Michael Hurd, his biographer, is himself not a poet or writer
by calling, but a musician; and we may be glad of that, at least
glad of his ability to place Gurney in the galaxy of English
song-writers between Dowland and Benjamin Britten.[1] With
Gurney's poems he does not manage quite so well. To introduce him biographically Michael Hurd should have quoted
more of his best poems, I consider, which are still not so very
familiar. But he understands. He places at the very beginning
that asylum poem — to give it now complete in its two stanzas —
which is at once simple and revelatory of this poet-composer:

The songs I had are withered
  Or vanished clean,
Yet there are bright tracks
  Where I have been,

1 *The Ordeal of Ivor Gurney* by Michael Hurd (1978).

And there grow flowers
  For other's delight.
Think well, O singer,
  Soon comes night.

"There are bright tracks where I have been" — it is an extraordinary brightness Gurney climbs to — that summit of his
Cotswold-Olympus, that vision of the cloud-piled Malverns,
that vision of his country as a portion of world glory.

Agony over the brightness which raised him, and the
brightness left by his passage through life interlock in so many
poems which cannot be read without pangs of delight and
dismay. I fancy that the brightness of bryony leaves, the shine
on them as leaves and prying vines wind upwards, will every
year recall Gurney to those who know that other brief poem of
his high hills recalled in bitterness, when the swiftness, walking
with clarity,

Like last year's bryony are gone.

They are hard to separate in a case such as Ivor Gurney's —
the pathos of the artist writing or deadened in madness, and the
exultancy of what he called the "making-passion".

It is the exultancy that matters, but for the pathos I shall
mention, from this introduction to Gurney's whole being, the
visits which Edward Thomas's widow Helen paid to him in the
comfortless asylum, as she describes it, at Dartford. For her
second visit she had had the good thought of bringing with her
some of Edward Thomas's ordnance-survey maps of the
Gloucester district — "Ivor Gurney at once spread them out on
his bed and he and I spent the whole time I was there tracing
with our fingers the lanes and byways and villages of which he
knew every step." This reminds me of Gurney writing in a
poem about his "dear lane/That holds all delightfulness there".

About Gurney's music, musicians so far have done more
than writers to advance his celebrity and memory. Perhaps that
is right, and would have given Gurney the more pleasure. He
said of himself, anyhow, that "the brighter visions brought
music, the fainter, verse".

Michael Hurd speaks of his "astonishing creative-pride". He
quotes, too, the composer Gerald Finzi, who championed
Gurney's music, on his family's shocking yet understandable

---

1 At the time of writing some of Gurney's songs can still be bought on disc.

attitude to Gurney, in his distress: "It has never been, nor ever will be possible to avoid such misunderstanding, when a radiant mind is born amongst sterile, unimaginative minds."

That is where the tragedy is so evident: in what extra triumphs, what completed extra triumphs, there might have been, had the creative pride not been snubbed by circumstance; — had Gurney's genetic inheritance, on the black side, not plunged him so deep into dismay.

1973

A Meaning of Auden

I was one of those who welcomed the young, first Auden, and now after nearly fifty years I sit down on a cold half-sunny morning, the summer over, to write him a goodbye. No, I was not one of his intimate friends, many times as he befriended me. I knew him on and off, loving him, fearing him a little, as we often fear — and perhaps should fear — the great artists encountered by us on the outside of their inexplicable work. I revered him — "him" including himself and his writing. I could offer my broad conviction that the English, and the English-speaking, are left now — only for a while, no doubt — without any master of verse, without a master in any kind of writing, of his wit, penetration and imaginative clarity. But I couldn't provide one of those confident surveys and assessments of the Land of Auden.

To be honest, their contemporaries are likely to be poor or only partial guides to the totality, including the middle works, and the late works, of great men. Contemporaries live most in the work they first recognized. I live — perhaps they are the best if not the most profound, profundity not being all — in the poems of his earlier books up to *New Year Letter*. I suppose that later on when he embraced more —

> How hard it is to set aside
> Terror, concupiscence and pride,
> Learn who and where and how we are,
> The children of a modest star,
> Frail, backward, clinging to the granite
> Skirts of a sensible old planet.

— he no longer composed so well.

Looking backwards then, I ask how do we first detect — or rather how do we so often miss — the new writer? The first poem I remember by Auden, never republished, and I have never hunted it out again, seemed to me to have risen out of an "Englishness" (he was English, after all) until then unexpressed or not isolated in a poem. Auden was reading English; English at Oxford involved him in Old English, which involved him in *Beowulf*. In the poem he saw the blood-trail which had dripped from Grendel after his arm and shoulder had been ripped off by Beowulf. The blood shone, was phosphorescent on the grass — or so I remember the poem (in the *Cherwell* perhaps?). It was as if Auden, this untidy, untied up, short-sighted, pallid person from Christ Church, had given imaginative place and "reality" to something exploited for the Examination Schools, yet rooted in the English origins. It was the same with many of his early poems; a measure suggesting fatality, assonances and alliterations coming together to make a new verbal actuality as it might be of rock or quartz, a milieu of the profound Midlands, half aboriginal, half soiled or damaged, half abandoned; the very palpable truth of something, emotions and attitudes included, both anxieties and satisfactions, at once recognizable and pertinent, autochthonic and not provincial (though intimated a little in Housman, and more in Hardy).

In smart Oxford, and the smart Outside, a fashion then was for the frothy, vicious, aesthetic, and selfish; an aesthetical, excluding snobbery re-exhibited for us in the detestable diaries of Evelyn Waugh. The contrast. This is England, this is man: this is Us, this is our sensation. We only are. From Auden I first learnt what the trolls in *Peer Gynt* were up to, and amounted to, when they said "To thyself be enough"; and how skilfully and suavely our trollishness disguises itself — like Auden's devil in *New Year Letter*.

Within a few years (*The Orators* and *The Dance of Death* and the first *Poems* already published) poems were coming to me from Birmingham or from the Malverns, and I was publishing them in *New Verse*. They came on half sheets of notepaper, on long sheets of lined foolscap, in that writing an airborne daddy-longlegs might have managed with one dangling leg, sometimes in pencil, sometimes smudged and still less easy to decipher. They had to be typed before they went to the printer, and in the act of typing each poem established itself. It was rather like old-fashioned developing in the dark-room, but more certain, more exciting.

At the far end of the enormous room,
An orchestra is playing to the rich.

— there at last on the white page, to be clearer still on the galley, the first entire sight of a new poem joining our literature.

Earth turns over, our side feels the cold . . . .

England of a new generation beginning to widen into the world, the anxiety and the concern of the English individual; Wystan Hugh Auden, beginning to encompass the anxieties of man.

August for the people and their favourite islands . . . .

Dear, though the night is gone . . . .

A new poetry, poems to appear again in that wonder-book, *Look Stranger!*, in 1936.

The "English individual" — what kind of a name was *Auden*? In the early Auden years I liked to think this name of his must be Old Norse, proper for a poet who knew about trolls running along the edges of the mind, like Morris's *Sigurd the Volsung*, read the sagas, and visited (I had been there before him, impelled, I suppose, by the same kind of reading) the "sterile, immature", cindery landscape of Icelandic dales and plains — the great plains "forever where the cold fish is hunted". The surname dictionary says *Auden* could be Anglo-Scandinavian, *Healfdene*, "half-Dane". That would do. But it could also be English, from *Ælfwine,* "elf-friend". That too, would serve for this Wystan Auden, the elf-friend, the magician, allowing that there are good and bad elves, good and bad magicians.

And "Wystan"? I found that as well as a parish called Audenshaw, in Lancashire, there was a parish in Shropshire — Auden's Shropshire of the deserted lead mines — called Wistanstow; and didn't the guidebook to Shropshire by the Reverend John Ernest Auden — Auden's uncle, I think — relate the martyrdom of Wystan, son of Widmund, grandson of Wiglaf, King of Mercia, who wished "to become an heir of a heavenly kingdom", not of an earthly one? Wystan's treacherous cousin — at Wistanstow — struck him down with a sword after giving him the kiss of peace. "For thirty days a column of light extending from the spot where he was slain, was seen by all those who dwelt there, and every year on the day of his martyrdom, the hairs of his head, severed by the sword, sprang up like grass."

Sentimental, beside any possible point, to connect the name-saint, the Half-Dane, the Elf-friend, the magician, the poet, and the poems? Well, this poet wasn't called Marmaduke Rees-Mogg, his names fitted his poems, they symbolized a depth of historical, local humus from which this poet could spread above and below ground from local into universal. For me more than a thirty days' column of light stood up from his poems:

In the deserts of the heart
Let the healing fountain start,

In the prison of his days
Teach the free man how to praise.

Picking through a folder, from the *New Verse* days, I found,
on the back of a sheet of *New Verse* notepaper, a statement
excerpted from Auden at this early time:

> When a poet is writing verse, the feeling, as it were, excites
> the words and makes them fall into a definite group, going
> through definite movements, just as feeling excites the
> different members of a crowd and makes them act together.
> Metre is group excitement among words, a series of repeated
> movements. The weaker the excitement, the less words act
> together and upon each other.

His feeling was already rising to its greatest power to excite.
And the early article in which he wrote that, when he was
twenty-five, to explain verse to children (and their parents), he
called "Writing, or the Pattern between People". Between
people — even then. Writers "would like to be read by
everybody and for ever. They feel alone, cut off from each
other in an indifferent world where they do not live for very
long. How can they get in touch again?" The wish for
company, the desire to make — these, he said, are the
respectable reasons for writing.

He had, when he began, no doubts of his vocation; he
accepted his gifts, learning and admitting as well where he was
limited or fell short. His Oxford tutor, Nevill Coghill, told me
once, on a night drive between Reading and Oxford during
which we talked the whole way of Auden, a story which might
have appalled the Auden of his middle or later understanding.
As usual Coghill had interviewed his new undergraduates, and
he had asked Auden his stock question, after a while:

> Tutor: "And what are you going to do, Mr Auden, when
> you leave the university?"
> Auden: "I am going to be a poet."
> Tutor: (since something must be said). "Well, in — in that
> case you should find it very useful to have read English."
> Auden: (after a silence). "You don't understand, I am going
> to be a great poet."

Not all of his writing — but who cares, except the pedant who
hates and misunderstands both the arts and the readers he
thinks he is serving? — is "great" or free of dullness. The
appalling uniqueness of each great writer includes the different

proportions in him of fudge and gold. And what writer, Tolstoy, Hugo, Baudelaire, Melville, Shakespeare, is not a warning against demands for a sustained perfection in literature, as if the great writer's graph ascended steeply and at the worst flattened to a long high level? Zigzags are his condition. And Auden had to write for a living, in our indifferent Anglo-Saxony which gets its poems but expects its poets to live on book-reviewing and the free provision of stale air.

"I am going to be a great poet" — in that early essay I mentioned, he spoke of the writer as being the soil and the gardener: "The soil part of him does not know what is going on, the gardener part of him has learnt the routine." Better to be a bad gardener than bad soil, he went on. His soil proved deep and extensive as the Fens. If sometimes he gardened poorer patches of himself, he was a supremely able, dedicated gardener.

Not all of his poems are kind, but most of them are, and he was — exemplifying the unshiftably true fact that the great writer is always, in the base and inside the total of himself — the good man. A book about Auden (though I cannot bear to read such books) which was sent to me from Australia, ends with a note by Rex Warner mentioning Auden's great kindliness and the way he inspired "great affection in all who know him". To be kind — not to be cruel — isn't to be evasive, and I see as inseparable from his kindliness Auden's much debated Christianity. It has upset old faithfuls, it repels new readers. For me it demands too much of an "as if" for intellectual assent; but I see it as wrung from Auden by his long look at the muddle, wickedness, goodness , and necessities of men; wrung from him by desperation about ourselves; not as backsliding, not as contradiction, but as an enlargement, accepted or no, of his first, limited Marxist cures for our discontent.

Aren't poets, in one form or another, naturally religious men, or nothing? His Christianity may not be what we want, it may disappoint us, it may not be what we suppose is most effective, or most enjoyable; but is it discreditable for a poet to find himself — allowing this to have been Auden's location — outside and beyond poetry in the end?

What Auden doesn't do is opt either from us or from our primary world. I see that is why he turned from, rather than against, Hardy. When old, Hardy wrote, in strict continuation, that he had not cared for life, but that since life had cared for him he owed it some loyalty; which must have seemed grudging, and more than half defeated. It was unkindliness — unkindness to man, who has to live, and in this world. The unevasive Auden I revere and love, conceived, like Pasternak, that we are guests of existence, which must be honoured with delight. If that is one reason why he has been a rhythm and a revolving or shifting fixture in our lives, I shall insist that Auden's Long Mynd and Malverns became the hills of the world. He saw man and the world as Langland saw them from the Malverns.

Our English fortune is to share particularities with him, as Americans share them with Whitman or Russians with Pasternak, or the French with Hugo. He is for everyone, for us he is extra, by language, by keepings, and milieu. In *A Certain World*, which he published in (and which by dedication was my ultimate gift from Auden), I was delighted to encounter so much, so late in him, of our primary world, whether, with everything else, in extracts from Cobbett, a winter and mountain poem by an Irishman of the tenth century, or a poem on roads by Edward Thomas. Who else would have known, say, about Ivor Gurney making delight of the world, in his distress, out of the Malverns or the Cotswolds:

Cotswold's farther early Italian
Blue arrangement. . . .

Up in the air there beech tangles wildly in the wind. . . .

If we follow him round, as he celebrates, investigates, discards, adds, re-attempts, we find in him, I declare, explicit recipes for being human. And implicit ones, in poems, stanzas, lines, again and again, which give us in sonority and movement the additional bonus of what their language cannot say — the bonus of great poetry.

1974

What Sins Gave Him Suck?

On the outside, on the jacket, this account of Swinburne[1] begins well. Little Swinburne, in colour, from Bell Scott's Balliol portrait of him, stands against (of course) the sea. What I suppose we must call a pair of sea-mews and not a pair of seagulls, fly away over across the surges. The dense wild mop of more than carrot-coloured hair, of blood-orange-coloured hair, surrounds a head large for the small body; against blue sky. Between quite large green eyes, a bird beak protrudes from a wide unlined face above a small red mouth not quite as thin-lipped as it was in fact. A fuzz of soft adolescent hair shows under the chin and above the lips. The eyes of this bird, described variously as a macaw, a hoopoe and a halcyon, look at nothing; or can be supposed to be staring forward into a self-projection.

A boy, said Henry Adams, meeting him two years later, when he had pushed his adolescence up to twenty-five.

> He resembled in action a tropical bird, high-crested, long-beaked, quick-moving, with rapid utterances and screams of humour, quite unlike any English lark or nightingale.

When this coloured bird-boy wasn't screaming or tirading, when he was reciting verse by himself or others, everyone was taken by something additional — his voice. It was gentle and musical, it was rich and like a flute.

The bird perched, the bird quivered and was still, and began, and there was Poetry, speaking or fluting, in a new exoticism.

It is important to know how people saw, heard and were affected by Swinburne, when he was young like this, in the 1860s. It bears upon the adjustment we have to make between his fame and reality. Here — how it thrilled them! — was new Ariel, a new spirit or sprite of Poetry, to be excused, if he was outrageous and aberrant, arrogant, insulting, passionate, or drunk in clubs. Learned, rapt, spontaneous, frail, liable to damage, at all costs this little avatar must be shielded and taken care of.

That was the situation after the first series of *Poems and Ballads* had zinged through London in 1866. Were the poems quite nice? They were not, but how passionate!

1 *Swinburne: The Portrait of a Poet* by Philip Henderson (1974).

Curled lips, long since half kissed away,
    Still sweet and keen;
You'd give him — poison shall we say?
    Or what, Faustine?

That was the coloured crazy alcohol required after too much
Tennyson. Ruskin, grand champion of moral elevation
through art, had read "Faustine" in manuscript. He had written
ecstatically to Swinburne, in a creepy-crawly phrase, that it
made him "all hot like pies with Devil's fingers in them".

How different from the effect of the ladies in Tennyson. So
Oxford undergraduates chanted "the heady lines of 'Faustine'
and 'Dolores', as they rolled, with linked arms down the High
at night", and young Thomas Hardy, up from Dorset in his
London architect's office, felt that it was as if "a garland of red
roses had fallen about the hood of some smug nun".

If not altogether unflawed, a remarkable triumph for the
time then. But what about the time after? Where I think this
biography fails is in arithmetic. What must be subtracted from
Swinburne? After that operation, what is there left which is
worth defending, explaining, celebrating? What is sterling in
this peculiar poet? Mr Henderson seems to me all too interested
in the childish junkyard of Swinburne's actual or fancied
aberrations and in his aberrant products as well. I admit that he
criticizes them; and that Swinburne is a problem for a
biographer. What can he do, for instance, with all those long
years of salvation, the years in which the once bright bird,
taken off the bottle, patters and flutters around Putney and The
Pines — "the little old genius and his little old acolyte, in their
dull little villa"?

It is no good balancing the voids with nonsense about
Swinburne's nonsense. Mr Henderson writes about Swinburne
as a critic, but Swinburne doesn't criticize, he only exclaims,
surely. He says (*Lesbia Brandon*, etc.) that clearly Swinburne
"had in him the makings of a considerable novelist". Even if
that were true, it is saying of a writer only that he wasn't a
writer. Pursuing him as a poet beyond *Poems and Ballads, First
Series*, he quotes, after, or before, saying *splendid*. That is his
favourite word. Splendid, splendid, splendid, he exclaims, like
Swinburne, never demonstratively in a persuasive way. He
thinks that Swinburne saw nature, just as an American
professor he refers to several times, with approbation, thinks
there is parallelism between Swinburne and late Turner, overlooking that late Turner is founded on early Turner, on seeing

nature precisely. Swinburne "saw", in not undelightful drowsy cadences, the ghostliness of the sea and his childhood's Isle of Wight (in "A Forsaken Garden") and the grey ghostliness of Suffolk by the sea (in "By the North Sea"), but he doesn't happen to be a poet we would go to for verbal pages out of a Turner sketchbook.

There have been some acute judgments of Swinburne's special nature as a poet, his qualities of copiousness and flow, his solipsistic and remarkable word-life. Studiedly or no, these are not mentioned. No mention of Eliot on Swinburne. No mention of Hopkins, who was sure of Swinburne's genius, but called his poetry — at any rate after "Atalanta in Calydon" and "Tristram of Lyonesse" and the 1866 volume — "a perpetual functioning of genius without truth, feeling, or any adequate matter to be at function on".

I see no point in writing the life of a poet without having established, and without implicitly or explicitly indicating, his best; for which all the bad and the worst, although acknowledged, is freely forgiven — allowing that "forgiven" isn't too moral a word. Life is too short to be bothered for long and in detail about which sins or shortcomings they were which gave Swinburne suck (see "Dolores", stanza 6), or to be made to hang too long round the bed on which the circus rider Adah Menken failed to get her tiny poet up to scratch, or around the door of the brothel in St John's Wood to which Swinburne went to be whipped.

As so often, we have to thank this literary biographer for sweeping together the facts, which will have to help us to our own re-exploration of the poems.

Andrew Young

What do entrepreneurs of intellectual or critical fashion do when faced with the peculiarities of Andrew Young (1885–1971)? It is an exclamatory question. The evident answer is they do nothing; or rather they do not allow themselves to be faced by a poet whose structures and substance — or apparent substance, quickly looked at and passed over — are not of the most intricate, and do not fit usefully into their scheme of relationships and their critical formulae. They leave him alone, outside argument, no doubt to be enjoyed, along with Herrick on tistietosties or Dorothy Wordsworth on fox-gloves, or Kilvert on blue hills and dog roses, or Dufy painting a regatta, by the unserious. And others take him up, and he is reduced to a simplistic property, to a "nature poet", owned, managed, proclaimed and interpreted or characterized in their own image by simpletons.

This won't do. But let us see how it has happened (not without some help from Andrew Young himself, it has to be confessed). Here was a clerical poet, from Scotland, on terms with nature. He liked flowers (a questing field-botanist or treasure-botanist of persistence and ability). So he was evidently rather Georgian and not disgustingly modern. He liked as well seeds, mushrooms, birds, quadrupeds, insects, slow-worms, crabs, snails, stars, feathers, leaves, seasons, snow, wind, mist, barrows, roads. signposts, quarries, hills, mountains, rocks, rivers. His poems had been full of them, delineated or indicated at once surprisingly, convincingly and evocatively, ever since they began to appear more than half a century ago, in pamphlets of the smallest circulation. Then in 1957, when Andrew Young was an old man of seventy-two and when he had nearly written himself out, a number of admirers united in a small book of tributes, entitled *Andrew Young, Prospect of a Poet*.

Setting the tone, the editor (who is also editor of the present final, or semi-final, collection[1]) told readers of this strong oddity of a poet that "it was as if the childlike, elfin hand of Blake had guided him on his explorations", that his poetry was

> refreshing in a world that is fast silencing the simple pleasures of men and will not stay to listen to the small

1 *Andrew Young: Complete Poems* edited by Leonard Clark (1974).

voices of mountain streams or the distant pipings of the hidden redbreast. For these it is compounded of the dewdrops which hang on damask roses.

One contributor, John Betjeman, did nothing but quote in Young's face, so to say, minor clerical poets, "gentle parsons" — as if tough and tortured Young was one of them — who had described the hills and woods of their parishes "through the eyes of a Salvator Rosa or a William Gilpin". (No wonder, after enough of this, that Helen Gardner would think it best to leave Young out of her new Oxford anthology, or that Philip Larkin — but they might both have been more percipient — would think it right to pick only a few of Young's slightest poems for his *Oxford Book of Twentieth-Century English Verse.*)

Other contributors used Young to mock or knock what they considered modernism to be. Young's quatrains and rhymes "must fill the younger prosodic rebels, the politico-literary malcontents with contempt". Edmund Blunden sent a poem from Hongkong intimating to this malcontent Young (only none of them noticed that he was a malcontent) that elves were to be met with behind rose-cottages in Sussex, in which county Young was living. Yet another contributor thought that Young's poems were descriptive and "might have been written centuries ago".

Only one of the fourteen tributaries, the poet Norman Nicholson, realized that their man was a writer of the twentieth century, in the curt activity and firm plasticity of his language and his conveyance of the subjective in objectivity. Only Norman Nicholson knew how much Young was admired by several poets in the wake of Eliot and Auden; and why. They realized that on the whole he rejected an easy, effete stylization. He rejected coy elves behind rose-cottages, they liked his use of concrete language both for the concrete and the elusive:

I climbed to where the mountain sloped
And long wan bubbles groped
Under the ice's cover,
A bridge that groaned as I crossed over.

Reading chronologically through his now assembled poems (and that means a kind of private re-editing, since the editor's arrangement is confusing), one sees how in fact Young had come gradually to his strength, how gradually he had discarded poeticisms. He abandoned ejaculation, he diminished the frequency of the iambic-inducing vocables, *the, as, like,* etc. The time came when he no longer strayed into such lines as

"Joyous in love's full flood", *o'er* got itself changed to *over*, he dispensed at last with such words as *tryst* (which had been a favourite), and he no longer rhymed *hush* with *bush* or pronounced *wind* with the long vowel of poesy. Life and language, he understood, admit and are enforced by conceits — "streams that quote the sky", an owl that snores "Till it grows dark enough for him to see", a spider which is "Villain of her Greek theatre" — but reject fripperies. Words were fitted by him to words, and made into poems of mosaic or of tile, the effectiveness of which outweighed brusqueness or awkwardness.

Every now and then it is of course possible to catch a whiff of origins, or rather of slight influences which helped Young to his ultimate strictness of authenticity and freedom — a whiff of Hardy, Housman, Crabbe, Bishop King, George Herbert, Lovelace, Spenser, Drayton.

Best poems certainly came in ones and twos, out of all periods of Young's reading and writing life, back to the earliest booklets; but the most assured collection of his brief poems was the last, *The Green Man* of 1947 (Young was then sixty-two); which is also the most disturbing.

Disturbance is his mark. It is everywhere. It can be detected in very early poems, in the *Boaz and Ruth* of 1920, for instance, where it already indicated a man with questions to ask, who was unlikely to be satisfied by answers. Some day biography may join the poems in supporting the likeliest account of this man's slow turmoil. Here was a Lowland Scot hedged as a child and as a young man especially — or so we may suppose — by the scrupulous puritanism of the Wee Frees; a strong sensualist, well-educated, spiritually inquisitive, inclined both to a freedom and a discipline of the senses. For a time, we are told by his editor, he was an art student — or at any rate a student of art — in Paris: "He became so interested in Fine Art that before leaving university, he went with a scholarship to Paris, living a life almost of penury in the Latin Quarter"; which is tantalizingly vague — whom did he know, what did he do, and see? He became a theological student in 1908, and a Free Church minister in 1912.

Was he both god-given and god-suspicious? The sensualist never quite reconciled with the discipline he imposed on the senses?

In that *Prospect of a Poet* there was one other valuable contribution (other than Norman Nicholson's). John Baillie, the distinguished theologian, and Professor of Divinity at

Edinburgh University, recalled the four years he and Young
had spent together in the theological college; he wrote of
Young being upset by the death of Swinburne, of his
philosophical and already mystical reading, his reading of
"yellow-backed French poets" (unnamed), his ecstasy over the
colours of nature — "there still rings in my ears his excited cry
of 'Oh, the colour, the colour!' as he re-emerged from a dive in
the sea" (they were holidaying in the Mull of Kintyre).

He was aesthetic, Professor Baillie remembered; yet he "was
always wary of the dangers of any kind of morbid
aestheticism".

Something else Professor Baillie did not mention — and
perhaps did not realize, clear as it may be in the poems from
the first, nearly, to the last — is that Young had, for whatever
reasons, a morbid fear of death:

> I fear the dead;
> For they sit always in a sunless place,
> Hanging their faces like pale flowers, and think
> Of us who are alive above the earth:
> And they are hasty in their minds and if
> One wrongs them any way they breathe a curse
> That rises upward in a thin blue smoke
> And, changing to a scorpion in the sun,
> Fastens upon the heart that sinned.

The speaker is Boaz in love with Ruth, in Young's second
collection (1920), and we may reasonably think that Boaz
speaks for him.

Poem after poem (his "oldest fear", also, was to be buried
alive) has to do with death or the churchyard, or with meeting
his own dead self — in *The Green Man* especially — until the
disturbance culminates in those two long final poems, "Into
Hades" and "A Traveller in Time", which bring Andrew
Young, or in which he brings himself, in sharper earnest, from
what he had called in one poem "playing at death", to the final
affront of being dead, and being buried in his own churchyard
in Sussex, from which he moves away as a ghost.

One churchyard image which recurs, is of

> that most bitter, abrupt brink
> Where the low-shouldered coffins sink.

It had appeared first in a poem — on the death of his mother?
— in *The Bird-Cage* of 1926. He had suggested in that poem
that the spirit shouldn't really be aghast at flinging off the

whole flesh. But aghast he was, himself. "Why is it no bird sings", he inquires in another poem, in the same book,

> But all birds sit silent as pine-perched cones
> And only stonechat flings
> Monotonous succession of sharp stones?

Why? Because Death the Hawk is around, overhead:

> when that bird drops down
> Tearing those leafy trees bare to the bone.
> What shall of us far-flown
> Be left? One silver bird-splash on a stone?

He is a glum poet at times; his visionary hills burnt out, he felt

> Here is nothing but black peat-bags
> Where a slow Lethe drags.

And this man who has to die, this man who fights with himself, is given, all the same — no, enticed all the same — to love of the earth, love of women. At first he is God's agent in the matter; it is all one love:

> Lord, who hast made the love of Thy earth's beauty
> My lovely duty.

But later is he quite certain about his Lord, all the time — this poet who once said that he read Hardy's *Collected Poems* right through every year?

What did he do, or reflect, when he came to poems in which Hardy took that Lord to account, and made him declare — and about time, too — his own demise, as a delusion which man had contrived for himself? And did Young recall Swinburne, and the "pale Galilean", the world having grown grey from his breath?

In the end, in the last section of "A Traveller in Time", he is sitting on the stone with Richard Rolle, in the autumn dale of rocks and trees, writing the *De Incendio Amoris,* the *Fire of Love.* A continent of a cloud — the Cloud of Unknowing — comes up and quenches the moon.

> Moses entered that cloud; Plotinus, too,
> Flew through it with the flight of a homing pigeon.

Will Young pass through the cloud to "the land with no horizon", "the imperishable 'Is', without where or when"?

> Was it appointed
> I should follow those athletes, cry with Meister Eckhart
> "Up, valiant soul, put on thy jumping-shoes
> Of love and understanding"?

His answer is "Soon I should learn". One thinks then of the elsewheres, in this and in other poems. He had been by a well:

> Shaped like a shrine, it was sacred to a Nymph.
> I felt her presence, and bending over the pool
> I saw myself in her arms. But I was warned
> The fancy was profane; a wild fig-tree
> Leaned over the well as though a holy Watcher.

He saw girls coming with offerings to this Well of the Nymph, "Great earrings jangling. Painted to the neck./Eyes like blue mussel-shells." He had seen himself, the dead knight after tilting for love, lying in front of the high altar of the abbey church, under a white pall, cornered by four candles:

> Fantastic lover,
> He, too, had been a religious, armour his habit,
> A casque his cowl, and in the end love's martyr.

Variously, through his many years, he had written love poems, he had written about "beauty and love" being all his dream (1920), he had written "The Sheaf" (1937), of the two rats in the sheaf of corn:

> With indistinguishable limb
> And tight tail round each other's head
> They'll make to-night one ball in bed,
> Those long-tailed lovers. . . .

He had written, in "The Archaeologist" (1939, revising an earlier poem):

> Though Aphrodite divine and godless,
> Helped by a rope, rise from the sea,
> None is immortal but Persephone.

And in "Autumn" (1935), this "new Teiresias and unreproved", who wasn't, he said, stricken by the goddess that he loved, had looked and had seen "the earth undress/With intimate and godlike carelessness".

What pursued Young — extra to that which pursues every one of us? A Calvinistic guilt, allied with the fear of death, leading him to desert harsh Scotland for gentler Sussex, leading

him eventually out of the Presbyterian community into the
Anglican priesthood?

> Something warns me everywhere
> That even in my land of birth
> I trespass on the earth.

Why had he called that last book of his short poems *The Green
Man*, unless he had been thinking of the spring sacrificial
victim, the nature victim, carved in churches, frowning,
agonized, and wreathed in the leaves of the oak or the may
which grows out of his mouth? (He knew about such things,
and one can imagine he would have read Lady Raglan's article
on "The Green Man in Church Architecture", which had
appeared in *Folklore* in 1939.)

He was the victim. Eventually he wrote, or had to write, this
lover of nature and the "amorous earth", this older edition of
"that young lover, Who pitched his tent in heaven and read
Plato", this poet who like Cowper, when he saw the leaves
falling off the willows, wanted to live for ever and ever here
and nowhere else, that

> All other loves,
> That in my trivial travels I had witnessed
> Were thin outcroppings of the primal love
> The creative Word imparted to the world
> On its six birthdays

—adding, all the same, that the new earth created by the very
Word was still "more veiled" (and less certain?) "than the
Word made flesh".

This life, or *that* life? Consider one poem in *The Green Man*:

> Finding the feathers of a bird
> Killed by a sparrow-hawk,
> I thought, What need is there to walk?
> And bound them on my feet;
> And as I flew off through the air,
> I saw men stare up from a street
> And women clasp their hands in prayer.
> "To Hades" was no sooner said
> Than a winged Hermes I was there;
> And though I peered round for the dead,
> Nothing I saw and nothing heard
> But a low murmuring from a bough,
> "Ah, who is wearing my poor feathers now?"

Does he or doesn't he take the side of living, here and not elsewhere? Yes and no, as this searching man searches and does not find.

We must — even if we cannot as yet explain it entirely — acknowledge the pull, now stronger one way, now stronger the other, out of which Young's poems were made; while also realizing that what an Edinburgh Calvinist — or a Claudel — might call a great villainy of the sensual, can have a greater, unvillainous issue in the arts. Young wasn't a Victor Hugo, though he was haunted; he wasn't a Pasternak, a conscious guest of livingness more freely able to be glad and to urge his readers to an unrestricted ecstatic thankfulness. He was a little short or uncertain, as some of the quotations illustrating this review will show, in the rhetoric and sound of verse; but from an outer province of our time he was a genuine, rewarding poet all right.

Should we be entirely thankful, then, for this *Complete Poems*? No. It is what a first posthumous Complete Poems shouldn't be. It is not complete. One or two poems are omitted, for instance Young's early "Memorial Verses" about his student friend Cecil Simpson, and the poem "Dartmoor" from *The New Shepherd*. Also, since Young altered and refashioned many poems, to give only the final versions deprives the reader of whole chunks, whole stanzas, of his writing.

So muddled is the arrangement — poems from one or other collection are scattered through the book — that it is difficult to discover how Young's style and thought and response developed. At one end the editor's introduction partly repeats the introduction he wrote years ago for that *Andrew Young: Prospect of a Poet*. Dates and sometimes trivial facts are added, with simple asseverations that poetry is poetry, that Young "saw nature in the larger setting of life itself, with that life always governed by the religious principles in which he firmly believed", and that he "was blessed with a profound awareness of life, death and resurrection". Etcetera. At the other end comes a confused bibliograhical note, much of it reprinted verbatim from a note prefixed to the *Collected Poems* of 1960.

If the texts are on the whole faithful to the earlier printings, this is still not the "definitive edition" which the editor calls it. Sooner or later it will have to be done over again, properly, without whimsy and shallowness.

1974

To Heaven with Mr Kingsley

Do you recall Arthur Hughes's picture *The Long Engagement*, in the Birmingham Art Gallery? It was painted in the very middle of the Victorian century, and it might do for the personal history of more than one eminent Victorian, Charles Kingsley included. In the picture, the not quite so young man with side-burns, apparently a curate, who hasn't managed yet to acquire a living, leans against a tree-trunk. He holds hands with a not quite so young girl. The strain shows in their faces — she looks at him, he looks away. Behind her — as if symbolizing the sweet youth which is fading away or is over — and framing her head, hang wreathes of dog roses. Beside them both the ivy of delay and the passage of time grows steadily and ruthlessly up the tree-trunk. There will be no solution until that living comes along, or a legacy, till his "prospects" improve, and opposition is withdrawn.

The first and really the most fascinating thing about Lady Chitty's life of Kingsley[1] is just how Kingsley and the girl he married acted in the same social, sexual and economic trap. *The Beast and The Monk*: how did Victorians inclined to the Monk subdue the Beast? Lady Chitty has had access to letters unrevealed before. It is true the actual engagement wasn't so long, a matter of three months. Kingsley, son of a clergyman of good family but little money — little at any rate by the upper-middle-class standards of the 1840s — met his well-to-do Fanny Grenfell when he was still an undergraduate at Cambridge. This is their time-table: they first saw each other in the parsonage garden one day in midsummer 1839. They were in love (Kingsley aged 21) by the New Year of 1841. Their association was opposed by Fanny Grenfell's elder sisters. It was sanctioned nearly three years later — a very difficult and tortured three years both for the lusty young Kingsley and Fanny, "a well upholstered young woman with a creamy skin, glossy brown hair and fine eyes" — and then came three months of engagement before they were married.

Time enough; in the course of which Kingsley had taken his degree, slept- with a prostitute, turned to religion, and been ordained into the traditional role of penniless curate. The fascinating thing is both the cultivation and control of the flesh,

1   *The Beast and the Monk: A Life of Charles Kingsley* by Susan Chitty (1975).

Kingsley sleeping on thorns and counselling hair-shirts, Kingsley and well-rounded Fanny Grenfell (in whom thwarted sex turned to illness) talking about each other's bodies, Kingsley making erotic drawings of the pair of them in strictly sanctified nudity.

Young Kingsley wrote to Fanny about the attractions for himself both of Catholicism and monasticism. "But there was one very serious obstacle to becoming a monk: Fanny's beautiful white body. Gradually Kingsley was becoming convinced that he was a creature who could not survive without a mate." And he wrote one of those so often missing confessional documents of Victorianism:

> Eventually he sat down and penned a detailed account of why celibacy was an impossible condition for him. That account was preserved in the small leather deed box in which he kept his most precious possessions such as the gloves that Fanny was married in and letters from Royalty. When that box was opened recently the document was found to be missing. No doubt some discreet relative had burnt it.

Not so long before they were married Kingsley the young curate wrote to Fanny suggesting that for the first month of their marriage she should remain in his arms only as a sister — "I wish to show you and my God that I have gained purity and self-control, that intense though my love is for your body, I do not love it but as an expression for your soul."

Well, well. Victorians — no, human beings — never cease to be surprising. "Kingsley assured his bride that by postponing their bliss. . . they would purify and prolong it, so much so in fact that when they reached heaven they would be able to enjoy uninterrupted sexual intercourse."

A curious vision of heaven, if you pursue Kingsley's intimation; and for Fanny — it is reproduced in this book — he made a drawing of the pair of them ascending to heaven together in airborne intercourse. (Fanny equipped with useless butterfly wings, Charles making the aerial lift on long and strong bird wings.) At least the old Adam does survive.

Of course this story of courtship and Adam's survival isn't more than an introduction to a life of Christian pugnacity and breeziness and breakdowns. Ahead lie Kingsley's Christian Socialism, his novels, his children's books, his poems, his appalling behaviour in controversy with Cardinal Newman, the uncertain matching of his actions and his convictions, his disappointments, his degree of trimming, his lively, jovial, genuine, yet somehow not very convincing immersion in natural history. Behind him, behind his solution of the poor man's marriage problem, are the wonderful years of boyhood at Clovelly, where his father was rector in the 1830s, and school at Helston Grammar School, the "Eton of the West", where his headmaster was Coleridge's son Derwent, and one of the masters — who became his friend for life — was C.A. Johns, the botanist author of *Flowers of the Field* and *A Week at the Lizard*.

About Devonshire Lady Chitty quotes frequently from the *Prose Idylls*, the last and I suppose the best of Kingsley's books, other than *The Water-Babies*. It is a book some publisher might think worth reprinting, though it does have to be admitted that Kingsley usually slips out of gear or out of genuine tune as a writer — yes, and as a man. Why is it that this shy, stuttering, breezy masochist seems unconvincing in the end? Why is it he seems hollow inside? He wrote poems we remember without quite wanting to remember them, *The Sands of Dee, The Three Fishers* (very much a Clovelly poem, or a western peninsula poem). He wrote *Airly Beacon*. He wrote *The Bad Squire*, in which the poacher's widow tells the squire—

> There's blood on your new foreign shrubs, squire,
>   There's blood on your pointer's feet;
> There's blood on the game you sell, squire,
>   And there's blood on the game you eat.
> You have sold the labouring-man, squire,
>   Body and soul to shame,
> To pay for your seat in the House, squire,
>   And to pay for the feed of your game

and adds—

> You may tire of the jail and the workhouse,
>   And take to allotments and schools,
> But you've run up a debt that will never
>   Be paid us by penny-club rules.

His heart was rightly placed. But perhaps not his whole heart. And he could convince himself where conviction should have been impossible (as in his controversy with Newman).Lady Chitty recalls an apt comment by Gerard Manley Hopkins. Hopkins did not admire Browning's poetry (a necklace of pearls without the string) and saw in Browning a reminder of Kingsley — "a way of talking (and making his people talk) with the air and spirit of a man bouncing up from table with mouth full of bread and cheese and saying he meant to stand no blasted nonsense. There is a whole volume of Kingsley's essays which is all a munch and a not-standing-any-blasted-nonsense from cover to cover."

He judged from Kingsley's books. Edmund Gosse judged from having known Kingsley, who used to take the small Gosses out trawling in Torbay — "a jolly presence" indeed, "although his hawk's beak and rattling voice frightened me a little". When Kingsley's Christian Socialism was strongest in him, Froude, the popular historian, who was to marry one of Fanny Kingsley's sisters, commented — "I wish he wouldn't talk Chartism and be always in such a stringent excitement about it all. He dreams of nothing but barricades and provisional governments and grand Smithfield bonfires where the landlords are all roasting in the fat of their own prize oxen."

Certainly there is much of the case against Kingsley in that "not-standing-any-blasted-nonsense", that rattling voice from a wide mouth below a beak of a nose, and that stringency of excitement. Is it fair to say he was more of an opportunist — and not a very successful opportunist — than he should have been? A poem I like by Kingsley is an unfinished set of sad elegiacs, in which he rides wearily and alone on the sands, no longer the "joyous knight errant of God, thirsting for labour and strife", no longer borne free through the ether "on magical steed" — "But like the hack which I ride, selling my sinew for gold."

He watches the wind sweeping the dry sand along, so that it drifts over shell and seaweed; he watches the seaweed and shell, like his dreams, "swept down the pitiless tide"; and says "Woe to the weak who, in pride, build on the faith of the sand." I suspect he could have reached a greatness had he lived in the admission of failure. But he could always cover up.

On the whole, this biography neither spares nor condemns him. But cover up is what it does not do, decidedly.

1975

I Who am Dead a Thousand Years

How "good" are Flecker's poems? In a sneaky way many of us who used to say them over to ourselves, have since behaved as if they were a childish taste to be concealed. They do not fit. Flecker had no right to introduce his own Parnassian reaction into that scheme by which things for ever divide into aestheticism, Georgianism Imagism, and then Hardy, and Eliot. But writing does not care whether it fits; and Flecker's poems remain "good" enough to compel curiosity about the man who made them.

In writing this new life[1] his nephew has had all the Flecker papers to work from. He could have made a whole very entertaining book out of the relationship between Flecker, or Flecker and his wife, and Flecker's parents. His parentage was bizarre. Both his father, clerical, headmaster of Dean Close, and his mother were Polish Jews transformed into bigoted Low Church Anglicans (Flecker was Herman Elroy Flecker; he changed Herman to James when he was an undergraduate, retaining the euphonious Elroy which was, in the Hebrew, the name of the Angel of the Lord, in Genesis 16:13).

These conforming parents repressed him, forced him and tried to keep him as their property, before and after his early death. Flecker had escaped into a sado-masochistic freedom, in which he was a failure precisely where his parents directed him to be a success. What one expects to be a full story of this declines to a sketch, though a fuller account might have stirred interest in the poet and so in his poems.

Something else comes out, the stimulus to Flecker of his Parisian-Athenian wife Helle, whom he met en route for his first consular appointment in the Near East. Mr Sherwood seems upset because they played about with canes and straps in making love. Everyone to his taste. In their few years of marriage, as he began to die of tuberculosis of the larynx, Helle was his life of mind and body, encouraging him, confirming him in his taste for the French *Parnassiens,* herself the living shelter within which he wrote *Hassan* and his best poems. She seems attractive, he does not. He combined a delight-giving talent with an uninteresting mind. But it was virtuous — though a virtue little praised or genuinely appreciated — to

---

1 *No Golden Journey: A Biography of James Elroy Flecker* by John Sherwood (1973).

have brought into English verse in the damp Georgian time some French objectivity and form. On top of dying young Flecker hadn't the strength or the poetic finesse of that tough *Parnassien* Leconte de Lisle, but to recognize the kinship of slighter to richer and more solid just read, say, de Lisle's "La Bernica" or "Le Manchy" and then say over to yourself celebrated poems or lines by Flecker in which there is a de Lisle element —

> the hidden sun
> That rings black Cyprus with a lake of fire

or

> A ship, an isle, a sickle moon

or in the Prologue for *Hassan*:

> We have rose-candy, we have spikenard,
>   Mastic and terebinth and oil and spice,
> And such sweet jams meticulously jarred
>   As God's own Prophet eats in Paradise.

In cadence and keepings very differently directed the only English poet more or less of Flecker's time who shared qualities with him was Edwin Muir.

Mr Sherwood asks what would have happened to him if he hadn't died at thirty. "Some of the possible answers make one tremble for him." Maybe that is right. Maybe it is forgetting the strength of Helle Flecker. Awkward fit or no, the poems exist, meanwhile: in our literature.

Comedienne, Sad, Glad, and Serious

1

Most poetry is as poor as most fiction or most biography, or most books. But it is often so aggressively, so conceitedly poor and undistinguished that readers cannot be altogether blamed for not bothering with the new books as they come out, and I am always hesitant to make them try. In some ways, but not in others, Stevie Smith, who died earlier this year, was the kind of poet who might break down such indifference. Here is her last book, named *Scorpion*[1] not at all inappropriately, since Stevie Smith was well able to straighten out her curled tail, her rococo tail, and sting.

Not sure if sting was right, I have just looked up scorpions, to find that "their structural peculiarities are the very large and powerful pedipalpi and the segmented abdomen ending in a flexible metasomatic 'tail' which carries the sting and poison-gland". I can see Stevie Smith enjoying that description, health-giving or corrective as her own poison may have been. She is Scorpion herself — with powerful pedipalpi — in the title poem. "Are you Mrs Briggs, dear?" she is asked in the Out-Patients Department. She answers, "No, I am Scorpion," going on to say that she would like her soul to be required of her so as —

> To waft over grass till it comes to the blue sea
> I am very fond of grass, I always have been, but there must
> Be no cow, person or house to be seen.
> Sea and grass must be quite empty
> Other souls can find somewhere else.

That is that, a lonely and self-sufficient metasomatic Scorpion, who is equally imaginable as a Chalkhill Blue or an iridescent beetle, in her own territory.

The very easiness or informality of her way could put some people off. *Scorpion* lightly stings the idea that poetry must be solemn. If she knew that Keats liked dirty jokes (he did), it would not have upset her. She was not one for the Poetry Voice. She mixes nonsense and its opposite. Can you say

1 *Scorpion and Other Poems* (1972).

which is which when a poem begins—

Lord Say-and-Seal, Lord Say-and-Seal
Why not for once say and reveal?

That is her tone, in poems of innocence or experience (I am sure no one ever read Blake more affectionately) which may be very much founded in life.

In this *Scorpion and Other Poems* try "Oh grateful colours, bright looks" (one of several poems written in the knowledge that she was soon going to die), beginning:

The grass is green
The tulip is red
A ginger cat walks over
The pink almond petals on the flower bed.
Enough has been said to show
It is life we are talking about. . . .

Also try the simple-sinister tale of Angel Boley, daughter of Malady Festing and wife of Hark Boley, an evil pair who kill children and are killed in turn by Angel — "Angel of Death" — who makes them a soup of "A. Phalloides", "a mushroom of high toxicity".

After *Scorpion*, the collection to read is *The Frog Princess*, which she published six years ago.

2

Appearing since her death, a *Collected Poems*[1] now encourages and warms us to a fuller delight in Stevie Smith. She was born in 1903, and dying in her late sixties in 1971 I doubt if she ever felt herself accepted as a poet of bizarre and unassailable accomplishment. I for one should have spoken more loudly and often for Stevie Smith than I ever did. Desmond MacCarthy, according to a modest preface by James Macgibbon, once remarked of her, rather patronizingly, that she possessed "a little nugget of genius". She would not have cared for Desmond MacCarthy. But then Little-Nugget-of-Genius played the game of words in a way which was witty, knowing, satirical, sceptical, ironic, wry, charitable, loving, and mournful; suggesting experiences of life which if imaginary, seem actual, and if actual, could be investigated only with a superfluity of impertinence.

1 *Collected Poems of Stevie Smith* introduced by James Macgibbon (1975).

There's the poem, there's its fact, of love or not-love.
Enough.

Certainly Stevie Smith was aware of herself. Thinking that
some money might help, I asked her on one occasion to write
some pieces for a contributed book of prose. She replied
politely — that the money was anyhow too small, and that she
was too serious a writer to waste her time.

She improved her poems, and herself. Early on you find
Stevie Smith occasionally siding with common prejudice:

He wrote *The I and the It*
He wrote *The It and the Me*
He died at Marienbad
And now we are all at sea.

That was "On the death of a German Philosopher", and might
have been written by some You-know-who in North Oxford
— how civilized we English are! Or — how uncivilized we
English are — Stevie Smith could also play to the opposite
prejudice:

This Englishwoman is so refined.
She has no bosom and no behind.

She got over feelings or temptations or expressions on that
level, firm in a category of poets among whom you find Lewis
Carroll, Edward Lear, Morgenstern, Prévert, and some
American comedian-critics. I would add to that list W.S.
Gilbert, but unenthusiastically because there was so much in
him of the majority-tickling cad; whereas the better poets of
the category share, like Stevie Smith, a lonely "I am, and it
can't be helped."

She is funny:

A dismal bell hung in the belfry
And clanged a dismal tune
And back and forth the bats did fly
Wherever there was room.

She parodies both life and poetry (another characteristic of
her kind). She is romantic, and guys her romanticism. She
exhibits the unrepentant fearless bad taste which belongs to
good taste in its good sense, afraid of many things, but never
afraid of laying them out, clear, in her unequivocal words. And
she never backed from seriousness — expressed in her
unserious idiom — when it demanded her feeling or her time:

Man aspires
To good,
To love
Sighs;

Beaten, corrupted, dying
In his own blood lying
Yet heaves up an eye above
Cries, Love, love.
It is his virtue needs explaining,
Not his failing.

She sided with life, she was tempted, but it was a devil's voice
which cried: "Happy/Happy the dead."

Don't underestimate this allusive, educated original; who
knew — and usually managed to step back — when she
skipped too near the park edge of the whimsical. She kept off
the grass; but poets of her nature get relegated to a kind of
wigwam outside official literature (what book on Victorian
literature takes genuine account of Lear or Lewis Carroll?).
Stevie Smith knew about art officialdom:

Let all the little poets be gathered together in classes
And let prizes be given them by the Prize Asses
And let them be sure to call all the little poets young
And worse follow what's bad begun
But do not expect the Muse to attend this school
Why look already how far off she has flown, she is no fool.

Poets like Stevie Smith are too awkward to treat academically,
and are left alone, as a rule. Few bother about the virtuosity of
their poems, even when they are inconvertible, incorrupt and
incorrodible and more consequential than inconsequential, as
hers were. But they are read, that's the point; or it seems they
are read.

Question, for an examination paper: *Give your thoughts about
poems which continue to be read, but are not discussed.* Alternatively
— *What do you find in common between the poems of Stevie Smith
and of Robert Lowell (N.B. "Nothing" is not sufficient answer to
this question); and which do you prefer?*

To a new reader my suggestion is that he begins by reading
"The Frog Princess" and the poems about the various Romans,
Tenuous, Precarious, Hazardous, Spurious, Posthumous,
Perfidious, Surreptitious and Finis ("My name is Finis").

1971–5

A Very Technological Matter

[*A review which John Gross, when Literary Editor of the* New Statesman, *refused to publish.*]

I find the first sentence of this book[1] extraordinary, and indicative of much banality to follow: Professor Davie says he has "taken it for granted that works of literary art are conditioned by economic and political forces active in the society from which these works spring and to which they are directed, forces which bear in on the solitary artist as he struggles to compose." I mean, how far is this meant to go? Allowing that his preparative and current life is affected by "economic and political forces", mustn't the writer attempt to correct in himself the bias which they cause? Isn't that to be a poet? Isn't "himself" the thing to be felt for? And which writer directs his writing to "society"? "Fit audience find, though few": is that fit and limited audience "society"? Or was Milton an ass? Or Ivy Compton-Burnett (conservative and semi-upper-middle-class rentier), who said: "I would write for a few dozen people; and it sometimes seems that I do so"?

Then Professor Davie continues, "This is a book about poetry," almost at once adding that it isn't a book about poetry but "an attempt to define the political temper of the educated classes in England on the basis of the literature which they have produced and responded to in the last fifty years." A thesis emerges: "that in British poetry of the last fifty years (as not in American) the most far reaching influence for good or ill, has not been Yeats, still less Eliot or Pound, not Lawrence, but Hardy." Well, that isn't disputable, it isn't a novel conclusion, or one which is worth re-enunciating with such a numbing impact of cliché.

If you can stand the way in which Professor Davie enunciates or if you can believe that anyone who writes as he does can have anything in the least profitable or delicate to say about the writing-art of Hardy or anyone else, you will go on, you will discover a stiffly pedantic view that Hardy does have virtues and that some American hoity-toitiness towards English poetry does need reducing. However, to reach that far, you must cross a coastal range, fighting through the craggiest of chapters on

1 *Thomas Hardy and British Poetry* by Donald Davie (1972).

Hardy as a Smilesian artificer or engineer or technologist and self-helper — a chapter in which a few poems are scrutinized.

I often notice in critics of verse both an abnormal insensitivity to tone, movement and disposition, and a sensual ignorance, as if they had grown up and continued inside an iron lung in the suburbs. Professor Davie scrutinizes "The Wind's Prophecy", one of the poems in which Hardy is said to exhibit himself as "the poet of technology, the laureate of engineering"; he sieves it for technological and industrial associations. Hardy: "Gulls glint out like silver flecks." Daviedian comment: "The gulls 'glint' with a metallic" — i.e. technological — "glitter". Hardy: Clots of flying foam break from the "muddy monochrome" of a distant verge of grey sea. Comment: "When the sea comes into sight, its muddy monochrome has a hint of the daguerreotype." Hardy: The tide makes noises "like the slam of doors/Or hammerings on hollow floors". Comment: "The sound the sea makes is a slamming and a hammering. These industrial associations gather until we wonder whether the huzzaing multitude of the penultimate stanza is not a dangerously mercurial proletariat."

What piffle! And it recurs. In Hardy's "Overlooking the River Stour" a moorhen darts out "planing up shavings of crystal spray" and swallows like little crossbows fly round in figures of eight. Comment: The virtuosity of this poem "is of a kind impossible before conditions of advanced technology", birds "are transformed into machines, the swallows into crossbows, and the moorhen into some sort of lathe". Is the familiar antiquarian shape of a *crossbow* (which is not a *Maxim gun*) an item of Victorian technology? Is this moorhen whirling round at speed? No, this moorhen is *planing*, like a *plane*; Hardy, like most of us (but unlike Professor Davie, snug inside his iron lung), having been familiar, from the carpenter's shop, with the smooth ripping forward thrust of a plane throwing up curled shaving after shaving of fresh wood.

Etcetera, in other directions. Hardly a sentence, a statement, which follows — except an occasional truism or reflection from a better mind — ever convinces me. Anyone, of course, with a reasonable intelligence and a habit of books can make sensible enough gestures in favour of art. But I am not convinced — I can only snort — when I read "in sheer accomplishment, especially of prosody, Hardy beats Yeats hands down" or that *Brigg-Flats* is "by any account one of the greatest achievements of English poetry in the last fifty years". I am not convinced by declarations that much dry, rightly neglected verse by particular living poets isn't dry, or rightly neglected. Nor does it matter to me if Hardy isn't Yeats, and if Hardy in fact wrote in the belief from Leslie Stephen that "the ultimate aim of the poet should be to touch our hearts by showing his own", while Yeats wrote differently in different beliefs. One poet is one self, another poet is another self. I don't believe in admonitions (of Hardy and his rather monotonously small follower Philip Larkin) against "selling poetry short". I am bored, bored, bored by sentences which begin "As Schniedau and others have hinted"; and if I read "So it is, at least if one is of those who hanker for the rigid in a world of flux," I wish that the monumental had more literate promoters. Illiterate is only just too strong a word for criticism so nearly of McGonagall quality. Also I hope Professor Davie's students don't always accept what he says — for instance, that Gautier was, like Hardy, "a late nineteenth-century poet" (nearly all his poems were published by 1852), or that Smeaton (who died in 1792) was a Victorian builder of iron bridges and railway stations. Also in a book groping among English poets I think I am rightly offended to find *honor* for *honour, center* for *centre* and *maneuver* for *manoeuvre*, etc.

Small Detective with a Bilberry Eye

Blake once advised Samuel Palmer to stare at a knot in a piece of wood until it frightened him. Palmer once remarked that to go for a walk in the country (what was then the Hampstead country?) with Blake was to be instructed in the soul of beauty, through the forms of matter. And Blake once examined Constable's drawing of fir trees on Hampstead Heath and looked up and said, "Why, this is not drawing, but inspiration." Constable's sarcastic reply that it was meant for drawing has always made me think slightly — but only slightly — the less of him. Tom Paulin's book[1] about Hardy, or Hardy's poems, is about vision. Hardy looks at the world, in which we are walking. And though "soul", I agree, is rather an old-fashioned or superseded word, he sees the soul of us, or realities of us (not always pleasant, and not usually comforting) certainly through the forms of matter.

But how far do we need to push statements like that? How much of an advantage is there, for us, as readers, in both criticism — of poems, or any other such thing — and a scholarly groping after the states of mind in which the works criticized were written or painted or carved or composed?

I would not like to deprive academics of their livelihood; but I become sceptical. I more and more remember Dryden saying about poetry that he was satisfied if it gave delight; I care less and less about — well, Thomas Hardy's relationship to, or accurate knowledge of positivism and Comte and Schopenhauer, and what he learnt from Leslie Stephen; less and less about which other poets influenced him in his poems. Because, after all, his poems are his, and no one else's.

As far as concerns me — and many or most other readers, I suspect — something follows: that a book on Hardy's poems such as this one by Tom Paulin succeeds or fails in its ability to introduce and celebrate; in its ability to quote the poems most worth reading.

The best things I ever read about Hardy's poems (Mr Paulin does not happen to mention them) were by the now venerable I.A. Richards, W.H. Auden and John Crowe Ransom, one critic, and two poets, who were, at any rate to begin with, Hardyists. In a tiny book, *Science and Poetry*, I.A. Richards discussed a number of the Hardy poems he admired: and these

1 *Thomas Hardy: The Poetry of Perception* by Tom Paulin (1975).

in consequence were the first Hardy poems, apart from the poems about Lyonnesse and the heaps of burning couch-grass, which I first read, and also admired. Then Ransom — this was thirty-five years ago — quoted Hardy's poem on the end of the First World War, on the armistice — no more shooting, no shells, no moans, no weft-winged engines blurring the moon's thin horn:

> Calm fell. From Heaven distilled a clemency;
> There was peace on earth and silence in the sky;
> Some could, some could not, shake off misery;
> The Sinister Spirit sneered: "It had to be!"
> And again the Spirit of Pity whispered, "Why?"

Auden, like Ransom, said much else, but he also quoted. He quoted "A ghost girl-rider", and "He was a man who used to notice such things", and that one robin which will "never haunt our two green covertures", and that "wind oozing thin through the thorn from norward", and

> Icicles tag the church-aisle leads,
>   The flag-rope gibbers hoarse,
> The home-bound foot-folk wrap
>   Their snow-flaked heads.

and — vision of fresh Plymouth and love of his dead wife:

> I reach the marble-streeted town,
> Whose Sound outbreathes its air
>   Of sharp sea-salts. . . .

I hope Mr Paulin will not chide or deride me too much if I say that a best characteristic of his book — nearly, if not quite the book we require on Hardy's poems — is that he also quotes well; which means that he quotes with a sensible tenderness; which means that he feels for ourselves, as we go through our existence; which means that he knows something of poetry. Andrew Young, a deeper, more tried, more devious and more Hardyesque poet than is generally realized, told me that he read Hardy's poems through once a year, discovering each time strokes he had missed or passed over on earlier readings — strokes of vision, no doubt. Portions of existence are to be felt in rhythms and pauses, in the vision of a stone or a tint (more even than Mr Paulin perhaps realizes, though he speaks of lumps of dead fact holding a trace of humanity, of experience saturating bricks and plaster).

What I am sure of is that readers who believe they know the

body of Hardy's poems will be caught up again and again in this account of them; and startled.

They will find as well — but it does not matter much — a little dutiful kow-towing to not very interesting authorities or reputations of the moment. Then they will suddenly find Mr Paulin commenting in exactly the necessary way on Benjamin Britten's setting of Hardy's *Before Life and After*, a setting in which — well said — Hardy's "sense of the cruelty of circumstances" and of the injustice involved in our consciousness and sensitivity "comes over with irrefutable power". And if Hardy says *snow* or *green* or *kingcup*, here is an appreciator who exists more than between the radiator and the bookcase, who knows what Hardy is referring to, without having to be evasive, dry, smart or too abstract. A commentator with senses which are open.

Mr Paulin slates me, as a Hardyist, for going back to some degree on my expressed admiration for Hardy, and having, he says, too shallow a view of him; to which I would reply that there are heights of experience and poetry to which Hardy did not rise. He was not Shakespeare, he was not Dante, or Hugo. But that is another matter.

Oddly it was a quotation, not from Hardy but from his Dorset mentor William Barnes (love of whose poems seems to me a litmus paper of the genuine), which pleased and surprised me most. It is from Barnes's poem *The Wold Clock*:

> Who now do wind his chain, a-twin'd
> As he do run his hours,
> Or meake a gloss to sheen across
> His door, wi' goolden flow'rs,
> Since he've a-sounded the last
> Still hours our dear good mother pass'd.

Mr Paulin's comment is "a beautiful vision", lines "really marvellous", lines "both Dutch and visionary". True. I cannot see many other academic critics of our time agreeing with him in so open a way. But the quotation and the comment epitomize his vision of Hardy's vision.

I came across another thing, a description of Hardy and a remark about himself which I did not know and which delighted me — from William Rothenstein's reminiscences. Hardy had been sitting to Rothenstein and remarked about the expression of his eyes in the drawing that he knew the look, "for he was often taken for a detective". Rothenstein went on that Hardy "had a small dark bilberry eye which he cocked at you unexpectedly". So I see him, this small untouchable man, with his fine hands and sombre dress, standing about like a detective enquiring into life on the ewe-lease, on the Weymouth esplanade, in one of the blue carriages of the Somerset and Dorset Railway, or on the other side of the closed shutters. A small great detective with a bilberry eye.

Half an Art:
Julia Margaret Cameron

Years ago, introducing Helmut Gernsheim's pioneering book on Julia Cameron, now revised and enlarged,[1] Clive Bell rather unwisely wrote "Her presentations are often luckily out of focus. She could do no better — or no worse."

He was wrong. Limitation was in it, but not luck, except at the beginning. Eccentric chemical-stained Mrs Cameron was conscious of herself as an Artist, was determined and knowledgeable. She knew how to deal with sitters in her chicken-house studio on the Isle of Wight, where Tennyson was her neighbour, whether they were nobs or nieces or domestics.

As for being in focus or out of it, she had artist friends, she knew about modelling and gradation. She wrote a now celebrated helter-skelter letter, in 1864, to Sir John Herschel, to whom she presented the album now in the National Portrait Gallery, and reproduced in Colin Ford's huge quarto,[2] about "that roundness and fullness of face and feature, that modelling of flesh and limb which the focus I use only can give tho' called and condemned as OUT OF FOCUS". And then she asked, with sense and spirit divagating into a perfect statement of the Victorian art ideal, in its over-pious terms, "What is focus? And who has a right to say which focus is the legitimate focus? My aspirations are to ennoble Photography and to secure for it the character and uses of High Art by combining the real and the Ideal and sacrificing nothing of Truth by all possible devotion to Poetry and beauty."

So much for luck. But then which of the kinds of Cameronian product had she in mind in that letter? I think both kinds, fancy pieces and portraits, without distinction. When she let go on lilies and young girls and her maids in extra-clothed poses from the Elgin Marbles, when she combined real and ideal· in the Kiss of Peace, or Prayer, or Romeo and Juliet, or dressed up her dull bearded poet Henry Taylor as King Ahasuerus or Prospero, her photographs are as ludicrous as anything of the kind which her painting friends sent every year to the Academy — except in one thing, the

1 *Julia Margaret Cameron* by Helmut Gernsheim (1975).
2 *The Cameron Collection* edited by Colin Ford (1975).

limit she accepted in the nature of photography. Plate and camera, broad lights and darks, limited or reduced the possible absurdities of a painting hand.

It is exactly so in the superb portraits. Often the portrait is, if you look twice, a fancy piece in headgear and clothing. Or Ellen Terry is Youthful Beauty, Darwin below his jettied Neanderthal brow is Science, Tennyson is Nobility (no wonder he didn't care to compete in the Nobility class with Henry Taylor, who had a smile, he said, like a fish).

But whether the sitter was fancifully chosen, clothed or posed, all that was beforehand. There is the point. When it came to the last moments in the chicken-house and to lifting off the shutter, Julia Cameron was face to face with a face. And what her plate recorded, wasn't to be touched up later. She was not like her adored Watts, who saw and drew and then modified afterwards to present whatever virtues were demanded or presumed.

Commentators on Mrs Cameron frequently misunderstand both the photographer's and the painter's process. Lord David Cecil in his elegant, suitably tempered essay which introduces *A Victorian Album*,[1] another of the collections Mrs Cameron gave away, talks of the "artist's creative faculty" showing in his power to "interpret his model", not understanding that painting a portrait — a good portrait — is seeing rather than interpreting or that "interpreting" as a rule produces falsification. Even Helmut Gernsheim, whose book is still the essential study, talks the layman's literary talk about Mrs Cameron having had "the real artist's faculty of piercing through the outward structure to the very soul of the individual".

Of course we can always be wise *ex post facto*. Looking at the face of Benjamin Jowett, plump or puffy and white, placed by Mrs Cameron above the vague, wide, white open vee of some great book, we could believe, Ah, she saw not only him, but through him; we could suppose she was treating us to something of a photo-parallel to

> First come I, my name is Jowett,
> There is no knowledge but I know it.
> I am Master of this college.
> What I don't know isn't knowledge.

---

1   *A Victorian Album: Julia Margaret Cameron and her Circle*   edited by Graham Ovenden (1975).

No, we can be sure that in fact Mrs Cameron was photographing Knowledge or Wisdom, but — the face was so, and Mrs Cameron utilized those limits of light and shade.

Lord David Cecil is tactfully right about the high posturing comedy of Mrs Cameron. Think of it in her insistence that Tennyson, her chief Exhibit, should go down to the beach and wed the sea with a garland of red and white flowers, a bridegroom as worthy as a doge of Venice, or in the story of short-sighted Tennyson holding a candle up to his Camerons at Farringford, telling "grimly humorous anecdotes" about the sitters and their capture, and setting his hair alight as he did so.

About this terror of a woman, and her family, and her maids, and Tennyson and so on, more is to be learnt from the way Virginia Woolf and Roger Fry introduced her half a century ago in their album of *Victorian Photographs of Famous Men and Fair Women* (1926). All the photos were by Mrs Cameron, who was Virginia Woolf's great-aunt, and the album is now republished and enlarged (two dozen new photographs) with notes explanatory and, alas, corrective, by the documentary film-maker Tristram Powell.

I say alas because Virginia Woolf's fun about Aunt Julia and the Camerons is now just a little impaired. Mrs Woolf began with a vignette in life and death of James Pattle of the Bengal Civil Service, father of Mrs Cameron, "a gentleman of marked but doubtful reputation, who after living a riotous life and earning the title of 'the biggest liar in India', finally drank himself to death and was assigned to a cask of rum to await shipment to England". Worse — or better — was to come: "The cask was stood outside the widow's bedroom door. In the middle of the night she heard a violent explosion, rushed out, and found her husband, having burst the lid off his coffin, bolt upright, menacing her in death as he had menaced her in life."

Tristram Powell sprinkles that rum tale with doubt, but if we lose Mr Pattle we still have Julia Margaret ruling the celebrated with the camera she was given at the age of fifty — Julia Margaret who said to a cousin, "If you ever fall into temptation, down on your knees and think of Aunt Julia"; Julia Margaret who "chased Tennyson into his tower vociferating *Coward! Coward!* and thus forced him to be vaccinated"; Julia Margaret whose parlour-maid posed as the Virgin Mary or Sappho while the guests answered the door-bell.

About the photographs, Tennyson as the "dirty monk", and the suet and priggery and snobbery of Jowett, and that photograph we have all been in love with, of the young Ellen Terry hooking two fingers over her necklace, and the photo of Browning looking so handsome, healthy and bouncingly optimistic, and the photo of Aunt Julia's bearded old philosopher of a husband, who went into fits of uncontrollable hilarity as she got to work — about these wonderful photographs is the ineluctable fact that they are photographs, and not art, *pace* all photographers, and all the prattle of Roger Fry in that Woolf and Fry album, and all the prattle — or pattle — of Mrs Cameron herself. That the finest photography really is and can really be no more than a demi-semi-art is something which should be more than ever insisted on just now.

But what a gallery!

The Poet Akhmatova

Eliot, who published poetry by others than himself and knew all about sales, once wrote ironically that we have a thirst "for words about poetry, and for words from poets about almost anything", which seems insatiable in contrast to our thirst for poetry itself. His remark does make me feel a little guilty. Here I am recommending a book written about the Russian poet Akhmatova,[1] whose writings most of us cannot read, whether we would like to or not.

Very well. There is in that thirst for words about poetry and poets at least a compliment to poetry. At least I can see, as well as taking it on trust from her peers, that Akhmatova was a rare heroine of her tribe — not because she survived purge and terror, not because she stayed, deliberately, in Russia, despising the status and self-solution of exile, but because, in silence and out of it, she became splendid in her sense of life and art. That much we can accept from all the inadequacies of translation and from all that has been said of this great writer by her associates. Also what nerve it took, what self-certainty, to write as this woman did, when she was thirty-five, the poem about the Muse coming to her in the night:

. . . she's here. Throwing back her veil
She looks attentively at me.
I say: "Did you dictate to Dante
The pages of the 'Inferno'?" She says, "Yes."

This poem "The Muse" is quoted in Amanda Haight's not very long, but always clear, and again and again moving sketch of Anna Akhmatova's life, from her childhood holidays on the Black Sea coast, where she was born in 1889, to her death in 1966. And it is in some degree a first-hand sketch, since Akhmatova in her old age and Akhmatova's friends were known to the sketcher.

My myth says that women poets are all beautiful. Then, unfortunately, I cannot think of many examples. But there is Akhmatova. The familiar face is the plump one of the fulfilled woman, or the resigned, or more or less peaceful woman halfway between seventy and eighty, double-chinned, grey hair wispy and undisciplined. Amanda Haight's book begins with a photograph of Akhmatova at twenty-three, and it would be

1 *Akhmatova: A Poetic Pilgrimage* by Amanda Haight (1976).

hard to imagine a girl who looked more beautiful — by our standards — and more in command of her vigour and herself — though she was described as looking more interesting than beautiful, "so interesting to look at that it would be worth while making a Leonardo drawing of her; a Gainsborough portrait in oil; an icon in tempera; or best of all, to place her in the most important position in a mosaic illustrating the world of poetry".

She was married by that time — yet inviolable. Before her husband enters the book, we are given a glimpse of this inviolable girl in her Black Sea holidays, a girl reading Verlaine and Baudelaire — a girl "more at home in the water than on land", who "wandered around in summer without stockings and just a dress over her bare body which she clutched to hide the rip all along the thigh". She inclined to jump into the sea from unexpected places: "When her aunt chided her for this, saying that if she were her mother, she would cry all the time, Anna replied, 'It's best for both of us that you are not my mother.'"

The young poet she married soon found, like lovers and husbands to come, that inside herself she was alone and determined to stay alone, possessed and defended by her own power. He said in a poem he had taken "not a wife, but a witch"; a witch with a word-purpose, but a purpose he recognized. For a change, it was a great woman insisting, instead of a great man, a great woman sad that she could share only a part of herself with any lover — but "who can refuse to live his own life?"

For me this book fitted the last brick to one peculiar story. After the war an English diplomat in Stockholm told me — with no names — how one of the British Embassy staff in Russia was asked to go and visit an elderly writer in Leningrad, who would love to talk to him about her past years in Paris and the west. He went; he found to his surprise a portrait of her, on the wall of her room, by Modigliani, whom she had known. She, in turn, was surprised to discover from him that this poor Italian in Paris, long dead, had become one of the celebrated artists of the west.

The story was embellished, heightened and romanticized; I used to feed on it, and it was years before I realized that the elderly writer was, of course, Anna Akhmatova. Here the story is told in full. The embassy official — temporary — was Isaiah Berlin, the year 1945. He was taken to Akhmatova's flat, and had not been there long before a call of "Isaiah, Isaiah" came up from the courtyard — from the oafish Randolph Churchill, of all people, who, in need of an interpreter, had discovered where Isaiah Berlin had gone: "It was a nightmarish moment. Berlin's only desire was to prevent Churchill from bursting in. He and the man who had introduced him to Akhmatova rushed downstairs and left with Churchill as quickly as possible. . . . For a Soviet citizen to meet a foreigner privately outside a place of public resort or without authority had for many years been almost synonymous with treason. The war had changed things slightly, but not much. Managed quietly with tact, a meeting might well have been 'overlooked', but to have the son of Winston Churchill shouting wildly in one's garden as one entertained another foreigner could hardly pass without notice." Courageously Akhmatova asked Isaiah Berlin back and they talked through the night; and Berlin saw Modigliani's drawing on the wall of Akhmatova's very bare room, in which there was little else but a chest of drawers full of poems.

That was one English contact with Akhmatova. There are others. Passing the Sheldonian, in Oxford, I can now think of Akhmatova inside, in the scarlet gown of a D.Litt., being compared by the Public Orator in his Latin citation to Sappho (not quite aptly, I would have thought, except that they were both women, and poets). Passing the Randolph Hotel in Oxford, I can now think of Akhmatova surrounded by flowers in her room, receiving her visitors "one or two at a time, as was her custom in Moscow and Komarovo".

Better, though, to think of the girl wandering without stockings on the edge of the Black Sea, the witch of genius; or of Akhmatova with her first husband —

You will hear thunder and remember me
And think: she wanted storms

— or of Akhmatova with Modigliani on a bench in the Luxembourg gardens, under an old umbrella in the rain, reciting Verlaine to each other. Modigliani's drawing of Akhmatova, the one Sir Isaiah Berlin saw on that dicey occasion in Leningrad, is reproduced in Amanda Haight's book, though it may not prove quite what you expect it to be, or hope it to be.

On Gertrude Stein, Alas

A most peculiar business, the works and being of Gertrude Stein. I remember her at Oxford, on an occasion described in Janet Hobhouse's sympathetic and somewhat equivocal biography[1]. She reached Oxford under the wing of Edith Sitwell, and spoke, or repeated herself, to a sceptical undergraduate audience. How bored and boringly mystified all of us seemed. Then it came to questions, and a few of that audience tried baiting her with ridicule. They received more than they gave. That self-obsessed, self-contented dumpy little Jewish American from Paris of the Arts displayed the devastating come-back sometimes to be experienced from a leonine three-year-old who has just mastered the power of talk.

We were a sycophantic or fickle audience; with Miss Stein we turned on the questioners who had expressed our own boredom and laughed against them instead of her. The Oxford meeting, though, was far from the "resounding success" Janet Hobhouse supposes it to have been, and if you ask whether Gertrude Stein's career was a success, the answer will depend on your view of living and writing.

Janet Hobhouse's account isn't undiluted praise. She gives room to some of what I should call the iron case for rejection, and even ridicule. She admits that the masters of the School of Paris and the Paris poets were not amused by the ineptitude and falsity of her recollections when she looked back at them in *The Autobiography of Alice B. Toklas*. She admits the rejoinders of Matisse; of Braque ("For one who poses as an authority on the epoch. . . she never went beyond the stage of the tourist". She saw Cubism "simply in terms of personalities" — inevitably, because her French was so bad, Braque recalled, that she couldn't have been party to the goings on); of André Salmon ("What incomprehension of an epoch. . . she understood nothing except in a superficial way"); of Tristan Tzara (the "lowest literary prostitution", stemming from a "clinical case of megalomania"). She admits that Miss Stein's brother Leo was astounded by her simple-mindedness and stupidity ("I doubt whether there is a single or general observation in the book that is not stupid"); and that Gertrude Stein, in her more

1 *Everybody who was Anybody: A Biography of Gertrude Stein* by Janet Hobhouse (1976).

typical work, is unreadable. Tedium numbs every reader, after
a celebrated sentence or two (such as "A rose is a rose is a rose
is a rose" or "Pigeons on the grass alas"). Janet Hobhouse
allows Wyndham Lewis his celebrated attack on Miss Stein as
one of the soft enemies of the hard intellect. She was "a
Monument sitting on patience"; a "huge lowering dogmatic
Child".

All that and more. I wouldn't dispute that something
remains. Janet Hobhouse quotes from her brother Leo that
Gertrude Stein's "massive self-admiration and in part
self-assurance" had enabled her "to build something rather
effective of her life and work". But I am not sure what that
something was; and by this book I am confirmed in thinking
that it wasn't much. A name? Dead for thirty years, she is still
a name. For what? Perhaps for no more than the magic
mysteries of Art. Unread, unreadable, the "cold suet roll" of
her work, said Wyndham Lewis, was "the same sticky opaque
mass all through and all along. . . weighted and projected with
a sibylline urge. . . mournful and monstrous", fat without
nerve.

This assembly of information, admission and claim leads me
to a triple conclusion. First, this Gertrude Stein was only an
ectoparasite on the modern revolution in the arts, a revolution
we do have to re-draw and purge of some of its nonsense.
Second, this Gertrude Stein in a way foretells our television
age, in which the crystal screen magically presents us with an
apparent something created from some actual nothing, or with
some virtual nobody or non-existence "interesting" for his
wild hair, or for his oiled Assyrian hair and his pink evening
coat. Thirdly, I conclude that, all said and done, the laugh has
been less on this Gertrude Stein of ours than on the gullibility
of a public, a vogue public, English and American, which so
largely accepted her, or even created her. Stuffed, Gertrude
Stein should be set on a perch, as a warning, in the Museum of
Pseudo-Modernity.

Janet Hobhouse has written rather more of a caution than she
realizes, perhaps.

Ideas of Place and Poetry

1. AN IDEA OF THE NORTH SEA

Do you nurse any special idea, any special feeling about the North Sea? If we say the Aegean or the Mediterranean, it is rather like saying Greece or Rome or Venice — the name carries an extra. A load of inherited feeling and affection and association is added to the mere label of sea or city. But the North Sea: for most of us, do those two words combining into a name mean anything more than a stretch of salt waters in the atlas, or a distance, which has to be crossed between Harwich and Hamburg or Gothenburg or Oslo?

My theory is that the sea-surrounded English do not like the sea, unless it happens to be blue and smooth and warm and distant in time and space, a halcyon image, a halcyon symbol, which, though elsewhere, can actually be visited and entered, up to the neck, in comfort. No scrotum-tightening sea, to borrow James Joyce's heroic adjective.

And to that, explaining an indifference to the North Sea, explaining a refusal to accord it a symbolical personality, I add a second theory: that the English, hash of Saxons and Angles and Celts and Norwegians and Danes and Normans, do not greatly care for their strictly English or Anglo-Saxon history, for strictly English or Anglo-Saxon origins on the other side of the North Sea, along the Frisian coasts of Holland and Germany. I suspect that, in a quiz programme, most earnest and brisk polymaths would do badly on Anglo-Saxon kings and queens and kingdoms and saints. If, on that account, we neglect an idea of the North Sea, I shall say that we miss some of the most powerful and sombre — certainly sombre — natural poetry, or poetry of place, which is available to us.

Can I point to a work of the imagination embodying an idea of the North Sea? Yes. George Crabbe, the poet, was born and reared at Aldeburgh in Suffolk, and Crabbe wrote the savage verse story of Peter Grimes, the North Sea fisherman who murdered his apprentices. Then Benjamin Britten — he was also born on the East Anglian edge of the North Sea — composed his opera of *Peter Grimes*. That makes two works of imagination with the North Sea moving inside them like fate.

If you want to hear the North Sea, dark and dark-clouded, swelling up into music which is ominous yet benedictional,

listen to the four sea interludes from *Peter Grimes*. If you want
the North Sea in verse which is both mournful and powerful,
read Crabbe, catching, in story after story, the way in which
low East Anglia merges into the North Sea, aware of the
shingles and the slow twist and crawl of tide-waters lapsing
back through the mud.

Crabbe is effective on the dangers of the North Sea along his
East Anglian coast. There is a tale in which he describes how a
picnic party sail out and make tea — with a shining tea-urn and
all — on a sandbank at low tide. The tide turns, their boat has
broken away and drifted out of reach, the tide rises higher and
higher, up the legs, the bodies, of the pleasure party, up to
their necks and nearly to their lips.

Knowing the dangers of the North Sea, Crabbe can describe
how tides driven extra high by a north-west wind can break
over the land. A girl watched, in her threatened farmhouse:

> And from her bow-formed window on the west
> Saw the broad stream for many a rood engulph
> The salt short herbage. Wider yet became
> The wat'ry waste, and billowy like the sea. . .

>   — it could not be
> But those wild waters in their strength would meet!
> All would be sea, and like a stranded ship
> Their house a wreck, and all it held a prey.

Then — very Crabbe-like — the clouds part, the moon
smiles down on the storm and the advancing flood-billows,
and Crabbe admits to "a strong enchantment in the scene".
The girl, gazing through her bow-window, feels a strange
delight:

> Made up by terror and astonishment!
> And admiration and religious awe
> That strove with fear, and made divine the event.

For me, such imaginings combine into the idea of the North
Sea, at any rate of the North Sea as I have experienced it from
the edges of Essex, East Anglia and Lincolnshire — threat,
terror, astonishment, strange delight, awe, a kind of divinity.

Dunwich, on the Suffolk coast, the place which was, and
isn't any more, offers this delight of the North Sea in a
particular concentration. I was there, in a cold February, when
the snowdrops were out along the last piece of a Dunwich lane
or street; snow showers were coming in over the sea. The

scour of the North Sea had cut the land back to the last
churchyard. Lumps of the church itself sprawled down on the
beach. It is along the shingles of Dunwich that the Suffolk
artist, Charles Keene, used to walk up and down at midnight,
alone, playing laments to the North Sea on the great pipes. On
the same shingle, one of my family, who is a bone
archaeologist, was walking with her husband, and talking of
fossil bones and the late post-glacial formation of the North
Sea. Her husband bent down and picked up a black leg-bone,
and said sceptically: "I suppose this is a fossil bone" — and it
was, not a human leg-bone, not the leg-bone of some
Dunwich mayor or alderman from the churchyard above, but
the fossil leg-bone of an ox, a *Bos primigenius,* washed in from
the more ancient, drowned lands of the North Sea.

Besides Charles Keene, various life-haunted men have visited
Dunwich, thinking about the medieval city which is not there
any longer. Thomas Hardy was one of them, another was
Henry James, a third was Swinburne. James, so rich in his
reaction to place and the enigmas of the ordinary or the
unusual, came to the crumbling cliff-top of Dunwich when
that last church was still erect, out on the verge, and found
some wonderful sentences on the very absence of the Dunwich
that used to exist. "All the grossness of its positive life," he
said, was now at the bottom of the sea. Dunwich was "not
even the ghost of its dead self; almost all you can say of it is
that it consists of the mere letters of its old name." "There is a
presence in what is missing."

Henry James mentioned "the verses of an extraordinary
poetic eloquence", in which Swinburne glanced at Dunwich.
He did not quote them, but I shall — from the long poem
Swinburne actually called *By the North Sea*, the "song the sea-
wind gave him from the sea". At Dunwich, Swinburne found
death and the sea, and all the end of all the glory of God:
"Dust, and grass, and barren silent stones". And dead like
God, he found the one hollow church tower (of which Charles
Keene made a desolate etching), as he walked among the
graves:

Now displaced, devoured and desecrated,
    Now by Time's hands darkly disinterred
These poor dead that sleeping here awaited
    Long the archangel's re-creating word,
Closed about with roofs and walls high-gated
    Till the blast of judgment should be heard,

Naked, shamed, cast out of consecration,
   Corpse and coffin, yea the very graves
Scoffed at, scattered, shaken from their station,
   Spurned and scourged of wind and sea like slaves,
Desolate beyond man's desolation
   Shrink and sink into the waste of waves. . .

Rows on rows and line by line they crumble,
   They that thought for all time through to be.
Scarce a stone whereon a child might stumble
   Breaks the grim field paced alone of me.

I don't say the sun doesn't shine at Dunwich. It does, brilliantly. Even then, I have always found Dunwich sunshine emphasizing, as it did for Swinburne. I am sure, that missing Dunwich, and emphasizing as well the North Sea, however lazily creaming on the Suffolk shingle, as a sea of mortality.

Swinburne came from Northumberland; up there, between Newcastle or Craster and the mouth of the Tweed, I make the North Sea of Dunstanburgh and Holy Island and low cliffs of ochre sandstone much more into an image of felicity.

In between, there is the Yorkshire North Sea, high cliffs, chalk, shale, and fossils along the coast; I don't know that stretch; I don't know that extensive curve before the Humber, from which the North Sea has sliced so many villages. But there still remains the Lincolnshire North Sea, the sea Tennyson used to visit from his rectory under the wolds. Caravans and huts or no, it is along this Lincolnshire coast that I have most felt the North Sea as image, according to place and circumstances, of power and splendour and endlessness. Sands and gleam — and Tennyson indulging himself and letting the wind into his black beard — at least when he came home in his bearded days — and asking "Why?" about himself in the world, and asking it aloud of the North Sea and the wind. The demilune of beach and dunes from Mablethorpe to Skegness has been deprived of some of its old poetry of the desolate, but holiday grab and sprawl cannot stop the North Sea performing grand Tennysonian gestures along this curve of

Grey sandbanks, and pale sunsets — dreary wind,
Dim shores, dense rains, and heavy-clouded sea.

Tennyson describes such gestures at night, under the moon:

As the crest of some slow-arching wave,
Heard in dead night along that table shore

Drops flat, and after the great waters break
Whitening for half a league, and thin themselves,
Far over sands marbled with moon and cloud,
From less and less to nothing.

And there is a story, which may be told again, of the young
Tennyson, walking from night to dawn along the shore
somewhere near Gibraltar Point or Wainfleet Sand, below
Skegness. It was 4 am, and he was wearing no coat, no hat,
when he met a fisherman, and said good morning to him, to
have the fisherman reply: "Thou poor fool, thou doesn't knaw
whether it be night or daä."

In from this North Sea coast are the Enderby villages, Wood
Enderby, Mavis Enderby, on the wolds, and Bag Enderby,
next door to Somersby where Tennyson grew up, reminders of
another Lincolnshire poet, and of what can, at a pinch, be
described as another North Sea poem — Jean Ingelow's "High
Tide on the Coast of Lincolnshire". The sea-wall breaks. The
high tide of the North Sea, or at any rate of the Wash, drives
inland over the Lindsey fens, and, to warn everyone, the
Boston ringers play the bell-tune, "The Brides of Mavis
Enderby", on the high bells of Boston Stump.

> The heart had hardly time to beat,
> Before a shallow seething wave
>   Sobbed in the grasses at our feet;
> The feet had hardly time to flee
> Before it brake against the knee
> And all the world was in the sea.

A disaster — a North Sea disaster all right, though every time I
re-read that charming never-to-be-overlooked Victorian poem,
I am almost surprised to discover again that it is about death
and drowning.

There is never any doubt of that kind about Crabbe. When
he edges towards doom, or North Sea doom, the doom is in-
trinsically there, in the sparkling glumness of his rhythms and
his scene.

First, the slow tide returning, then the sea, at Aldeburgh:

> Beneath an ancient bridge, the straiten'd flood
> Rolls through its sloping banks of slimy mud;
> Near it a sunken boat resists the tide
> That frets and hurries to th' opposing side.

The lines slope down to the thud or not quite so hard thump of
the last rhyming word:

> Here on its wiry stem, in rigid bloom,
> Grows the salt lavender that lacks perfume;
> Here the dwarf sallows creep, the septfoil harsh,
> And the soft slimy mallow of the marsh;
> Low on the ear the distant billows sound,
> And just in view appears their stony bound.

There you have the ominous North Sea, or its low fringe: the
North Sea which, sorrowful but less mournful, if also less
masculine, Tennyson (who much admired Crabbe) gathered up
in that exact adjective "heavy-clouded". "Dim shores" — it is
worth saying it over again — "dim shores, dense rains, and
heavy-clouded sea". Once I looked down from the graveyard
at Dunwich, on the edge of this heavy-clouded North Sea, and
saw flakes of snow settling on two skulls — husband and wife,
do you think? — which had come to a temporary rest halfway
down the dribbling clay and sands of the cliff.

2. AN IDEA OF THE DAFFODIL FIELDS

The young John Masefield, long ago in 1913, published a
poem, a tragic story poem, a tragic love poem, which he called
"The Daffodil Fields"; and though he talks of his tragedy
taking place in Shropshire, I am pretty sure that he was
picturing all the while the daffodil fields which I have in mind,
and which I think of, partly in relation to a few poets other
than Masefield, as a kind of *hortus conclusus*, an enclosed garden,
if a wild one more or less, a kind of secret earthly paradise of
the kind all of us need.

In earlier springs, before heedless picking of the daffodils was
stopped, it was possible to find the way to these daffodil fields,
a few miles north-west of Gloucester, by following the broken
daffodils which had dropped from huge bunches tied to the
carriers and handlebars of bicycles. The trail of wild daffodils
led to Newent, first of all, then towards the parishes of
Dymock and Kempley, near the border which divides
Gloucestershire from Herefordshire. It was just over the
border, in Herefordshire, at Ledbury, that John Masefield was
born in 1878. I suppose this daffodil district which is enclosed
between the Severn and the Wye, and sheltered to the south-
west by the heights of the Forest of Dean, and to the south by
the broad, far-visible height of May Hill, was itself forest at

one time. It is still heavily wooded, and it is speckled with old
woodland place-names. Awkward, rather narrow little roads or
lanes traverse it, tarred lanes which are given to turning sharply
at blind corners. Plenty of small streams run about under the
trees and round tree-edged or tree-enclosed meadows.

Anyone familiar with these Gloucestershire and
Herefordshire daffodil fields will see them in the first stanzas of
Masefield's poem. He starts with a cold hill-spring, which
bubbles up and flows away, and turns and babbles and is
trodden by cattle, and passes woods. Then:

> Under the road it runs, and now it slips
> Past the great ploughland, babbling, drop and linn,
> To the moss'd stumps of elm trees which it lips
> And blackberry-bramble-trails where eddies spin.
> Then, on its left, some short-grassed fields begin,
> Red-clayed and pleasant, which the young spring fills
> With the never-quiet joy of dancing daffodils.

Accurate, at least. Masefield describes the daffodil leaves
dotting the grass with blue-grey, the way the nodding beauty
of the daffodils "shakes along the ground":

> There, when the first green shoots of tender corn
> Show on the plough; when the first drift of white
> Stars the black branches of the spiky thorn,
> And afternoons are warm and evenings light,
> The shivering daffodils do take delight,
> Shaking beside the brook, and grass comes green,
> And blue dog-violets come and glistening celandine.

Daffodils, even if nowadays fenced and gated off, come up
everywhere. That red-clayed soil of the Old Red Sandstone is
right for them. They advance from woods into meadows, they
grow up between roots, they occupy little promontories or
bare earth or black mould round which the streams curl. They
are as natural through this daffodil country as bluebells or
wood anemones elsewhere.

In any case, this low but not level country seems shut in and
secret, on the way to nowhere, revolving on itself. Whether he
meant them for this area or no, all Masefield's descriptions will
serve for it; and certainly Masefield, telling his "tale of woe
among the daffodils", thought of his special area as one of
difference, signed and summed by the delight of its
Shakespearian rather than Wordsworthian flowers — a wild
hortus conclusus suitable to love, with which Time, the daffodil-
picker, interfered.

In the end, after absences and desperation and returns, the girl's two lovers kill each other, one with a bill-hook, one with a stake, on a field of those wild daffodils. "You come to tread a bloody path of flowers," says one dying lover to the girl. "All the gold flowers are covered up with blood."

I would not claim that Masefield's poem is entirely successful, but it is worth trying it — in his *Collected Poems* — for some good touches, at least, and especially if you make a visit to the daffodil fields. My extra point is that another group of poets, including two of a more authentic power, Robert Frost, the American, and Edward Thomas, lived for a while among these daffodils, or in these daffodil parishes, and must, I imagine, have partaken of that same surety — though not one of them was a native of the locality, like Masefield — of enjoying a spring garden of the mind and the emotions, as if it were known only to themselves. Besides Frost and Edward Thomas, the others were the inconsiderable poets Lascelles Abercrombie and Wilfrid Gibson, two northerners by origin.

My suspicion is that Masefield, or at any rate the particulars of his "Daffodil Fields", must have had something to do with the coming of these poets to the secret garden. It is said that Abercrombie settled here in the daffodil country, in 1913, the year in which Masefield's poem came out, only because his sister was already established a few miles from Dymock, as wife of a well-to-do farmer. The Abercrombies were followed by the Gibsons. Then came their friend Robert Frost, with his wife and his four children. Edward Thomas, who knew Frost (and Masefield), and who could be called a collector and experiencer of sympathetic countrysides, stayed off and on with the Abercrombies, and became intimate with the neighbourhood. He stayed with the Frosts as well, in their cottage near Ledbury; and it was in this secret garden that Robert Frost prodded Edward Thomas, critic, often fierce critic, of poetry, into becoming Edward Thomas, writer of poems.

When the Frosts arrived at Dymock in 1914, it was April, and the daffodils were out; and apple trees, pear trees and plum trees, this being part of the orchard country of the Vale of Severn. But there is not much direct influence of the locality — why should there be? — in poems by Frost or poems by Edward Thomas. Reverence, all the same, for Thomas (who is the more stylish poet, in my view) and respect for Robert Frost (and for Masefield as well) are extra reasons for coming to the daffodil fields in the right month — March or April — on the right kind of day. Thomas wrote, though not in a poem, that hereabouts the fields were so small and the trees along the hedges so many that a distant view suggests solid woodland. There are records of meetings with black-mopped W.H. Davies and Rupert Brooke, beautiful as a large girl, and aware of it; records of outdoor parties along the Leadon, the small stream which flows down from Ledbury between Little Iddens, the brick-and-timber cottage rented by the Frosts, and The Old Nail-shop, the brick-and-timber cottage which housed the Gibson family. There were long evenings of discussion, and long walks were taken together by Edward Thomas and Robert Frost.

Frost, in one poem written years later, remembered how the two of them, walking home from the Malverns, in the north, through an evening drenched with water-mist, saw to their wonder a small prismatic bow ahead of them, caused by the moon. I am not quite sure what phenomenon these two poets witnessed in fact. Was it a fog-bow caused by an intensely bright moon behind their backs, or was it a halo round a moon in front of them, a halo which seemed low in the sky in the peculiar circumstances of their descent from the Malverns? This "Iris by Night", as Frost called his poem, this bow, became a prismatic circle enclosing them:

> It lifted from its dewy pediment
> Its two mote-swimming many-coloured ends
> And gathered them together in a ring.
> And we stood in it softly circled round
> From all division time or foe can bring
> In a relation of elected friends.

Such was the closeness and indivisibility of the brief yet extraordinary friendship between these two poets, English and American, occasioned by these few months or few occasions of a companionship they had neither of them experienced before in their lives. And I have wondered, though perhaps this was not quite in the line of these two poets of man in nature, if they ever went together into the small Norman church of Kempley, Old Kempley church, by the side of a brook a little way out of Dymock, and interested themselves in the paintings inside, a fourteenth-century wheel of life, and a Christ on a rainbow, of the twelfth century. Perhaps — though I think that these now restored paintings were not so striking or so visible in their day.

To me, that small isolated church, painted from end to end, now seems integral to the daffodil fields, to be visited again whenever the fields are visited, as if it were a chapel standing in the corner of some medieval illumination of a *hortus conclusus* or of the spring season in a Book of Hours.

For these Dymock or daffodil poets, here in their brief enjoyment, before the war which sent Robert Frost back to America and killed Edward Thomas in France, the only irritations were the Earl Beauchamp's bullying and interfering gamekeeper — he once threatened Frost and Thomas with his gun, and was visited in his cottage by Frost, who told the gamekeeper that he would come and "beat the daylight out of him", if he repeated his behaviour — that and the egotism and conceit (Frost's description) of W.H. Davies on a long visit. The tramp-poet kept fairly sober, but would upset Frost and disgust the Gibsons by talking of the tarts he slept with. Still, he was a better poet than little correct Abercrombie or flat pedestrian Gibson. Frost must surely have admired some of his tougher, blacker, less sentimental poems, though he declared that Davies didn't "really know nature at all".

For Masefield, the snake in the paradise of daffodils was Time, who brought the farmers to death and poverty, and lovers to dismay and murder. "Daffodil picker Time took from their lives the glow", just as the pickers from the towns picked the glow off the daffodil fields, and trod down the blue-green leaves. It was a trouble even then, the inordinate daffodil-picking for money, and it is curious to read of what we regard as a modern evil already plaguing the country sixty years ago. Masefield's double murder takes place by

> an old farm where always the wind grieves
> High in the fir boughs, moaning,

a farm which people call The Roughs:

> And there the pickers come, picking for town
> Those dancing daffodils; all day they pick;
> Hard-featured women, weather-beaten pram,
> Or swarthy-red, the colour of old brick.

He doesn't like them at all. An old shepherd, or old carter, regards them as they rest and eat, and Masefield calls them a "gaugrel tribe" — "gaugrel" meaning beggar or vagabond — a tribe of beauty-destroying gypsies, or didakis — half-gypsies. I wonder if he ever saw the daffodil fields at weekends in the full age of cars, the vast picking, crushing, heading and destroying, that went on and came to a climax a few years ago, when at last the daffodils began to be wired off and protected? That was done by the gaugrel tribe of all of us, not even for a living.

The daffodil fields are uniquely worth knowing, I would affirm, even now, wire or no wire. Yet I am glad to have seen them in something of their ancient freedom, before barbed wire and locked gates became necessary, and before they began to exemplify one of the problems of an overpopulated, over-motorized island.

At the end of Masefield's poem, which cannot be read without tears, at least for the girl, her in-laws hear her singing and moving in the night, in the room with her two dead. They break in, and find the singer on the floor beside the dead man she really loved, still "singing her passionate last of life away".

> White flowers had fallen from a blackthorn spray
> Over her loosened hair. Pale flowers of spring
> Filled the white room of death; they covered everything.
> Primroses, daffodils and cuckoo-flowers.
> She bowed her singing head on Michael's breast.
> "Oh, it was sweet," she cried, "that love of ours,
> You were the dearest, sweet; I loved you best."

In 1976, the spring landscapes of England, the flower-landscape of England — or do I say this because I am no longer young? — don't quite so readily prompt us to love or to images of love, the *hortus conclusus* being over-trampled.

3. AN IDEA OF A BORDER

With devolution in the air, should I say that England is blessed, or cursed, with border territories? I mean, either way, it is a kind of mental advantage to have ambiguous areas along the border with Scotland, which is half a Celtic border, and the border with Wales, which is entirely a Celtic border, and then along the little Celtic border, along the Tamar between England and Cornwall.

It is a scenic advantage, too, the borders — at least, the two long borders, running through wild, strong country. The border I shall talk about is the Welsh one, or as the Welsh, I suppose, would say, with equal legitimacy, the English one. I am thinking of it not just as scenery, not as a wriggling line, not as Offa's Dyke, but as a band of ambiguous country on either side of the line, along which two histories, two cultures, two peoples, two sentiments, two states, of light and dark, interpenetrate — even two enmities, if you think of the past. Border territories have a kind of electricity (perhaps not something to say in these days of East and West Germany) which is stimulating. You meet in them familiarity blended with unfamiliarity; you remember — and, as well, you look for — the differences. You recall old invasions and raids and greeds and savageries which were not to the credit of either country.

As between the Scotch border (I am English, and I say "Scotch" and not "Scottish"; I believe strict Scotchmen also prefer to say "Scotch") — as between the Scotch border and the Welsh Marches, there is first of all one geographical, topo-graphical, symbolic dissimilarity to observe. The border is a matter of North and South, the Marches of East and West. North stands, in northern estimation, for Spartan or tartan energy against effete Southerners, who have taken a different view about northern barbarity: it is oatcakes against the wheat loaf. East, in an English view, can stand for light — that's where the sun rises, after all — and West or Wales has stood, the sun going down beyond the mountains, for a strangeness and darkness. In the Scotch lowlands, Englishmen have reflected, they at least speak an Anglian English more or less understandable. The other side of the Wye, the Severn, the Dee, they speak — if you go in deep enough — a language of a now restricted world few Englishmen can catch hold of; though Englishmen may be assured by translations that masterly verse, heroic, amatory and satirical, was written in that language as far back as history goes. And I think at once, in translation, of a delightful poem of the fifteenth-century Welshman who goes to an English wedding at Flint, altogether too English a town for him, hoping to make some money by singing to his harp. The shifty Saxons prefer an English bagpipe, a devil's pouch which makes a noise like a dirty, diseased and pregnant goat.

However, since I should be talking about place, in one way and another, not about the past, I should like, even a little devilishly, to take you up to a high place, to which you may not have climbed, in order to exhibit my English sense of relative light and relative dark. I am beginning with my favourite road to the Marches and to Difference, to the southern lands of ambiguity — not through Hereford, which itself is always a reminder of ambiguity, since it means the army ford, one way or the other — but through Ross-on-Wye, and Owen's Cross and Broad Oak, and over the Monnow past Skenfrith Castle, White Castle and Grosmont Castle towards Abergavenny.

The highland zone is beginning, the hills broaden and mount up and reveal blue shoulders; and before descending to

Abergavenny, I make you pull in below Ysgyryd Fawr —
Great Skirrid — a bilberry ridge rising to about 1,600 feet,
several hundred feet above the roadway. On top, where there
are a few stones left of a chapel of St Michael, the archangel of
high places and isolated hills, who was a great favourite of
mediaeval Welshmen, mediaeval Cornishmen and mediaeval
Bretons, I exhibit my feelings about — from the English pole
— east and west, and light and dark.

I assume a dark day with a south-west wind which nearly
blows you away. I assume clouds, black clouds, close down,
hurrying towards England. You look east (I also assume that
the day is getting on): the sun is lowering itself in the other
direction and putting light on an England, a Herefordshire of
sheep pastures which look green. You look west — and
mountains, the Black Mountains and the Brecon Beacons, are
black against sinking light, throwing vast shadows forward,
which are blacker than the fast clouds overhead. Looking
westward, it may seem home to a Welshman: to an
Englishman, the black, western view can seem formidable and
discomfiting. It may look different on a nice day, early, when
the sun is in the east, and is illuminating the border.

But that will do for the moment. You are on or in the
nervous strip; and you will be on it still for some miles, if you
go and take this favourite road of mine beyond Abergavenny
towards Brecon, and Tretower (which is one of the most
rewarding mediaeval houses to visit in all Britain) and Grongar
Hill and the Tywi and Carmarthen. I am proposing another
stop after you pass the turning to Tretower, and before you
reach Brecon, precisely where this valley road, running along
with the river Usk, comes to a corner, at a church with a yew
tree among its surrounding graves; the church of Llansant-
fraedd-juxta-Usk, the church of St Freda, or St Bride.

Under the yew tree there is a large flat gravestone,
introducing now a metaphysical border, or a metaphysical
aspect of the border. The grave is that of Henry Vaughan, the
poet, the Swan of Usk, inscribed by his wish in Latin: "Here I
lie, a useless servant, and the greatest of sinners." I am not
lecturing on Vaughan's poems — I am only pointing to special
ambiguities involving Vaughan and his poems of wonder, and
a country of wonder, of stream, rock, mountain, light,
shadow, foxgloves and dog-roses.

Descended from the Vaughans who owned Tretower, Henry
Vaughan was born — in 1622 — only a mile or so down the
road in a house called Newton. If you clamber up to Newton

(it is marked on the one-inch map), on the side of a hill called
the Allt, you see Vaughan's earthly world, the Vale of Usk
below, the great black Brecon Beacons beyond. The
ambiguities are those of a poet Welsh and yet English, English
and yet Welsh, who grew up speaking both languages; a poet
of the extraordinary landscapes around him, and of mental
visions of eternity and the happiness of a descried and
meditated heaven. He wrote metaphysical poems, yes, but
images and poems were suggested to him by the gleam of
water, by the morning lights and the moonlights of these
Breconshire hills and mountains. For instance, behind the Allt,
at the back of Vaughan's house, hides a lake — Llangorse Lake,
rather a peculiar, indeterminate, misty extent of blue or grey
surface. Vaughan must have been thinking of this lake when he
wrote a poem he called "The Shower" — though perhaps he
ought to have called it "The Cloud". Anyhow, it begins:

'Twas so. I saw thy birth: That drowsie lake

— and drowsie is just the word —

From her faint bosome breathed thee. . .

> But, now at Even,
> Too grosse for heaven,
Thou fall'st in teares, and weepst for thy mistake.

Another poem likens his blood, his spirit, to the river Usk in
flood. When there have been storms, the Usk comes down red
from the Old Red Sandstone soil it cuts through. Vaughan sees
the red river tearing along below his home: he knows his blood
"is not a sea",

> But a shallow, bounded flood
>   Though red as he,
> Yet have I flows, as strong as his,
>   And boyling streames that rave
> With the same curling force, and hisse
>   As doth the mountain'd wave.

Genuinely, if in conventional terms, this Anglo-Welsh poet
maintained his content in his extraordinary Welsh environment. He translated a Spanish euology of the country life,
which says that hapy is the countryman who lives away from
the court and the law, "and in the shadow of some fair wood
with unspeakable delight contemplates the beauty of fields,
meadows, fountains and rivers. . . daily delighted to hear" —
this is very Welsh — "the bleating of his sheepe and lambs".

Moving about this big countryside in all weathers, Vaughan was the local doctor, given to solitary devotions and much thought about living and dying, and light and darkness — though it was on the side of living and light that he always came out, in the end. He translated one of the Welsh "Verses of the Months":

In March birds couple, and new birth
Of herbs and flowers breaks through the earth,
But in the grave none stirs his head;
Long is the impris'ment of the dead.

As if he was thinking of his own poems and this surrounding neighbourhood, he wrote in one of his now, I suppose, little-read devotional books or small treatises: "There is no object we can look upon, but will do us the kindnesse to put us in mind of our mortality, if we would be so wise as to make use of it. The day dyes into night, the spring into winter, flowers have their rootes ever in their graves, leaves loose their greenesse, and drop under our feete; where they flye about and whisper unto us."

From the frozen valleys of the Usk, in December 1647, Henry Vaughan sent the copy for his second book of verse up to London, to St Paul's Churchyard, to the fashionable publisher, the Faber and Faber of the time, Humphrey Moseley, who had published Milton's first book two years before. He started off with a Latin poem announcing himself, saying that he was a child of Wales, born where Father Usk wandered through spreading valleys under airy mountains. Then he gave Usk a poem for himself, praising his sands, his clear waters — they are still clear — and his wild roses; adding the Usk to the other rivers of other poets, to the Hebrus, the Tiber, the Moselle, the Thames, the Severn, and then saying something I think we should remember — that

Poets (like angels) where they once appear
Hallow the place, and each succeeding year
Adds rev'rence to't, such as at length doth give
This aged faith, That there their Genii live.

That is not a bad sentiment — that a place retains something of the genius or being of an authentic poet, an authentic painter who loved it, each — place and poet — having something to reveal of the other. This Breconshire neighbourhood — reading and enjoying this neighbourhood — shows something

of what may be found in Vaughan's life and poems; the poems
— reading and enjoying them — show something of what an
attuned reader and walker may find in explorations around the
Usk and Llansantfraedd and the Brecon Beacons, both poems
and neighbourhood illuminating views of human life.

It fits that up and down the Welsh-English border there are
other districts where penetration of English and Welsh, and the
meeting of the highland landscape and the lowland landscape,
have had metaphysical consequences.

Such consequences are visible in the nature mysticism of the
poet Traherne, living in the country outside Hereford, in the
English area of this ambiguity of the border. They are visible in
visions of landscape and life in the journals, written down in
the last century, of Francis Kilvert, living not so far away at
Clyro, on the Welsh, the Radnorshire, side of the Wye, near
Hay-on-Wye, under hills rising towards two thousand feet.

Then, if you move north again up the Marches you come,
once more on the Welsh side of the rivers, to an Englishman in
ecstasy in the Vale of Clwyd — to the poet Gerard Manley
Hopkins looking towards the Snowdon range and shaping an
ecstatic, religious uprush of landscape feeling in poems of an
immense felicity.

Felicity is Traherne's word. He found immense felicity, the
highest essence of his religion, in everything revealed by the
sun. He said felicity was so wonderful a bird of paradise that it
couldn't fly among men without dropping some feathers, and I
don't think it fanciful to detect the border scenery he knew,
westwards from Hereford towards the Brecon Beacons, the
Black Mountains and Radnor Forest, in his remarks that the
sun "illuminates the World to entertain you with prospects",
that the sun "surroundeth you with the Beauty of Hills and
Valleys", that "the Mountains are better than solid diamonds".
The wonderful ambiguities of this border country were at
work — it is more than coincidence — in Vaughan, Traherne,
Kilvert and Hopkins across the centuries; though I suppose we
are rather more likely to feel some of those darker ambiguities
of the border country which I mentioned to begin with.
Certainly the experiences and preferences of poets can direct us
to the landscapes likely, in one way or another, to have most
effect on us. Certainly the good poet is tied to the environment
he prefers.

4. AN IDEA OF THE CENTRE

The centre of England, that country — try it with a pair of
dividers and an atlas — where you can never be more than 50
miles from the sea, is reckoned to be in the parish of Meriden,
between Coventry and Birmingham, in the county of
Warwickshire. In that rich central county there are specialities.
In Stratford, Shakespeare; on the butcher's counter, white
puddings; on the banks — "I know a bank where the wild
thyme grows," and so on — a plethora of summer
nightingales; slow, on the whole clean, rural rivers, and dead
or dying elms, in astounding number.

I shall come back to the dead and dying elm trees, which
might be taken as a symbol, and remark, meanwhile, that
Shakespeare, who reflects Warwickshire upbringing in
hundreds of lines and details, is not the only Warwickshire
author, that other writers from this centre of England also
suggest a centrality of English experience, English image-
making; and that, *per contra*, some explorers or appreciators
have found a too-muchness in this green county and its cattle
meadows and its mansions. Henry James appraised
Warwickshire with the fresh, sympathetic but sceptical senses
of someone who was half a foreigner or half a stranger. He felt
its centrality. He felt a ripeness, he hints at an over-ripeness in
its "large, lawn-like meadows", in lawns, domestic ones,
outside territorial homes and castles, which were, he said,
"delicious to one's sentient boot-sole". The adjectives with
which this most admirable observer establishes his account of
Warwickshire are adjectives of praise which can also be taken as
a little less than praise — "fat", "cushiony", "ordered",
"mellow", "conservative"; to these he adds even "bovine",
and "ovine", and "asinine", as if he found some pretensions in
Warwickshire which were ridiculous.

I pick out one extraordinary image. He strolls from the
garden of a spacious and easy Warwickshire rectory, where
"younge fresshe folkes" are playing tennis on the inevitable
lawn, into the churchyard alongside, around a small Norman
church. The sunset is "red behind a dark row of rook-haunted
elms", and James goes on:

> The stillness seemed the greater because three or four rustic
> children were playing, with little soft cries, among the
> crooked deep-buried gravestones. One poor little girl, who
> seemed deformed, had climbed up some steps that served as
> a pedestal for a tall, mediaeval-looking cross. She sat perched

there and stared at me through the gloaming. This was the heart of England; it might have been the very pivot of the wheel on which her fortune revolves.

The children playing among the graves, the deformed child on the pivot of the wheel of English fortune. . . . All things change; and one may wonder in what extraordinary sentence James would fix the moribund elms of Warwickshire, if he could drive through the county today.

Of course, Henry James was well aware that Warwickshire belonged to George Eliot as well as to Shakespeare, that this central county was the land of *Middlemarch* and *The Mill on the Floss* and *Adam Bede*. George Eliot: the Warwickshire land-agent's daughter; Shakespeare, the Warwickshire yeoman's or butcher's son — two central authors, in fiction and in poetry, from the central county.

Of course, he was well aware of Shakespeare's Stratford. He found no contradiction between the "nutritive suggestion" of Warwickshire scenery, and the ripeness, health and humanity and "underlying morality" of Shakespeare. At Stratford, he said, Shakespeare planted, "to grow for ever, the torment of his unguessed riddle".

The swans still float along the Avon, but I think now, in 1976, I would go elsewhere in Warwickshire to feel at least an English centrality. Henry James complained slightly, in the now far-off 1870s, of the "cockneyfication" of English romantic sites. Employing a milder word, or, at least, a word which is less conscious of class, it is fair enough now to complain of pressure, the pressure of many backs, fronts, and shoulders, packs and prams, everywhere.

Today, if you go to Stratford Church, to see Shakespeare's ledger-stone and that prim bust above it on the chancel wall, you find yourself in a long, slow river of people, guided and hemmed by soft ropes, which prevent you from stepping into the chancel.

For my English centrality I would go nowadays to a different town, and into another church — to Warwick itself, the county town, and into St Mary's, Warwick. Let me tell you, if you don't know, and remind you if you do, of what is to be found in that church; and then ask a question: why isn't this church one of the special shrines or cultural holy interiors of England, acquaintance with which no one can avoid?

Crossing the main street, avoiding the Midland traffic, and walking past some bland town-housing of the eighteenth century, you enter the church (most of which is itself no more than a reasonably distinguished rebuilding, over a Norman crypt, of a medieval church burnt down in the seventeenth century), past the white marble bust of the poet Walter Savage Landor. That is the first point. He has a nice, fresh face, this very independent, rather outrageous, undisciplined man, who was born farther on down the hill, in Warwick, and who wrote most of the best and most disciplined epigrams in the English language.

> Triumphant demons stand, and Angels start,
> To see the abysses of the human heart.

That is Landor, and so is this:

> When I gaze upon the sky
> And the sea below, I cry
> Thus be poetry and love,
> Deep beneath and bright above.

And:

> Here lies Landor
> Whom they thought a goose
> But he proved a gander

(though this clear poet of the central county is not buried in St Mary's, Warwick, but in Florence — there is something not inept in a life passage from Warwickshire to Florence, where Landor hoped to be buried, at Fiesole, under the shadow of four mimosas planted by the woman he most loved).

After passing Landor's bust, the next thing to do in the church is to walk to the far end and step down into the Beauchamp Chapel — which escaped the fire — into the late Middle Ages, and contemplate what I suppose to be the most serene and moving funereal effigy in any English church, of Richard Beauchamp, Earl of Warwick. He died in 1439, and he is described, I hope correctly, in the *Dictionary of National Biography*, as "a brave and chivalrous warrior in an age of chivalry". At any rate, this soldier and statesman, who, in his day, made the pilgrimage to Jerusalem, where "he performed his vows, and set up his arms on the north side of the temple", lies there, on a tomb chest, a long figure of polished and gilded brass with a long face. It is the face one remembers — it is said not to be a portrait, which I don't believe — the face and the fingers of elongated brass, the two brass hands which he raises to a boss of the Virgin Mary in the vaulting overhead. A wonderful image, altogether, of dignity and mortality, of an unbumptious, unaggressive confidence.

The Earl of Warwick's great effigy is not the last of the memorable things in St Mary's, Warwick. After the Beauchamp Chapel, you come into a chapter-house. This also survived the fire, and it is almost filled with a black monument, a black, stone coffin, canopied with black, cornered with black obelisks. The date is just after 1628, the black, Calvinist taste of the monument is disconcerting, it has a black, negative grandeur, an ostentation of the funereal; and it is to another poet, Fulke Greville, Lord Brooke. The stark inscription is rather a goodbye to the world, than a humble if confident knock on the gates of heaven. But it has its own worldly dignity and simplicity — saying this, and this only, in an epitaph written by Greville himself, "Fulke Greville, Servant to Queen Elizabeth, Councillor to King James, Friend to Sir Philip Sidney", then adding, as the required knock at the heavenly portals, the words *trophaeum peccati*, "monument to a sinner", which seem almost an afterthought.

There is not a word about the worldly dignity and pride of this epitaph in *The Buildings of England* guide to Warwickshire, no mention that Greville was a poet, which is pushing indifference to anything except architectural shape just a little too far.

But there he is: another Warwickshire poet, another poet of the central county, in which he was a territorial grandee. He and Philip Sidney went to school together at Shrewsbury. If he was not as good a poet as Sidney, he wrote at least two wonderful love poems.

One, which Coleridge greatly admired, is a sonnet of goodbye to love and blind Cupid—

Farewell, sweet boy, complain not of my truth;
Thy mother lov'd thee not with more devotion;
For to thy boy's play I gave all my youth,
Young master, I did hope for your promotion.

Now he is going to turn to more serious, or less disappointing matters:

I bow'd not to thy image for succession,
Nor bound thy bow to shoot reformed kindness,
Thy plays of hope and fear were my confession,
The spectacles to my life was thy blindness;
But, Cupid, now farewell, I will go play me
With thoughts that please me less and less betray me.

The other love poem is unlike much Elizabethan verse in its indication of place and actuality; it is a love poem, you might say, of green Warwickshire footpaths and stiles and large, lawn-like, comfortable meadows and rook-haunted rectory or churchyard and elms, which Henry James found a little too much. The girl has left him or given him the push—

> . . . I, that on Sunday at the church-stile found
> A garland sweet with true-love knots in flowers,
> Which I to wear about mine arm was bound,
> That each of us might know that all was ours:
>   Must I now lead an idle life in wishes?
>   And follow Cupid for his loaves, and fishes?
>
> I, that did wear the ring her mother left,
> I, for whose love she gloried to be blamed,
> I, with whose eyes her eyes committed theft,
> I, who did make her blush when I was named;
> Must I lose ring, flowers, blush, theft, and go naked,
> Watching with sighs, till dead love be awaked?

—and so on for two more stanzas, in one of which Greville talked of this girl, Myra,

> Washing the water with her beauties white.

In St Mary's, Warwick, you can have thoughts about fatality and life, about Walter Savage Landor still writing poems at eighty, about the strength, courtesy and gravity of the Earl of Warwick in the chapel where they were to offer endless masses for his soul, and about the youth and death of Fulke Greville, who was brought to his black monument after a servant murdered him in his old age. And you can have such thoughts more or less alone in this church, without that dense pressure which now defiles Shakespeare's church at Stratford. This Warwick church is not trodden in the same way by queues which stretch down the street.

All Warwickshire suffers, not quite in the manner which Henry James seemed to foretell. Warwick in the middle, it suffers from Rugby to the north-east, Coventry to the north, and enormous Birmingham to the north-west. Its towns, its villages suffer from the incessancy of lorries. Detergent floats down its rivers — some of them — like sugar-floss, which gets held up in the weirs; as it does, for instance, on the Avon, below Warwick Castle, which Fulke Greville rebuilt or refurbished, and which, for Henry James, was "the very model of a great hereditary dwelling — one which amply satisfies the imagination without irritating the democratic conscience". The tone of villages and towns has been altered, in a suburbanized style. Paths, corners, nooks where cars can pull in, are over-used, and made shabby. There is too much asphalt in Warwickshire, wearing also into holes. In the gardens of Warwick Castle, the moulting peacocks tread around on asphalt. Add to all this now, to all this alteration of tone, that strange irony of elms killed on their feet by the beetle-spread virus of elm disease; and can you say still in Warwickshire that you are "interviewing the pastoral Britain", or that the county remains a full image — another Jamesian phrase — of the "richly complex English world, where the present is always seen, as it were, in profile, and the past presents a full face"?

I suppose not. I don't like to think of this new Warwickshire as altogether a new, more than geographic, centrality, an image of what our country must become in many different ways, with much destruction and replacement of values. But the changes are fascinating. In the modern exploration of the Midlands, and Warwickshire in particular, losing out against what another Warwickshire poet, Drayton, in the sixteenth century, called "the lothsome ayres of smoky cittied towns", there is a cultural masochism, a curiously entertaining apprehension.

1976

Montale on Art and "Copies of Men"

Eugenio Montale was awarded last year's Nobel Prize, so these three booklets have appeared in celebration.[1] The one to buy is *Poet in Our Time*, a translation of Montale's anxious reflections on culture and poetry. Before coming to these reflections I should dispose, as kindly as possible, of Professor Singh, or rather of his translations — with introduction and notes and a buttressing article by F.R. Leavis — of some of Montale's later poems. Dr Leavis says the translations are "admirable". However, these English versions, by a translator and expositor who thinks that *data* and *juvenilia* are singular nouns, commits such solecisms as "we weren't he" and defines Piranesi as the "author of *Le Carceri*", are always out of register, without any compensating or satisfying felicity. Each "poem", therefore, is like something seen through a bottle. Montale is turned into almost nothing.

Nice of Professor Singh to have tried. But really he should have faced an Italian text with a literal English, if he could have managed that much. The Leavisian note, mostly about Montale's poems on the absent presence of his dead wife, congelates registered facts, profound impressions and the playing of decisive parts, concealing the fairly obvious in Leavisian complication of manner. Eliot and Valéry are knocked, a word is slipped in from Lawrence, Professor Singh's not very fortunate comparison of Hardy's and Montale's poems of bereavement is adjusted; and Montale is awarded an A-level.

Poet in our Time, translating *Nel Nostro Tempo* of 1972, is described by Montale as a collage of notes he has made in the last fifty years (he is now eighty) — notes on poetry, life, culture and crisis, expressing attitudes partly (and rather more hopefully) echoed in *E ancora possibile la poesia* — Is Poetry Still Possible? — which he delivered as his Nobel address. Individuals and multitudes are his obsession — the poet, necessarily alone, inevitably unique, and the men to whom communications are made *en masse*; whereas in a real sense "Only

---

1   *Poet in our Time* by Eugenio Montale, translated by A. Hamilton (1976); *Eugenio Montale: New Poems* translated by G. Singh (1976); *E ancora possibile la poesia* by Eugenio Montale (1976).

the isolated communicate", the mass communicators of our world doing nothing — in spite of those grand Latin words in the hall of Broadcasting House in London — but repeat and echo and vulgarize. Montale says that mass communication isn't addressed to real men, but to copies of men. He accepts his age, but hopes rather plaintively that the open-eyed individual be extinguished. The static centre has vanished, men have woken up to shame at being men, which is the worst basis for humanity. They renounce responsibility, they adhere for comfort, drugged with the pseudo-arts of dumb passivity and thumping repetition.

Pasternak's Modesty and Pride

When Pasternak is speaking, this book is wonderful.[1] But first, though with real gratitude, we have to get rid of Alexander Gladkov, who is the tape-recorder — on tapes too gapped and too short. This dramatist (he died last year) revered Pasternak for his poems, his wisdom, and his character. Pasternak's poems hit him when he was a schoolboy, he met Pasternak first in 1936, and then he ran into him many times in the remaining years of Pasternak's life, most frequently in the war winter of 1941 and 1942, when with other members of the Writers' Union the young Gladkov and the middle-aged Pasternak had been evacuated to Chistopol, a small frozen river port five hundred miles east of Moscow.

Gladkov reminisces, for all his devotion, in rather a skimpy way. Pasternak is handsome. Pasternak has white teeth, and one tooth is missing in front. Pasternak's voice, when he reads his poems, has a "deep nasal timbre" and he draws out his vowels. He looks young, always young, for his age, even if his hair, every time they meet, shows a little more grey. About other writers he is given to praise, or else to saying nothing about them. Although he is gauche on some public occasions, he is "graceful, benevolent, trusting, absorbed in himself and his work".

Gladkov does go on. He goes on about Pasternak liking him, and giving him signed copies, and praising his musical comedy. He has to pad, I suppose, to fill out even a *samizdat* manuscript, which was to go the clandestine rounds (this is translated from a Paris edition of the manuscript). Still, Gladkov's touches of description add to the idea we already have of a decidedly and splendidly Superior Person. We see a little more of a man who trusts in his egotism, a man both modest vis-à-vis history and life and sure of his own worth. Gladkov once discussed Pasternak's blend of modesty and pride with the Russian critic Grigor Vinokur, a very intelligent man, we are told, who knew and admired Pasternak. "I am never sure," Vinokur said, "where modesty ends and supreme self-esteem begins."

There is nice self-assurance in Gladkov's best story about Pasternak. To the Theatre Association in Moscow, in 1943, he

---

1 *Meetings with Pasternak* by Alexander Gladkov, translated by Max Hayward (1977).

gave a reading of his new translation of *Antony and Cleopatra*, and at the end of the scene in which Enobarbus tells the story of Cleopatra and her love for Antony, the audience interrupted with sudden applause. Pasternak smiled, took off his glasses, gave "a rather awkward little bow", and said, "Just wait — it gets even better." Everybody laughed, and Pasternak laughed, then put his glasses on again and continued the reading.

A charming story of that self-esteem. But then Pasternak always demanded, and seems usually to have exacted, the best from himself, which was his justification; and charm deepens into something else when Pasternak is allowed to speak for himself — when the table-talk begins, and when Gladkov isn't describing Pasternak's funeral or telling us why he has a low opinion, after all, of *Doctor Zhivago*.

Pasternak was at all times — if the listener was sympathetic — ready to pronounce, aphoristically and seriously. Out come the convictions:

> The first mark of talent is boldness. . . boldness in the presence of a blank sheet of paper.

> Nothing is more spurious than outer freedom if one lacks inner freedom.

> A genius is a qualitative extension of a mankind which is homogeneous in quality. The distance separating a genius from an ordinary man is imaginary, or rather non-existent, but this supposedly intervening space is crowded with all those "fascinating" people who make a point of letting their hair grow long and wearing velvet jackets. It is these — if one grants that they have any place at all in history — who embody the concept of mediocrity.

> Truth has need of few words.

> I have to work every day, or I feel ashamed of myself.

> I saw it as my task [against the "easy victories of travelling stage performances", as nugatory in Russia as they are in England] to revive the idea of poetry, printed in books, on pages which speak with the power of deafening silence.

And so on. We don't have to agree, supinely, with every aphorism which is pronounced with austerity and authority; but it is sensible to consider them, and to be provoked by them, and, if we dissent, to justify our disagreement with them. They do not need to be original, but our need is to relate them to the speaker. And really, in the way of criticism, poetry-criticism, I cannot believe there is anything which energizes and enlightens us more than poetry-talk of that kind — by Jonson, Goethe, Coleridge, Novalis, Hopkins (in his letters), Valéry, Eliot (bedded circumspectly in his essays), Auden: or Pasternak. Few poets try it without a well-founded conviction of their right.

I realize that Pasternak's *obiter dicta* may put him far out of fashion in either of two present circumstances, the circumstance of an excessively idle and spineless poetry (but then "poetry" is always in such a condition) and the circumstance of more and more book-length criticism, English as well as American, which is remote from everything palpable, sensual and structural in poems. But like Pasternak ("memory is history, and memory is art. . . art is really crystallized out of chaos"), each poet ought to see in himself history continued.

Two Books of American Verse

A broad peculiarity of American verse is a yearning for Elsewhere, a poetry of immigrants or the separated, lamenting lost origins. Poem upon poem extends itself to England, Rome, Greece, the gods; and in this new Oxford Book,[1] title upon title indicates as much — The Sphinx, Merlin, Bacchus, Xenophones, Chaucer, To Helen, The Coliseum, The Attic Landscape, Lear, Sestina: Altaforte, Homage to Sextus Propertius, Ave Caesar, Little Gidding, Priapus and the Pool, Mr Pope, Aeneas at Washington, Orpheus, Two Pieces after Suetonius, Four for Sir John Davies, Dolphin, Persephone, Oxford, Gulliver.

That about covers the procession, for more than a century—

I hold in my own hands, in happiness,
Nothing; the nothing for which there's no reward.

This Elsewhereness has been the condition of successful, touching, even wonderful poems, among them Ransom's "Philomela" (there he is, at Oxford, all the way from Pulaski, Tenn., in Matthew Arnold's Bagley Wood — where else? — listening for Grecian or Anglo-Grecian nightingales) or Wallace Stevens's "Sunday Morning"; but Elsewhereness also leads to a monotone of dissatisfaction instead of celebration, too much pretension, and too much irony.

And then in some of the At-Home or More-or-less-At-Home poets Elsewhere, and Elsewhen, provoke another peculiarity, often the same lamentation but in flat, loose, American-modern, unshaped modes; and I shall add that it is both risible and disgusting to observe English poetry-journalists and poetaster-professors rattling their beggar's tin to poetry of the kind, either on behalf of poetry in England or else to send it up.

In this anthology the Goldsmith's Professor of English in the University of Oxford bends to every puff of his native American fashions. As far as Frost, that defiant, at times understandably malign At-Home poet, he has the guidance of time, though is American poetry so rich that he can properly omit "The Tuft of Kelp" by Melville, or "The Fisher's Boy" by Thoreau, or Conrad Aiken's "Annihilation"; and all of

---

1 *The New Oxford Book of American Verse* chosen by Richard Ellman (1976).

Leonie Adams, Elinor Wylie and Edna St Vincent Millay? (With the last two Professor Ellman shirks a dutiful exploration of the sugar sack.)

He stuffs in too many of Emily Dickinson's verselets, too many cuts from the endless rolls of Victorian poetry. When he stays long and properly in the universe of Whitman (whose At-Homeness is universal) he prefers Whitman's generalizations to standing still with him and watching "Bivouac on a Mountainside" or "Cavalry crossing a Ford". No room also — we must be serious, serious, serious, and cultured — for America's delightful light versification; for a poem or epigram by Phyllis McGinley, for instance.

Onwards from Frost, through Pound, Williams, Olson, into the flats — oh, how vanguard we must be, giving no offence and playing safe, into disaster — good poems occur, of course they do, but also every kind of thin, loose nullity. Also to a poor academic ear, which accepts doggerel and jumble, and a poor academic eye, add, in Professor Ellman's introduction, the apologetic stance in poor academic writing: "American poetry, once an offshoot, now appears to be" — come, Professor, is it, or isn't it? — "a parent stem. . . . Such clustered enterprise makes persuasive the claims of this poetry to have a distinctive and national character."

Q — Quiller-Couch, first Oxford Book editor — used to write like that, aeons ago; and I prophesy that in ten years this collection will seem — beyond as much as it contains of the needful — stuffed, dusty, tatty and dated like an Untermeyer anthology of the Twenties or Thirties. To show the real force of American poetry this Oxford Book should have been shorter by a third, and inhabited by fewer poets, and edited by a poet.

No reading, no exploration — and I have been at it a long while — certainly none of the promotional activity which continues in and out of American embassies and American universities and latterly English universities, persuades me that America has, in fact, produced any considerable and greatly agreeable poet since Ransom.

Ransom published his best poems more than forty years ago (he died in 1974), so that means a long nullity, if I may repeat the description. But then we can be sure that it is fiction, not poetry, in which, so far, the Americans have excelled, and which has saved their writing from provinciality.

An unpopular judgement, I know, from someone who is neither an American chauvinist nor an English chauvinist; an idiosyncratic judgement, though why shouldn't an apparently idiosyncratic judgement be the correct one? Some must disagree, obviously; among them salaried agents of American literature, and English academics anxious for a profitable turn in American universities. Anthologists will disagree, whether Professor Ellmann or Professor Moore, who follows Professor Ellman's Oxford Book with a fat Penguin waddling the same curious course from Anne Bradstreet in the seventeenth century to Williams, and Olson.[1]

In writing it is achievement which matters, not history, not succession. So it sickens me to find Professor Moore (an American at the University of Hull who instructs our cisatlantic young on transatlantic literature) saying he is giving us a "representative anthology", which is also a "teaching anthology". No poem can represent anything except itself. Nothing but the enjoyable and the enlivening deserves pushing under any nose.

To my knowledge the good American poets have never yet had the anthology they deserve, or one by which they are not insulted. Rubbish would have to be lopped and dropped, first of all, in such a collection, whether it is rubbish again by Anne Bradstreet or rubbish by Emerson (a versifier whose ineptitude is amazing). Only then would there be room at least for all the proper poems by those unlikely coevals Longfellow (not such an inferior poet, after all) and Poe, by the poetically small Thoreau and by the huge Whitman, and so on to Masters, Lindsay Robinson, Frost, Marianne Moore, Eliot, Ransom and a few more of various size.

This right American anthology would not be enormous, it could not swell to Professor Moore's 560 pages of verse, or Professor Ellman's 1,060 pages. It could be impressive all the same.

But then lopping away ineptitude means recognizing ineptitude by strict reference to poetry as an art, as artifice difficult in the making. Round the imperatives of art it is no good taking the easy way of supposing or pretending that art has changed its nature. That way is the conceit of a modernism travestied and vulgarized, it is the now popular treason of clerks kowtowing to an *ex post facto* ninnification. Intent upon an ultimate frying of more and more watery catfish Professor Moore pauses in his introduction at Emily Dickinson, and to exalt her has to cry down Christina Rossetti; irresponsive to life

1   *The Penguin Book of American Verse* edited by Geoffrey Moore (1977).

or art, he has to pronounce that Christina Rossetti's poems are "trifling", though they do have "a pleasing musical element".

There you have edging towards the kowtow — to explaining that of course, and why not, the new American poetry isn't "musical in the traditional English sense"; as if the universal "music" of poetry, harsh, violent, sweet or calm, whether of Sanskrit poetry or Chinese poetry or Greek poetry or English poetry, could be discarded and disregarded for the first time in three thousand years or so.

After his idle swank of comparison and chauvinism Professor Moore's crasser inclusions and exclusions did not surprise me.

Early Auden

Grateful for the collection[1] — at last — of Auden's early writing, some of it not published before, I have first to say how much I resent the title. It implies that if Auden were English at the kick-off, he became American, in substance, before half-time. Did Handel, or did Henry James "become" English in that sense? I think Auden too would have resented the title and this division of himself. He wasn't a Wernher van Braun captured and self-sold to the victors.

Also he does insist, among extracts from an unpublished aphoristical book of 1939, how much we are the same from infancy to old age; after which statement he went on to an explanatory account of his own childhood and cultural and religious circumstance and schooling, and — in spite of false starts — of his basically unpolitical ego.

The second implication of the title is that middle if not later Auden surpasses earlier Auden. With that we may largely agree: the Auden who went to America wasn't dead or addled, he is not to be denied his maturity or that sense of glory he was to give out before long, in his *New Year Letter*, for instance. But this middle or later Auden doesn't have to be distinguished as "American".

What Edward Mendelson does, as a generally sensible and always devoted, if rather muddling editor, is to present, in the best early texts, Auden's poems from 1927 (he was then twenty years old) to 1939, together with a closing selection from his essays, journals and reviews.

Antique devotees like myself will be glad of younger devotees coming at last to the first full text of "The Witnesses", that *tour de force,* beginning, as it appeared one week in *The Listener* in 1938 (I can see in memory the whole pages and their lay-out),

> You dowagers with Roman noses
> Sailing along between banks of roses.

I am glad of the republication of two sonnets Auden gave me to print in *New Verse* in the same year, one of them opening, very Audenesquely

> At the far end of the enormous room
> An orchestra is playing to the rich.

1 *The English Auden* edited by Edward Mendelson (1977).

I am glad to see again the knockabout verses of "A Happy New Year", printed in 1933:

> In the middle distance a title whore
> Was distributing trusses to the ruptured poor. . .
> Lord Baden-Powell with a piece of string
> Was proving that reef-knots honour the king. . .

—glad also for a first reading of such notebook scraps as

> The glories of the English nation:
> Copotomy and sodulation

or for such a sample of Auden's power to sweep us into strange inhabited topographical images as

> We were to trust our instincts; and they came
> Like corrupt clergymen filthy from their holes.

But then Auden knew that his word prodigality, his image prodigality too, had to be kept on a leash. He is to be found in the selections from his prose warning himself against the temptations of verbal dexterity, preferring to the picked word and to rhyme discoveries what he calls "the manipulation of common abstract words"—

> Where you would not, lie you must.
> Lie you must, but not with me.

Yet he knew, as he explained, in 1936, that poems are variously solemn and light, comic and serious, pure and obscene, and that appreciating one kind only is like appreciating only archdeacons or only barmaids.

What is visible in the sequence of prose in this *English Auden* (as well as in the verse sequence) is Auden discovering where a genuine revolution begins, internally; Auden finding more and more unbearable the role put upon him as "court poet to the left". He was to be positioned in man, not in man left or man right. In 1932 he wrote that modern education failed because "nobody genuinely believes in our society, for which the children are being trained".

Mustn't that always have been his view? And doesn't it explain the entire folly of the state patronage of the arts, which he loathed, as by the Arts Council?

A Guide Examined

I prepared a brief exam paper, somewhere between O-level and A-level, for this Literary Guide,[1] and told the Guide to sit down and tell me what writer —

1. climbed Little Skirrid, near Abergavenny and admired the primroses and wood anemones?
2. wrote of the bluebells in Hodder wood, in Lancashire?
3. took hold of a girl's hand behind her back, in a revelation of impossible love, by Scale Force, in the Lake District?
4. was buried in the abbey graveyard at Strata Florida?
5. was married in the priory church at Edington, in Wiltshire?
6. gave his name to a most noble view of the Lune and the fells?
7. listened to nightingales in Bagley Wood, near Oxford?
8. also listened to nightingales in Bagley Wood, with disgust, some eighty years later?
9. was embarrassed by girls in Llanbadarn Fawr church, near Abergavenny, and wrote a famous poem about it?
10. described epitaphs and graves in the churchyard at Laugharne?
11. was heard howling and moaning in the cloisters of Chichester cathedral?
12. frequented Mablethorpe in Lincolnshire and wrote of the slap and thunder and hissing of the North Sea on the Mablethorpe sands?

The Guide sat there and chewed its biro and turned in an empty paper. Not a mark, not a pass. Yet the associations involved (answers in a minute) I should call fair ones of the kind which should fill a literary guidebook.

I don't despise "associations", especially between places of charm or peculiarity and writers of imagination — poets in particular. I don't quarrel with Vaughan writing that poets — or some poets — "where they once appear hallow the place"; and I am not denying that this literary guide, the latest of what is generally rather a debased kind of vade mecum, does contain a store of information which will surprise most readers (did

1 *The Oxford Literary Guide to the British Isles* edited by Dorothy Eagle and Hilary Carnell (1977).

you know that Erasmus was rector of Aldington, in Kent?).
Only the compilers leave too much out, put in too much about
the minimal, and make mistakes, and their store is rather a cold
store, refrigerated. A place is often in no way linked to the
warmth and reality of the writer's writings or personality.

Often the essence of a place isn't distilled. Take the entry for
St Juliot in Cornwall. Yes, Hardy went there about church
restoration in 1870. Yes, he met Emma Gifford at the rectory
(though she wasn't "the rector's sister"). But does the guide
mention the great St Juliot love poems? It does not; and that is
a whopper, among many whoppers.

As for my dozen questions, the answers are (1) Henry James,
(2) Hopkins, (3) Coleridge, taking the hand of Sara
Hutchinson, (4) Dafydd ap Gwilym, greatest of Welsh poets,
(5) George Herbert, (6) Ruskin — "Ruskin's View", beyond
the churchyard at Kirkby Lonsdale, (7) Matthew Arnold, (8)
John Crowe Ransom (see his poem "Philomela", which I never
tire of recommending), (9) Dafydd ap Gwilym again, (10)
Coleridge — not Dylan Thomas, (11) William Collins, (12)
Tennyson.

The lesson is that such a guidebook needs to spring from an
enthusiastic appreciation both of literature and place.

Elfins

If you have ever read — and of course Sylvia Townsend Warner has read it — "An Essay of the Nature and Actions of the Subterranean (and, for the most part, Invisible) People, heretofore going under the name of Elves, Faunes and Fairies, or the lyke", written in 1691 by Robert Kirk, "Minister at Aberfoill", and published by Andrew Lang as *The Secret Commonwealth*, you will know that these Other People were not small and airy-fairy; and you will have just an inkling of what to expect from the latest book[1] by that extraordinary veteran, Sylvia Townsend Warner.

Robert Kirk translated the Psalms into Gaelic. Miss Warner translates fantasy into sharp and delightful English, in a collection of stories as unlike Maeterlinck or *Midsummer Night's Dream* as you can imagine. She is a Dean Swift, a Deaconess Swift, of her various Elfin Kingdoms across Europe from Scotland and Suffolk to Holland, Brittany, Austria and Germany. Like Swift she is undeluded, worldly and sardonic, only genial and lyrical, ungiven to *terribilità*. Without employing a Gulliver, she takes the lid off the green hills and the other castles of the Elfin Kingdoms, and there they are, these Other People, in lives of a difference which illustrates our own living.

Like Swift, Miss Warner speaks from our world all the time, in a sharp contemporary voice that made these tales at once apt and unexpected contributions to the *New Yorker*.

First of all, that business of size. "It is commonly supposed", she says in one story, "that fairies, or elfins, are trifling little beings, always on the wing and incapable of dying. This mis-apprehension has come about because they prefer to live in invisibility — though they can be visible at will, by means of an automatic mechanism rather like the *una corda* pedal or a gearshift."

Elfin Kingdoms have paralleled human kingdoms. Flying — though all elfins have wings — is left to the lower orders: "In fact they are about four-fifths of ordinary human stature, fly or don't fly according to their station in life, and after a lifespan of centuries die like other people — except that as they do not believe in immortality they die unperturbed."

1 *Kingdoms of Elfin* by Sylvia Townsend Warner (1977).

There you have two innocent examples of the varied way in which Miss Warner ensures delight. She is given to the tickle, the sting, the slap in the tail of a paragraph which translates the bizarre into the familiar — the gearshift for flight; or contrasts elfinity with humanity — no fear of death because for the elfin there is no question of an after-life.

There is a logic in these contrasts. Propound a fantastic situation, and what follows from it unfantastically, realistically, logically? The mode is varied several times in the third and one of the best of the stories, *Elphenor and Weasel*. Elphenor is a Dutch elfin blown off course into Suffolk, where he is employed in visible shape by Master Blackbone, "a quack in several arts, including medicine, necromancy, divination and procuring". Elphenor encounters a green Suffolk elfin of great charm named Weasel (Miss Warner is well aware that although weasels are not very nice — from a rabbit's point of view — they are very beautiful little creatures from our point of view, each with a face like a seal in miniature). Weasel smells like elder-flowers, a bit sexy and over-sweet. Weasel is described, as Elphenor first sees her; and you think Miss Warner is coasting the whimsical. But wait — till the last word:

"She was a very pretty shade of green — a pure delicate tint, such as might have been cast on a white eggshell by the sun shining through the young foliage of a beech tree. Her hair, brows, and lashes were a darker shade; her lashes lay on her green cheek like a miniature fern frond. Her teeth were perfectly white. Her skin was so nearly transparent that the blue veins on her wrists and breasts showed through like some exquisitely marbled cheese." Weasel was like cheese.

There are plenty more contrasts in Weasel. "Though invisible, she might not be inaudible, and her voice was ringing and assertive as a wren's". The Weasel who sings like a wren.

Or the habits of this elfin: "They breakfasted on wild strawberries and a hunk of bread he" — i.e. Elphenor — "had had the presence of mind to take from the bread crock. It was not enough for Weasel, and when they came to a brook she twitched up a handful of minnows and ate them raw."

That reminds me of a curt throw-away, in another of the stories, about the stealing of human babies who are brought up as pets inside the green hills or other Elfin castles, after a conditioning process analogous to our neutering of tom kittens. Two of these humans, now adult, re-named Morel and Amanita (Miss Warner knows all about fungi, of course) brawl in a smelly, unseemly way in the Queen of the Fairies' bedroom, on May Morning. Soon everything was in order again: "Morel and Amanita had been strangled and their bodies thrown on the moor *as a charity to crows.*" Always a surprise.

Back to Elphenor and Weasel. They shack up for winter in a splendid East Anglian church with winged angels down either side of the roof. Elphenor as quack's apprentice "had learned some facts about the Church of England, one of them that the reigning monarch, symbolically represented as a lion and a unicorn, is worshipped noisily on one day of the week and that for the rest of the week churches are unmolested". They settle in, and then — "He woke to the sound of Weasel laughing. Daylight was streaming in, and Weasel was flitting about the roof, laughing at the wooden figures that supported the crossbeams — carved imitations of fairies, twelve feet high, with outstretched turkey wings and gaunt faces, each uglier than the last. 'So that's what they think we're like', she said. 'And look at *her*!' She pointed to the fairy above the pulpit, struggling with a trumpet."

I shall indulge myself with one more quotation, from the story of some discontented and discarded Elfins ("One day in early spring the Queen was bitten by a mouse. The result was totally unforeseen" — but that is not the quotation), who are given to philosophy, take to a deserted temple of Aesculapius in Greece, and become the beloved guests of a fat pederastical Turkish bey. This marvellously inventive tale begins:

"Wirre Gedanken was a small Elfin kingdom, never of any importance and now extinct. In the Austrian section of Countess Morphy's 'Recipes of All Nations', *Wirre Gedanken* (translated 'Troubled Thoughts') designates a kind of fried bun; but there does not seem to be any historical connection." A beautiful inconsequence. And there's the tone, the weave of these stories, light and serious, sardonic and learned. Miss Warner's judgement is so good, not stopping short, not overdoing it. And her writing is so good.

After reviewing this in the pannage season of literary prizes, I comment that prizes do not go to such books as *Elfin Kingdoms*. They go to short-lived, fish-finger packets precisely with a sub-bourgeois taste of cod, flour, bread crumbs and batter.

Romany Flash

1

If you are curious about Augustus John, not as a painter (that I think would be unreasonable) but as a name, a noise, a rumbustiousness, through many years, then here are the facts, illuminating and depressing, in this — good heavens — *first* volume of a life of him by Michael Holroyd.[1] The facts illuminate not only John but the old self-delusion and insularity of the English art world which lasted into the Thirties, and seems in this book to be revived. For this fashionable public, unsympathetic to changes or verities in art, John's function was to be the Bohemian, the Romany rye wild with the girls and exalted in the swish of the pencil and the bravura of bright pigments.

The social ambiguities of his origin and upbringing contributed. We are told about a mean, dull, pretentious father, Edwin John, a Pembrokeshire lawyer, not at all the gentleman, and therefore anxious, in the latter mode of the nineteenth century; about a generally absent, slightly superior mama, who sketched and died young; about soul-saving aunts, and drably respectable homes, in grey Haverfordwest, then in Tenby.

Michael Holroyd sees into this milieu, into its effect, he sees how John, having escaped to the Slade, speedily became the empty unveracious exemplar of Bohemianism, accepting what society required him to be

Early on he writes:

> To know Augustus John was to know not a single man, but a crowd of people, all different, none of them quite convincing. . . . In later years everyone else would recognize readily enough the manly and melodramatic form of Augustus John — but he himself did not know who he was. His lack of stylistic conviction as a painter, the frequent changes of handwriting and signature in his letters, his surprisingly passivity and lack of direction in everyday matters, the abrupt changes of mood, the sense of strain and vacancy, the acting; all these point to that central lack of identity.

1 *Augustus John*, Vol. 1: *The Years of Innocence* by Michael Holroyd (1974).

Then why go on? "His lack of stylistic conviction as a painter" — doesn't that mean he painted badly? The only excuse for going on would be to study the social aetiology of the polite world's affair with John or of John's affair with the polite world. That wouldn't do (though it might have made a valuable book), and I have to conclude that in selecting his subject the biographer was on the look-out for semi-popular sensation, in a pseudo-serious attire.

"His womanizing brought out in him a satyr-like quality." Possibly — though he was a mawkish satyr, on the evidence of his love-letters. Anyone like myself, who has had friends from among John's earlier and later intimates, will have heard first-hand tales of a blundering, clumsy lover, amusing enough as gossip, but not really the stuff or part of the stuff of a worthwhile biography, and it strikes me that Michael Holroyd's double standard soon confuses him; and will confuse the reader.

"This is a biography: it is not an art-book." All right. But it is a book about an artist; and I find no authority in Michael Holroyd's comments on painting. All he seems to know about it might have come from skimming through the annual picture book of the Royal Academy, with a glance at Clive Bell, and the local amateur art exhibitions.

Having made that early admission about John's lack of identity and stylistic conviction, he takes it back when it suits him, i.e. when he has to, if proceeding with the book isn't to be absurd. For instance, Augustus when old wrote of his sister Gwen John and her work: "Fifty years after my death I shall be remembered as Gwen John's brother." A correct prophecy, I am sure. Maybe John always appears to have had more energy than intelligence, at least more energy than sense, but he knew something about pictures in general and in particular, he knew his sister, that wonder out of the same muck-heap, he knew and felt her grave, delightful genuineness, yet Michael Holroyd dismisses his remark about Gwen as "admiration curdled into a sentimental concoction".

Michael Holroyd sees, but twists. That's the answer, I believe. And perhaps this false posture, this pretence of importance where it never existed, explains the fluent vulgarity of his own style in this biography, so choked by "long-term effects", "latter-day disciples" and "narrow channels" and "ir-resistible lures". "The key to Edwin John's character was a form of acute anxiety that apart from stifling his intellectual curiosity, dammed up his unexhausted physical passions and diverted them" — oh dear — "along the narrow channels of avarice".

I realize, however, that Michael Holroyd's accumulation of items will help to instruct ourselves and our successors in a period and in the genuine achievements of others (such as Gwen John) — which is the use now of the old dead two-decker biographies of such as Millais, Frith or Watts O.M.

The Art of Augustus John,[1] in which Michael Holroyd collaborates with Malcolm Easton, also faces towards and away from the truth, with an equal and easy blandness. Anyhow it coincides, as an aide-memoire; in eighty-two plates of John in his various avatars — John as Velasquez, as the quattro-cento portraitist, or the Late Renaissance draughtsman, as Puvis de Chavannes, or Rembrandt, or Blue-Period Picasso, always the acceptable *pasticheur* gesturing towards popularity or notoriety. Such was the future of the boy whose student drawings, Sargent exclaimed, were beyond anything that had been seen since the Italian Renaissance.

Wyndham Lewis, who was at the Slade with John and stayed surprisingly, if amusedly, loyal to him, used to praise John defensively as at least an Eye, and the Eye took it in and the hand obeyed. Then under pressure Lewis would admit — what else could he do? — the absence of imagination, the uncreativity and impersonality of the drawing.

In this *Art of Augustus John* the owners are listed, and it will be seen that none of the pictures reproduced belong to the lesser or greater European galleries or collections; which is not surprising.

2

Again, what is the worth of Augustus John? His oils, save for a lyric or two of his earlier time, are now so evidently flashy and inferior and his drawings so clearly simulacra of the genuine that to argue *de gustibus* won't do. *Non est disputandum* — except by those who have betted on John and by Michael Holroyd,[2] who maintains an ambiguity — that John made inferior use of an inferior talent. But then he was egged on: he was large, noisy, arrogant, vigorous, vulgar, aggressive, heartless, and given to falling on women — the incidents are paraded in Volume Two as in Volume One. And that a moneyed Philistia saw in his work a dying kind of art which they supposed to be

---

1 *The Art of Augustus John* by Malcolm Easton and Michael Holroyd (1974).
2 *Augustus John*, Vol. 2: *The Years of Experience*, by Michael Holroyd (1975).

art eternal. Here it was being practised, in its obsequies, with a sudden swagger.

No truck with Paris. Astute Augustus soon realized that his *beau monde* maintained a pedestal for one large Bohemian licensed to stand for art. He mounted, and posed on it, in his beret, penis, beard, and legend.

A biographic situation, then, of some piquancy, depending on the biographer's recognition of art and life and their Siamese-twin relationship. Not being foolish and proclaiming the wonderful man who painted the wonderful pictures, the biographer could say: this is how society behaves, how an artist now and then manipulates society. That could be valuable. Or he could say: well, I display a man who deluded others more than himself, who grew up in a loveless, insecure home, and behaved like an animated Priapus with a scarlet member from a Roman garden, and treated wives with selfishness, and children with the severity and indifference he had endured himself, all inside the art-uniform of gypsy and Bohemian.

That too could be interesting, with encouragement to the slightly sickened reader to brood over artists who were different — Pissarro, let's say, or Constable or Corot or Cézanne: have a long, cleansing stare at the Montagne Ste-Victoire.

Mr Holroyd's way is none of them. He displays the hollow artist always more conscious of having nothing inside him, nothing to exteriorize in paint. He pursues him to the last incident. John is eighty-three, a daughter is staying with him. One night he fumbles to her room, wearing his beret, and heaves in: "Thought you might be cold," he gasped, and ripped off her bedclothes. He was panting dreadfully. . . . He lay down on the bed. . . . "Can't seem to do it now," he muttered. "I don't know."

About pictures Mr Holroyd will say "bad", and the word is hardly typed before he says "important". He arranges his card-index — how industrious he is. 843 notes, 198 books in a Select Bibliography, and at the beginning 502 helpers thanked for their help — and then deals the cards out with a dead-pan impartiality, which looks like sobriety of judgment and in fact is equivocation. A kind of ambiguity, of supine neutrality, is the best I can say of the process, reflecting about the case of John that seldom has such nastiness been inflicted on others for so slight a return in the durability of art.

Mr Holroyd states (he has reached 1917 — nearly half a century to go): "Suddenly he was an artist with a past and little

future. The future lay with those who were abandoning
Naturalism and tradition and who demanded a new art
modelled on the functions of the machine in place of the
organic forms of nature." Which side is he on (apart from the
ignorant nonsense of his formulation), art's, John's, or the side
of the social swimmers and splashers?

He quotes: "A natural king among men. . . . A visionary
gleam pervades these rocky shores, these windblown skies;
through the eyes of the majestic figures, the soul gazes out lost
in a reverie. This blend of the earthly and the spiritual in his art
expresses the essence of the man who created it. . . it was
sacramental." Does Mr Holroyd approve this insufferable
rubbish (written by Lord David Cecil)? He doesn't let on. That
is Mr Holroyd's mark, not letting on. And, once more, how
poorly he manages it, for ever used by words in pre-existent
order — "the mellow brick", "the field of art", "he seemed
poised between two worlds". Toadying jobs of this kind will
kill biography.

1974–5

The Wrong Revivalism

1

I am no admirer — and it is not my fault — of the writing, the taste, the learning, the judgement, as displayed so far in his books, of Dr Roy Strong. But then his earlier books seemed to me imitative romps in corners so little frequented that they did no real damage, except to Dr Strong as critic or authority.

About his new book[1] I am not so sanguine. He has left the iconography — what a grand vocable, of which he is so very fond — of Tudor portraits and celebrity pieces for the iconography of Victorian story pictures. To love of the Virgin Queen he adds love of the Matron Queen. He considers, inter al., *The Boyhood of Raleigh* by Millais, and Dyce's *George Herbert at Bemerton*, and Yeames's "never-to-be-forgotten" *And When Did You Last See your Father?* (his title picture and jacket picture), as well as history pieces by Derby Day Frith; and he proclaims his respect for them all. "I happen to like this sort of painting." "I feel that these pictures should leave us" — as they leave him — "with a sense of awe and wonder."

Yet these are slightly exceptional sentences. Swimming in the stream of Victorian revivalism he expresses his delight in some of the vulgarest catch-client canvases ever painted, though in what I have to describe as rather a cunning way.

He sidles iconographically to rubbish, he explains that since this rubbish conveys a Victorian attitude to British history and heroism, it is deserving of celebration, historically.

Saying great, as art, he avoids or he manages to say it and not say it. He is, after all, director of one of the most splendid of the world's museums, and no doubt has to stand up at times to other artmen of equivalent status round the globe, as well as to his own colleagues; he has to keep some words in reserve somewhere — but where, so far? — to evaluate genuine masterpieces such as those in his own guardianship at the Victoria and Albert.

Thus if he made too much of his more than historical admiration for Yeames or Frith, what words would Dr Strong still have available for the Raphael cartoons, or Duccio's *Madonna and Child, with Angels*, or Constable's oil sketches, or

1 *And When Did You Last See Your Father?* by Roy Strong (1978).

Millet's *Woodcutters*, or Bernini's *Neptune and Triton*? So we find him writing, for example, of Sir William Allan's slightly pre-Victorian *Murder of David Rizzio* (National Gallery, Edinburgh) that it is "his masterpiece in mariolatry" (worship of Mary Queen of Scots), "not only a triumph of historical reconstruction but one of the most powerful evocations of the martyred queen".

To the innocent, to the inexperienced, who will go to the current exhibition of Great Victorian Paintings, what must his praise suggest except that they should bow — authority tells them so once more — to a picture which in fact is badly composed, badly drawn, and theatrical? Or that they have been right all these years to prefer *The Monarch of the Glen* or *The Wreck of the Schooner Hesperus* to a Bonnard or *The Wreck of the Deutschland*?

Very depressing. Here is the director of an expressly educational art museum confusing, for sentimental purposes, superficial icon with deep value, and encouraging others to do the same, in a book which is to be equated intellectually with current astro-archaeological fantasies, or with newspaper horoscopy; and which is an act of *trahison des clercs* — if the term *clerc* can be employed.

And how soon I gave up — there were so many of them — listing words Dr Strong has used without understanding them (eg loadstone, format. saga, exotic, seminal — "seminal roots"), and astonishing solecisms, and the number of times this or that was "crucial" to something else, and the occasions on which "threads" were "tackled" and brushes "occupied" or "inspired".

No honorary O-level, then, for this author, who does not make one statement or one suggestion about the nature of art (or about history) which surmounts the commonplace, and few which avoid the pretentious.

Is this absurdity of a book — I am not sure — too absurd to deceive anyone? Certainly it was disagreeable to see reactionary Dr Strong posing under the pennon of change or advance, and to find him scoffing at art historians (and at artists really) who have helped in the long rescue of art from just the salon pictures and academy pictures he so admires. What I will affirm — without risk, on my halidom — is that no head of a great art institution has ever before, in my time, allowed himself to be quite so unwise in print.

2

What are the elements of the extraordinary case of G.F. Watts,
Order of Merit? Shortly, from the evidence of this new
biography[1] and the previous biographies, here was a talent such
as might have led to the art mastership of a public school or
some mild sinecure in a corner of the art world. The vehicle of
this talent was a humbly born, illiterate, agreeable, rather good
looking, not over-sexed or determinate young man, astute,
compliant, ambitious and able to delude himself. After an early
piece of luck, he could be safely patronized. When he was
twenty-six, he won a first prize in the cartoon competition for
frescoes in the new Houses of Parliament. So Lord Holland and
Lady Holland could adopt him, in the conviction of helping a
genius. He was enveloped by the Victorian century. He exuded
ideal art. He painted high-sounding Thoughts: and in time
assumed that velvet skull-cap of spurious old mastership,
earning — when he took to sculpture — Lord Leighton's
comment that he was "England's Michaelangelo".

Ruskin, who ordered him to paint "like Titian", once told
him his botany was wrong in one of his pictures: "Forget-me-
nots do not grow on graves: *Anywhere* but on graves." Later,
when Watts was in his sixties, he told him he had "never made
an entirely honest, completely unaffected study of anything".
True. But society often requires a representative Poet, and a
representative Painter; and there are always candidates to
conform.

Moral idealism was required. Watts supplied it. The whole
fake (from which his portraits cannot be excepted: his principle
in them was to subordinate the individual to the idealization.
Tennyson to the Poet) may be summed in Watts's reiterated
invocation of Pheidias. "I learned in one school only — that of
Pheidias," "Pheidias, my adored Pheidias, shall reign
throughout" (throughout his *Alfred Exciting the Saxons to Resist
the Danes*) as if anything at all by Pheidias had come down
from antiquity.

Since the fake in these monstrous cases is double, fake of
supply, and fake of acceptance, we shouldn't, as we look back,
be too conceited about ourselves, having our minor Wattses,
for certain. All the same how can the high art of this vain
man's obvious allegories have been so accepted? How could his
friends and patrons have overheard such obiter dicta from

1 *England's Michelangelo: A Biography of George Frederic Watts* by Wilfrid Blunt
   (1975).

Watts as "Bury your sorrows in the garden and they will come up as flowers" or "The Utmost for the Highest" without recognizing — even if they had never looked at the way he pushed his pigments around — that the painter they exalted was an ass?

A "middle-aged lukewarm gentleman" was how Shaw described the Watts, the Idealogue, to whom Ellen Terry was offered as a sixteen-year-old sacrifice in 1864. How is he characterized as person and painter by Wilfrid Blunt? Ambiguously. Mr Blunt giggles a little; he says bad, then he says good; he says lofty; then he says flat. Some of his chapter-headings are "Muffins and Misery", "Three Acres and a Brush", and "The Importance of being Earnest".

He lays out facts. If we can add them up usefully for ourselves, he offers few convictions of his own about life, art, or Watts. But then he is the Curator of the Watts Gallery outside Guildford — of the shrine; which must be the least comfortable position for a biographer of Watts.

And Chesterton?[1] And Professor Bell? Chesterton's brief cooking up of Watts, which first came out in 1904, in a Popular Library of Art, is several times quoted by Wilfrid Blunt — not to much effect. I remain uncertain which is the more futile — Professor Bell's preface, the characteristic verbiage and provincialism of Chesterton ("He followed the gleam"), or the publisher's blurb ("This masterly book") or indeed the publisher's revival of an ethical disquisition about Watts which comes near the forms or the physical colours on Watts's canvas.

"It would be very absurd to suppose that a good art critic can distinguish good paintings from bad ones." Professor Bell can't be allowed that easy way out. A good critic must try: he must act as if there is an eternal verity or rightness, and by his attempt he will be judged. Pushing Victoriana may be left to dealers and auctioneers, and the Victorian Society.

1   *G.F. Watts* by G.K. Chesterton, with an introduction by Quentin Bell (1975).

The Creative Rebel

The Tamar dividing Devonshire from Cornwall is one of the more delectable of the small rivers of England. There were, above its woods and declivities, mines which yielded lead, silver, copper and arsenic. The arsenic ovens — for a while the most extensive in the world — did foul damage along the river, about which a Devonshire poet wrote, in an old-style poem,

> And where the blossoming orchards bless'd the view
> Tremendous ARSENIC its fatal fumes
> Has breath'd and vegetative life has ceas'd
> And desolation reigns.

The poem was published in 1826. Eight years after, in 1834, William Morris was born in far off Walthamstow, then a village where prosperous businessmen of London lived and bred their young in suave Georgian houses. Morris and arsenic, Morris and copper, had their connection. Cynics — who have never quite ceased to sneer at the politics of William Morris and at most things he did — may enjoy the fact that it was Tremendous Arsenic, poisoning the *hortus conclusus* of the fruit-growing Tamar valley, which smoothed the progression of William Morris from Walthamstow to medievalism, poetry, design, and a revolutionary communism. When he was a boy Morris's father, an already well-to-do discount broker, acquired by accident more than a quarter of the £1 shares of the richest of the Tamar mines, the Devon Great Consols, of which arsenic was a product. This holding of 272 shares jumped in value, in a few months, to more than £200,000. The income floating the Morris family — at any rate when Morris's father remained alive — must have been of the order of £20,000 a year.

Morris himself became one of the directors of the mining company. When at last he resigned his directorship, he came home from the board meeting in the City and placed his top hat on a chair and sat on it, a gesture in Morris's impulsive physical style.

That was in 1876. By then, at forty-two, Morris had written most of his poems, founded, conducted and taken over the art firm of Morris, Marshall, Faulkner and Co., "Fine Art Workmen in Painting, Carving, Furniture and the Metals", made himself expert in pattern designing of the freshest originality, and concluded his journeys to Iceland; he was entering the last twenty years of his life, in which he was to be the avowed communist, on paper and on platforms.

Did Morris ever visit the mine? Ever sniff the fumes of his money? There is no mention of such a visit. But it might be said that in all he did Morris was making restitution for the poisonous source of his livelihood; which has left behind, still visible, and not quite the memorial to associate with Kelmscott Manor or the Kelmscott Chaucer, "a vast broken landscape, extending for two miles along and above the Tamar", given to foxes, adders and buzzards.

The Morris family wealth gave the child Morris, in many things, but not everything, the happiest of humus and circumstance, which may be evidenced in his praise of Chaucer as "the summer poet and his master"; and in one atom of recollection in Mackail's *Life of William Morris* (1899), to which E.P. Thompson's revised account of him is one of the supplements and correctives — "to this day," he said, "when I smell a may-tree I think of going to bed by daylight."[1]

At Walthamstow, eldest of eight children, Morris lived from six to fourteen at Woodford Hall, a manor house in its own part of fifty acres, separated by a fence from Epping Forest, an up-and-down extent of clay in which fallow deer shelter in the bracken, below hollies and pollarded hornbeams, the small snipped leaves of which filter a peculiar light.

Here Morris imagined evil knights ambushing the virtuous among the hornbeams (see his early poem "Shameful Death"), here began that entry into the past, and that love of the earth Morris was to celebrate to the end of his incessantly vigorous life — roots of his hope for mankind in a recovered environment and in a happiness of art and peace:

> To what a heaven the earth might grow
> If fear beneath the earth were laid,
> If hope failed not, nor love decayed.

In his childhood paradise the thorns were the coldness or aloofness of his Evangelical parents, and then exile from Walthamstow and the Hall and his sisters when Morris reached thirteen and was sent to one of the new middle-class "public schools" — Marlborough College, in Wiltshire.

He hated that school; which he called a "boy-farm", by analogy with "baby-farm". E.P. Thompson excerpts a letter of Morris's later time in which he looks back to Marlborough, and to the parental shortcomings at Woodford Hall: "My parents did as all right people do, shook off the responsibility for my education as soon as they could; handing me over first to nurses, then to grooms and gardeners, and then to a school, a boy-farm, I should say. In one way or another I learned chiefly one thing from all these — rebellion.''

That unlocks a door to Morris's projective and creative life. There was trouble at Marlborough. It looks as if the always determined, direct and violent-tempered Morris was asked to leave (or was expelled? Only someone who has endured one of the English public schools will appreciate the force and shame and prospect of life ruination which used to be packed into the words "expelled" and "expulsion").

In Mackail's *Life*, sentences seem to be covering something it was unseemly to recall or record: "Under the elaborate machinery and the overpowering social code of the modern public school the type is fostered at the expense of the individual: with a boy like Morris the strain would have been so great that something must have snapped." Whatever snapped, Morris remained in exile at Marlborough only until he was sixteen; and we are the inheritors of the sepsis of that school, of the generative force of that rebellion. The school was at any rate surrounded with delights of past and present, of positive contradicting the negative. The Marlborough Downs, rolling sheep walks roofed with cloud shapes, came up to the school, "wide, wild houseless downs" (in the phrase of a Jacobean poet) marked by an evident yet vague and mysterious history, in round barrows and long barrows and the circular complex of the ditch and the rampart and standing stones of Avebury, for which "Druidic" was then the word.

Rebellion persisted. Rebellion turned generously against excluders, destroyers, scrapers of ancient beauty, the makers and purveyors of shoddy, against exploiters, and — when life is the only wealth — against the greed ex-President Ford has lately called with satisfaction "the name of the American game". Morris, in rebellion, is soon asking why his kind alone were privileged to enjoy willows and rivers and "Gothic" churches and the inheritance of the seemly and beautiful. Soon he writes poem after poem bringing evil to book, and mourning youth murdered or defiled in the white may-tree season, or wives and widows despoiled. *Deus est* — or *Deus* ought to be — *Deus pauperum.*

Rebellion-directed, Morris is driving to the loom and the dye-vat, to his proclamations of environment uncontaminated and society regenerated; and last of all he comes to his private joy, which has proved not so private after all, of the Kelmscott Press and his Kelmscott Chaucer, the ultimate payment of his debt, finished as he declined towards death.

If we destroy in our time, we also preserve, the thought of preservation comes easily to us. Morris had to establish and teach that concept *ab initio* at a time of the most poignant destruction of the past. That has to be understood for the total understanding of Morris. Mackail quotes Morris's lifelong friend Ned Jones — Sir Edward Burne-Jones as he allowed himself to become, in contradiction — on the Oxford where Morris and Jones first met as undergraduates in 1853: "On all sides except where it touched the railway the city came to an end abruptly as if a wall had been about it, and you came suddenly upon the meadows." In the poorer streets "there were still many old houses with wood carvings and a little scultpure here and there".

From this now unimaginable Oxford, Morris, in 1854, in his second Long Vacation, had his first view of Rouen: "No words can tell you how its mingled beauty, history and romance took hold on me; I can only say that looking back on my past life, I find it was the greatest pleasure I have ever had: and now it is a pleasure which no one can ever have again: it is lost to the world for ever." So Morris, founding his Antiscrape, his Society for the Protection of Ancient Buildings, also became the courageous, if at times despairing champion of the world's architecture.

All or most of this is well understood by E.P. Thompson, Marxist historian and author of *The Making of the English Working Class*. But Morris would have his strictures on this other book, surely, as a portrait of Morris; or as a study of Morris (Thompson's description). Just over two hundred pages take Morris from childhood through his reading of Carlyle and Ruskin, through his poems, and his art designing, and his marriage, and, via Kelmscott and Iceland, to his crossing in 1883, when he was fifty, of what Morris called the "river of fire" beyond which would be found the inseparables of the new art and the new life. On the brink hesitated the fearful of the English middle classes, Matthew Arnold, and Morris's own friends; and there they stayed.

After that, shortened indeed from the 1955 edition of Thompson's book, there follow no fewer than four hundred pages of Morris across-the-river, Morris in the revealed history of the Socialist League and the limping progress of socialist thought and activity in England; Morris in his revolutionary communism. "The transformation of the eccentric artist and romantic literary man into the Socialist agitator may be accounted among the great conversions of the world."

It is not at all that Thompson despises Morris the poet, the romancer, the designer, the maker, the good knight of Antiscrape, only that for his vision, they need no more than brief, not always very acute, consideration as the winding path to the climacteric value.

In view of English condescension to Morris, bred of gentlemanly disdain for his determined passage of that river, Thompson's treatment is understandable. It plumps the record where it has been left thin. But will it do? To me it seems reasonable — and respectable — and necessary to estimate Morris in a different way; to assert that if his political determination crowns his life logically and honestly, the work which we distinguish as "Morris" is, all the same, the best of his verse, the best of his prose, the best of his pattern designing; in all of which scintillated those qualities which made Yeats, one of his prime unfaltering devotees, proclaim Morris as his "man of life".

From rebellion at Woodford Hall, rebellion at Marlborough, the shape and substance of Morris in his work develop consistently. Here is Morris on himself, in 1894, two years before his death: "The hope of the past times was gone, the struggles of mankind for many ages had produced nothing but this sordid, aimless, urgly confusion; the immediate future seemed to me likely to intensify all the present evils by sweeping away the last survivals of the days before the dull squalor of civilization had settled down on the world. This was a bad look out indeed, and, if I may mention myself as a personality and not as a mere type, especially so to a man of my disposition, careless of metaphysics and religion, as well as of scientific analysis, but with deep love of the earth" — there it comes again — "and the life on it, and a passion for the history of the past of mankind."

Horrified as he may be of what is done to life, fearful as he may be of worse that may yet be done to it, what is any artist worth who is not, in his work, in what he makes, and separates from himself, such a basic lover of earth, grateful for his presence here, as a guest of life among its other guests? Two who would have understood each other are Morris and Wen I-to —

You must stuff my mouth with sand and mud,
If it can only sing about an individual's welfare

— or Morris and Pasternak (see Pasternak's *Letters to Georgian*

Friends, passim, Pasternak on loyalty to life, on "love of people and gratitude to the past for its brilliance", and "concern for repaying it with the same kind of beauty and warmth"; Pasternak on "happiness as it should be, serious, profound, fathomless and sad"). If Morris is to be known, it is in the crystallization of himself.

The fact is we have just about reached the possibility — if only the right biographer turns up — of a proper critical life of this great man, in whom a combination of grandeur and almost naive directness and combativeness have been so disconcerting, to some. We find him accounted for now in most of the compartments of his unity — in his socialism, with a final clarity which the haughty, scholarly and otherwise sympathetic Mackail could have achieved in 1899 only by a miracle, and in his designing, whose relationship to modern art is now recognized and appreciated.

As we thumb through *William Morris and the Art of the Book,*[1] the catalogue, with essays, of last autumn's exhibition at the Pierpoint Morgan Library, it may be ironic to reflect that, being rare, Morris objects have become desirable to the rich, to realize that so much of him as illuminator and as maker of books should end up in the treasure house of the villainous old Morgan. But then Morris books at the Morgan, Morris fabrics in the Victoria and Albert Museum, or on the walls of his own Kelmscott Manor can be seen quite clearly to exert the freshness and force of art. But what about the writings?

Here is a fairly recent estimate:

> Morris, William (1834–96), London-born English Socialist and founder of the Kelmscott Press, was associated with the Pre-Raphaelite brotherhood, and was a designer and craftsman as well as writer. His epic and lyric poems reveal an interest in Greek, Scandinavian and medieval legend. His prose works include *News from Nowhere* (1891).
> — from a handbook to English and American poets (the second edition of 1970). Ignorant, yes, and perverse, ludicrous even, but fairly typical of a neglect which began long ago as an undermining of Morris's once great literary reputation, a literary-bourgeois retaliation for his political and social apostacy.
> To go back to an early sample, Robert Bridges, who could, for all his later urbanity, vent a snobbish insolence on writers

1   Edited by Paul Needham (1976).

it seemed safe to despise, was calling Morris an ass, in June 1877 (and earning a rebuke from his friend Hopkins — Morris's recent translation of Virgil was "very likely a failure but it cannot be said that Wm. Morris is an ass, no"). Bridges's reasons for calling him an ass seem plain. A month before Morris had published *To the Workingmen of England*, his manifesto against the prospect of war again with Russia. Already on the way to his socialism, his conversion, he had not been polite. Those who were leading the English to danger and dishonour were, cried the manifesto, the "Greedy gamblers on the Stock Exchange, idle officers of the Army and Navy (poor fellows!), worn-out mockers of the Clubs, desperate purveyors of exciting war-news. . . and lastly in the place of honour the Tory Rump" — under Disraeli, with his "empty heart and shifty head". The month before Morris had been scalping the clergy of England for their ignorance and philistinism in the restoration of churches.

From this gentleman who was clearly an ass and a cad to speak in such a way, from this poet who would never be Poet Laureate, never be corrupted, much more was to come in the next dozen years. Socialist devotees of Morris who claim that he has never been forgiven, or that rounding on him has left behind it a habit of denigration, are right.

Still, when every weakness is urged against Morris's verse and prose, when all objections have been taken to his intermittent indulgence in the century's literary archaism, for instance, when the facile has been subtracted from a huge *œuvre*, poems and prose remain which are pleasurable, strong and direct, poignantly fresh as his Kelmscott may-trees, revelatory and reverberant; writing, too, which has also had its forward influence.

This ultimate, ideal, very much endowed critical biographer whom Morris needs, will have to take into his new judgement Hopkins on the "deep feeling" of Morris's early poems, Yeats in praise of Morris's "Golden Wings", Eliot on his poem "The Blue Closet", Edward Thomas wishing at times to be that "writing man" Morris and no one else, and loving his noble pieces of humanity, Auden caught as well by *Sigurd the Volsung* and by *The Hollow Land* and its lyrics. He will have to make many revaluations (realizing, for instance, that some of Morris's strongest writing is to be found in his *Icelandic Journals*, a mille-fleurs tapestry of the exquisite details of the Icelandic environment coupled with its wide brutality and lack of pity, and its relationship to the courage of a small society through a thousand years). But if Morris's new biographer is sufficiently polymathic and sensual and has enough feeling for human destiny, his book should be one of the grand biographies, very rich in pointed anecdote, in pathos, energy and hope, and finally in a special peace and benediction. E.P. Thompson, even if his literary judgement isn't very sharp, says in this reissue of his guide to political Morris that we may see in him, "not a late Victorian, nor even a 'contemporary', but a new kind of sensibility". And then: "If he sometimes appears as an isolated and ill understood figure, that is because few men or women of his kind were then about — or have happened since." Exactly.

1977

Melodious Tom Moore

Did Tom Moore, the Dublin grocer's son, sell out to the English who had so lately destroyed Irish independence and hanged the rebels of 1798? He did. Were the songs which Tom Moore wrote sentimental and artificial? They were. And have his countrymen rejected him? They have, according to his new Irish biographer[1] — just the one Tom Moore required — who explains how and why this little Irish snob, singing for his supper to the Whig aristocrats of England or to their ladies, was one of the most charming Irishmen ever to cross from Ireland to England.

First we are given the portrait of this poet, "little in stature and great in wit". He was five feet tall. He had fine dark eyes and curly hair, his mouth, said Leigh Hunt, was "generous and good-humoured with dimples". A radiance shone from him. Women, says his new biographer, detected in him the unspoilt child; he was meant to please, not to fight, not to be a martyr, or a hero. His voice (Leigh Hunt again) from being a little hoarse in conversation softened "into a breath like that of the flute" when he was singing.

Everyone, nearly everyone, loved him, and wanted to cherish him, including Sydney Smith. "By the Beard of the prelate of Canterbury," exclaimed Sydney Smith, "by the Cassock of the prelate of York, by the breakfasts of Rogers, by Luttrell's love of side dishes, I swear that I would rather hear you sing than any person, male or female. For what is your singing but beautiful poetry floating in fine music and guided by exquisite feeling?"

Sydney Smith was to call the middle-aged Tom Moore a "superannuated cherub" — no insult intended, he was a cherub still, if an older cherub; and after Tom Moore had been staying with him in his parsonage at Combe Florey, in Somerset, he wrote him a letter, occasioned by Moore's forgetfulness, Moore's absence of mind (except for people), which preserves as if in a small reliquary the feeling his friends had for him. The date is 7 August 1843, and Moore, famous above most writers, is in his sixty-fifth year:

Dear Moore,
The following articles have been found in your room and forwarded by the Great Western. A right-hand glove, an old

1 *Tom Moore* by Terence de Vere White (1977).

stocking, a sheet of music paper, a missal, several letters apparently from ladies, an Elegy on Phelim O'Neil. There is also a bottle of Eau de Cologne. What a careless mortal you are.

God bless you.

It says much, that "God bless you".

This biographer seems to walk round and round his subject, quoting the right things, a dab here, a dab here, a repetition when necessary, in the business of reconstituting his careless mortal, outwardly and inwardly, in a likeness altogether credible.

Terence White states, and does not excuse or explain away. Why *did* Moore at thirty-two rather improbably marry his Bessy Dyke, the sixteen-year-old dancer? Maybe because he had compromised her, and he was caught, and her mother insisted.

Once they are married, Tom Moore gradually admits that he has a wife (how is a wife, so young, so unsophisticated, going to be taken by all his grand lady friends, who are so much older than himself?). He does keep Bessy at home in Sloperton Cottage (but that is where she wished to be) while he is off to Lord Lansdowne's Bowood and all the other houses of the great. He does push away sorrow, does seem a little heartless at the death of his children — but then "Moore did not hug grief. It lighted on him and took off after making the bough tremble." He was not superficial. Terence White says that superficial is the wrong word, too obvious, too pejorative: "He was a song bird; not an eagle, not a dove; and he was untrue to his essential nature when he tried to be an owl."

About the songs of his song bird, his *Irish Melodies*, the temptation is always to be heavy — and wrong. Hazlitt was over-serious about them. He said Moore "ought to write with a crystal pen on silver paper". Good. But then "If these national airs do indeed express the soul of impassioned feeling in his countrymen, the case of Ireland is hopeless. . . . Mr Moore converts the wild harp of Erin into a musical snuff-box."

The wrong comment, and we are still singing Moore's impossible lyrics. "*The Last Rose of Summer, Oft in the Stilly Night* and *Believe me if all those endearing young charms* are almost embarrassingly sentimental; but they are irresistible". Terence White asks who of us "has not got the first lines, at least, of half a dozen of his *Melodies* by heart?" And he asks, "how many poets have written better *first* lines?"

"It is not a critical test; it will not pass in the academies, but who, given the choice, would rather have an existence in the foot-notes of scholars than in the hearts of living men?"

I fancy myself that the *Irish Melodies* lodge in the outer heart, as the seat of affection, rather than inside the heart as the seat of love. But I am not complaining. (My favourite is one nobody talks about or sings — "Thee, Thee, Only Thee":

The dawn of morn, the daylight's sinking
The night's long hours still find me thinking
        Of thee, thee, only thee.
When friends are met, and goblets crown'd,
    And smiles are near that once enchanted,
Unreach'd by all that sunshine round,
    My soul like some dark spot, is haunted
        By thee, thee, only thee. . . .

Was it written about Bessy Moore? The refrain and the movement make its emotion valid, I think).

What is not so well remembered — or celebrated by Terence White — is a contrary side to Tom Moore in the satire he wrote. The cherub, the five-foot sweet-singing cherub as satirist — how improbable a combination of two active beings in one. It was W.H. Auden, that, among so much else, deep explorer of English verse (or verse in English I had better say in this context), who gave me a first clue to Moore's rather overlaid satires, guiding me to *The Fudge Family in Paris*; and if English readers may especially enjoy Phil Fudge and then the Tom Moore of "Fum and Hum, the Two Birds of Royalty", the Moore of Hum the Prince Regent in his Chinese palace at Brighton going off to bed with "His legs full of gout and his arms full of Hertford" (Lady Hertford), Irish readers may revise a contempt for what they may think was Moore's national apostasy when they read him in various poems on Castlereagh or in his "Pastoral Ballad, by John Bull", on the despatch of five million rounds of ball-cartridge to Dublin in 1827:

I have found out a gift for my Erin,
A gift that will surely content her;—
Sweet pledge of a love so endearing!
Five millions of bullets I've sent her. . . .

To turn back from satire to melody, Terence White's final judgement is that in the centre of Tom Moore there existed "an ineradicable sweetness". Exactly so. And the image I am left with is one Terence White mentions, but then passes by rather quickly. Once, in the very happy first years of the marriage of Tom Moore and his Bessy Dyke (who was a very beautiful as well as a devoted wife) they started out to a dinner party and then realized they were going to arrive too early. So to fill the time "the Moores set to practising country dances, in the middle of a retired green lane".

There we may leave them, dancing together — in spite of Dr Leavis — on the Wiltshire grass; which is something to remember should you ever visit Bromham churchyard, nearby, where Tom Moore and Bessy Moore and two of their children are buried, on the cold north side of the church, under a monstrously tall, pseudo-medieval Irish cross.

"How Moore would have hated it!" Terence White insists. But I do not think he would have hated this new memorial, this new life of himself by this other Irishman, who is responsible and civilized, who says in his introduction that he found Moore's "very Irish character" of intense interest, recognizing all of Moore's failings in himself.

John Masefield Between Middle and Low

Masefield I have thought of as a simple good man who imparted in a few lines out of many poems, and in a few adventure stories, a feeling that the wonderful might be just around the corner. We are told in this[1] biography that the sophisticated Mario Praz went to see him on Boar's Hill in 1923 — Masefield was then forty-five — and found "a rather wooden-looking little man, dressed a little like a porter on Sunday, with short nut-brown trousers above his ankles and an impossible collar". Mrs Masefield (that remarkable ex-housemistress from Roedean) did the talking and answered the questions, while Masefield nodded his head up and down "in the manner of a papier mâché donkey, and said something or other, it is true", which "might have been said by anyone". Such descriptions exist of visits to Hardy, but then poets at tea and poets in print are not identical.

More to the point, and also quoted, is J.C. Squire making Masefield say, when everyone was reading his early story poems,

> Dogs barked, owls hooted, cockerels crew,
> As in my work they often do
> When flagging with my main design
> I pad with a descriptive line.

He pads, yes. He does break into a sudden emptiness, he inserts putty, just when a fullness ought to appear. Miss Smith, in her account, also pads; or she babbles too much in the socio-literary trivia of Masefield's life. What can be said, what has been said, against Masefield's poems she rather brushes away. What was the evident spring of Masefield she mentions — because Masefield mentioned it — without seeing its relevance altogether, or detecting its insufficiency.

Looking back to a childhood, in a family of sisters and brothers, in comfortable Herefordshire, on the edge of those daffodil fields which for a while also enshrined Edward Thomas and Robert Frost, Masefield wrote in his old age (as if he had been reading of another Herefordshire poet, Traherne), "I was living in Paradise, and had no need of the arts, that at

1 *John Masefield: A Life* by Constance Babington Smith (1978).

best are only a shadow of Paradise." He was a little over five
when one day, "looking north, over a clump of honeysuckle in
flower", he felt himself entering into what he calls "a greater
life" — "something much more beautiful, very near and almost
to be reached" — which at the same moment was entering into
him, "with a delight that I can never forget".

A culturally conditioned description, you may object, but
the experience occurs, and what I find sad about this
sad-looking and "wooden-looking little man", with —
afterwards — his rather ordinary sensibility, is that the
experience raised so little of his verse. He caught flicks of it
everywhere and often, when (after family disaster) he was
pitched into the Merchant Navy, when he had deserted ship in
New York (aged sixteen), and was in turn hobo, barman, and
employee of a carpet factory.

He clutched at that glitter, that illumination, in his New
York reading of Malory and Chaucer's *Parlement of Foules*. It
beckoned him, during his London days as a bank clerk, in the
insubstantiality of *Lavengro* and *The Romany Rye*, which he
knew by heart, then more brightly in the work of artists he
loved, Dürer, Cima, Bellini, Piero della Francesca, Millet,
Corot, Theodore Rousseau; then, too, in the stories of William
Morris's *Earthly Paradise* and in poems by Yeats, whose friend
he became.

Yet in nearly all his verse, if he describes, his description is
not an image of all actuality (a page of Dante explains the difference). The Paradise he experienced only dwindles, as a rule,
into such words as wonder or beauty. Of course it is true that
the not very good poets are never to be dismissed without
careful inspection; but then it is also true that his biographer
seems quite unable to inspect with care or certainty. She is
given to say, "Masefield was always a countryman at heart" or
"Jack's avid reading bore rich fruit"; and it appears to me quite
the oddest thing that she hardly mentions the work by
Masefield, the adventure stories in prose, which succeeds by its
genuine tone of the wonderful, of the about to happen. "A
story for children, *The Midnight Folk*, which was to become a
classic" — that is all she says of one of his best fictions; not a
mention of *Lost Endeavour*, or *Jim Davis*, or *The Box of Delights*.
I think often of a children's poem by Robert Graves (in *The
Penny Fiddle*) in which the piercing light and delight of what is
happening and will happen next are imparted as much in
movement and metre as in narrative. In a like way Masefield,
in his best prose tales, conveys wonder as much by that tone as

by incident or story.

Clues in this biography are scattered and not followed — clues, for instance, that there was something too nice, too respectable even, about John Masefield; clues also of how he pursued a poetry beyond his power or nature. He remarked already in his twenties that by and by he might be able to write properly of the bitter miseries of common life at sea, the "bite" of which had "lost its fang" in him, if only he could abstain from his "romantic dreams of John Silver, the Spanish Main, and all the Tropic Island palm tree business". Abstention didn't work, and really his business was to make something new and viable of his "dreams". His tough writing, his "closhy put" and "bloody liar", seems weak, if not fake.

As for his niceness, his wife, so much older than himself, whom he loved so much (having lost his mother when he was six), wrote in her diary, after the publication of his steeplechasing poem "Right Royal", that "he could never be vulgar even if he tried, though he can write of people as vulgar as you like". But once he had taken to his unromanticism, rightly or wrongly, some cut, some vulgarity might have helped.

When he reached America in 1916, famous for *The Everlasting Mercy* and *Dauber*, on an official war-time tour, he was surprised at the acclaim for *The Spoon River Anthology* by Edgar Lee Masters, behind which — how wrong he was — "there was nothing deep enough. . . to atone for it or make it human". What Masefield, nice man, could not do was write a poem as strong as Masters's epitaph on Editor Whedon who scratched dirt over scandal for money, and now lay in the graveyard near the dump where "abortions are hidden." Or can you see Masefield writing a poem as black and as bleak and critical as the one by the now neglected W.H. Davies in which the dead baby, "a knowing little child", seems to wink at the jurors, hinting: "Perhaps my mother murdered me?"

Not a bit of it — publicly. Only in private could Masefield forget — occasionally — to be quite so nice; as when he referred to his vicious Aunt Kate, his guardian, who sent him to sea, as "a repulsive hag so dead to the requirements of decency, courtesy and reverence"; or when he wrote in his pocket-diary a couplet about the Oxford lunch given to Honorary Doctors, himself included, after the Encaenia of 1922:

> With squeaky wit the light, improper verse
> Falls on the heavy lunch and makes it worse.

How often did he throw off such impromptus or near-impromptus as that, or as the epilogue he added to his life and to the last edition of his complete poems:

> I have seen flowers come in stony places
> And kind things done by men with ugly faces,
> And the gold cup won by the worst horse at the races,
> So I trust, too —?

The Rossettis

There are times — especially when yet another book about the Pre-Raphaelites slides into the bookshops — when we feel, or should feel, distinctly plagued by Pre-Raphaelitism — by the very word. Hippolyte Taine looked at pictures by Pre-Raphaelites when they were almost new and decided that English painters in general — the more or less modern ones — blunted and distorted their optical sensuality by so prodigiously concentrating on morality. "I do not believe that pictures so very disagreeable to look at have ever been painted. Impossible to imagine cruder effects, colour more brutal or exaggerated, more violent and gaudy discords, harder or falser juxtapositions of colour." That responsive Frenchman was thinking in particular of Hunt and Millais (e.g of Millais's "corpse-green" lady in *The Eve of St Agnes*) and Arthur Hughes's *Home from Sea*: "As for their landscapes blood-red poppies like holes in parrot-green lawns, flowering apple-trees in which the hard white of the petals against the blackish branches is painful to the eye: a meadow green graveyard in full sunlight, with every blade of grass provided with a high light and shining like a pen-knife blade."

Taine was writing in the 1860s, a long, long time ago, but still we forget his *Notes sur l'Angleterre,* we forget every other judgement, homebred or foreign, still we murmur Pre-Raphaelite, and persist in rather a brutish admiration. How adroit they were! *How accurate!* How much we are prepared to fork out for them at Sotheby's! And how seldom we admit that the initials PRB get in the way, when they should dissolve into their proper place in history. Pre-Raphaelitism drags on us still — another and another exhibition, another and another book — as if were a kind of everlasting Gilbert and Sullivan.

In seeing how Pre-Raphaelite lives — at any rate the lives of the more and less Pre-Raphaelite Rossettis — are treated, and by an American professor,[1] let's refresh ourselves first with a little recapitulation.

As a principle, this Pre-Raphaelitism was precociously brooded in 1847, by Holman Hunt, aged twenty, and John Millais, aged eighteen, with some not entirely convinced help from Dante Gabriel Rossetti, aged nineteen. Then a year later the Pre-Raphaelite group or movement was hatched. Hunt says that he and Millais, his pupil, were resolved "to turn more and more devotedly to Nature as the one means of purifying modern art". They found an inadequacy of nature in Raphael, or at any rate too little of the truth of nature in the subsequent strains of art by those who blindly insisted on the supremacy of Raphael. Hunt was also to write that he and Millais used to stand in front of the Raphael cartoons (then at Hampton Court) and judge them fearlessly, also that they condemned Raphael's *Transfiguration* (which they had never seen) "for its grandiose disregard of the simplicity of truth, the pompous posturing of the Apostles, and the unspiritual attitudinizing of the Saviour".

In their final estimation *The Transfiguration* "was a signal step in the decadence of Italian art".

> When we had advanced this opinion to other students [at the Royal Academy schools], they as a *reductio ad absurdum* had said, "Then you are Pre-Raphaelite." Referring to this as we worked side by side, Millais and I laughingly agreed that the designation must be accepted.

So the celebrated, all too celebrated, label was fashioned, first applied, and accepted not too seriously.

In 1846 when these young men came together with their imprecise aims of renewing or revitalizing English art, Holman Hunt considered that their inspiration, their determination to work, in their way, from nature, would best be described by this word "Pre-Raphaelite". Rossetti wasn't so sure. His preferred term was "Early Christian", but Hunt argued that "Early Christian" would link them with the German Nazarenes, in whose pictures the natural was absent. They accepted, all the same, Rossetti's other suggestion that they should be brothers in their new art, in short that they should be "P.R.B.", each a Pre-Raphaelite Brother in a Pre-Raphaelite Brotherhood of which knowledge should be withheld from the public. The trio now enlarged their Brotherhood, enrolling other sympathizers; and in that kinship Millais and Hunt worked on new pictures which they signed "J.E. Millais P.R.B." and "William Holman Hunt P.R.B." (the pictures were Millais's *Lorenzo and Isabella*, from Keats's poem "Isabella and the Pot of Basil", and Hunt's *Reinzi Vowing to Obtain Justice for the Death of his Young Brother, Slain in a Skirmish between the Colonna and the Orsini Factions*, from a popular novel by Bulwer-Lytton).

These two canvases were hung in the summer exhibition of the Royal Academy in 1849; and no doubt they would have added the secret conspiratorial letters, the monogram of their revolution, to later pictures had the meaning of P.R.B. not been disclosed by a Scottish journalist with a taste for the comic, and ridiculed.

Having a position to make, Hunt and Millais at once altered their strategy, but not their new-found principle. For the exhibition of 1850 they settled to pictures of religious storytelling instead of medieval storytelling. Hunt — he was one for long sententious titles and inscriptions — to his *Converted British Family Sheltering a Christian Priest from the Persecution of the Druids,* Millais to his *Christ in the House of His Parents.* Hunt's modernity, Hunt's fidelity to nature, in detail, was once more to paint an outdoor picture and to give his priest and his Britons faces of the day instead of faces out of painting — out of Raphael, for instance; pointed faces for round faces. Millais, in his modernity and fidelity, set his modern-faced family, in slightly Near Eastern undress, in a very English carpenter's shop, across the floor of which curled a plenitude of fresh wood shavings. (Elsewhere in that year — but the comparison is too obvious and too cruel — the thirty-one-year-old Gustave Courbet, rooted in his Franche-Comté and his respect for Velázquez, exhibited his *Casseurs de pierre* and his *Enterrement à Ornans*.)

And Rossetti, of the original Pre-Raphaelite trio?

Stanley Weintraub, in his group account of the Rossettis — the four children of the scholarly Italian exile who reached London from Naples in 1824 — won't be found telling the reader how badly, if in a different way, Rossetti painted, how meretriciously he wrote. But he does display, as if without intention, how un-Pre-Raphaelite this No. 3 of the Brotherhood was, this art-drugged Gabriel Charles Dante Rossetti who so speedily and romantically reshuffled his names, dropping the Charles and putting the Dante first.

For a while the young Rossetti did assent, with mind and not feeling, to Hunt's and Millais's notion of natural truth. He tried it, in one or two pictures which he no doubt thought of as "Early Christian". But very soon he began to fabricate his initial shortcuts to the effects of art. Rossetti's aversion to nature as his friends saw it and struggled with it (and as Dante saw it in his exact similes) is entertainingly evident in an exchange of letters — not mentioned in this book — between himself and Ruskin, after well-to-do Ruskin had declared himself as a champion and defender of the Pre-Raphaelites and of going to the fern or the moss or the ivy leaf, detail by detail.

Would Rossetti — if Ruskin were to pay — take a run to Wales and make "a sketch of some rocks in the bed of a stream, with trees above, mountain ashes, and so on, scarlet in autumn tints"? Rossetti demurred — whether or no a little drawing, a little accuracy from nature would be good for him or for the morality of his art. Wouldn't Ruskin pay for him to go to Paris?

Dear Rossetti,
   You are a *very* odd creature, that's a fact. I said I would find funds for you to go into Wales to draw something I wanted. I never said I would for you to go to Paris, to disturb yourself and other people, and I won't. . . .

That Rossetti went to art, to his choice of art, while they went, in their way, to nature, adding sharp-coloured accuracy to accuracy in their strident subject pictures, wasn't of course unrecognized by Rossetti's one-time Brothers in Pre-Raphaelitism. They were faithful, he was not; they were morally in the truth of art — in nature, that is to say — while Rossetti was none too morally in the grip of his senses and appetites. They reverenced women, Rossetti mixed reverence and whoring. They were respectable, under the Victorian gaze, Rossetti — well. . . .

Holman Hunt, pompous, though his pompous language was not always false, was to write that "in his designs as in his poems" Rossetti's mind "expressed itself, in a form independent of new life and joy in Nature", that Rossetti was indifferent "to the subject of a poetic image", and was dominated by "the finished phraseology, the mode of delineation". Millais, rebel long changed to orthodox hero of the United Kingdom, came to speak of him as "the mysterious un-English Rossetti", queer, dogmatic, irritable, with aims and ideals in his art quite different from those of Pre-Raphaelitism. He complained strongly of the way Rossetti's later work came to be spoken of as Pre-Raphaelite, and Rossetti himself as the former leader of the movement: "At least when he presented for our admiration the young women which have since become the type of Rossettianism, the public opened their eyes in amazement. And this, they said, is Pre-Raphaelitism! It was nothing of the sort." Millais too insisted that the Pre-Raphaelites — i.e., himself and Holman Hunt — "had but one idea — to present on canvas what they saw in Nature"; so such productions as those of Rossetti "were absolutely foreign to the spirit of their work".

Of course; but is there much to choose — perversions either way — between Millais and Hunt's Pre-Raphaelitism, and Rossetti's Rossettianism? That Rossetti gets in the way of Millais and Hunt, that Millais and Hunt get in the way of Rossetti, that all three are so mixed up historically does not matter; but it matters that between them they occupy so much room, it matters that the large portmanteau falsity, the large portmanteau concept "Pre-Raphaelitism", gets in the way of so much else by being made ineptly inclusive.

Barbarously as it is written (so that hardly a paragraph can be read with comfort), I should therefore respect Professor Weintraub's fourfold biography of the Rossettis rather more if it showed some suspicion at least of the existence of that falsity, and the way it interferes; if in other words his book was concerned genuinely, if incidentally, with the arts of painting pictures and writing poems.

Taking it, in a now *outré* way perhaps, that literary biography or painter's biography should evidently be undertaken for the sake of the writings or the pictures, I can correctly say that Rossetti's poems are neither the worse nor the better, nor any more interesting, because Rossetti's model and wife Lizzie Siddal died of an overdose of laudanum in brandy, in circumstances of doubt, or because many of his poems, in a manuscript book, lay between her cheek and her golden hair in the coffin in Highgate Cemetery until the coffin and the body were exhumed and the book was recovered. But over again we are given a potted account of the drying and disinfection of the poems, and a potted *réchauffé* of the wombats and Fanny Cornforth the luscious, and Howell the Portuguese cad, etcetera; all for their sakes, or Rossetti's sake, a biographical hot-pot, with no accompanying estimate, no celebration of the worth of Rossetti's poems and pictures; unless by writing at all of Rossetti Professor Weintraub implies — I suppose he does — that of course the poems and pictures are wonderful; though by now we have the measure — I think, I hope — of Rossetti's intolerable poeticism in either art.

A next question is how much does Dante Gabriel Rossetti elbow out Christina Rossetti? Does Professor Weintraub contrast Dante Gabriel's poems and Christina's poems usefully, or at all? Does he see the difference in kind and quality?

In Rossetti's poems even anguish — and he was anguished often enough — speaks for the most part in cliché of word, phrase, and movement:

Sweet Love — but oh! most dread desire of Love
Life thwarted. Linked in gyres I saw thee stand,
Love shackled with Vain-longing, hand to hand.

In Christina's poems —

Come back to me in dreams, that I may give
Pulse for pulse, breath for breath:
Speak low, lean low
As long ago, my love, how long ago

— anguish (or happiness) finds a variation of forms and a
delicacy of movement which are *sui generis*, and a language free
enough of literary pretension in its Victorian kind, free almost
of time. Professor Weintraub quotes from her poems now and
then, making them point to the biography, not to themselves.
"Erotic" is one of his adjectives for them (though he does risk
the conventional statement that the poem beginning "My heart
is like a singing bird" is "deservedly one of the great love lyrics
in the language").

Maybe Christina Rossetti's real life is concealed beyond
discovery — except as much of it as makes the poems; maybe it
was less mousy and dim and pious than it appears to be, and
more dramatic. (Professor Weintraub mentions and discusses
and dismisses a story that the still more obscured sister Maria
Rossetti once crouched for seven nights on the doormat of the
family home in London to save Christina from eloping with a
married man.) But I think the morbid dramatics in Rossetti's
life, which are described in so many books, do get in
Christina's way, even now; in the way of her just celebrity as a
poet. And Rossetti's verse, or the false estimation of it, also
gets in the way. When *Poems by D.G. Rossetti* was on the verge
of being published in 1870, eight years after the death of Lizzie
Siddal, and a year after his manuscript book had been
exhumed, Rossetti campaigned for his poems and his fame (see
the account in Oswald Doughty's life of Rossetti) in an extraordinary way, arranging reviewers and favourable reviews, and
planting advance copies wherever helpful opinions might be
expected. From that manic exercise his poems are perhaps
benefiting still, a hundred and seven years later, rather to the
detriment of the poems of his retreating but greatly more gifted
younger sister.

It is true that Rossetti acted for her, and pushed her poems
on to Macmillan the publisher. But he arranged no campaign
for them, and alongside the many collected editions of D.G.R.

there has been one, and one only, collected (and incomplete) edition of Christina's poems, in a bad text, edited by her steady and respectable brother William (of whom Professor Weintraub can give no more than an inevitably dull account), and published — though reprinted several times — as long ago as 1907.

In the end Macmillan also did their worst for the subtleties of Christina's art by corseting the poems two columns to the page, so that lines turn over, shapes are distorted, and hardly a poem can stretch and breathe in isolation (a selection worth looking at is the one which was made in 1930 by Walter de la Mare, one master of tone and movement in appreciation of another).

On the strictly P.R.B. episode of 1848 and a few more years Professor Weintraub writes only a chapter, with another chapter about *The Germ*, the Pre-Raphaelite magazine — "Thoughts towards Nature in Poetry, Literature and Art" — which ran to four numbers in the first months of 1850. Certainly a real need, which shows up in every book touching the P.R.B., is to restrict our application of "Pre-Raphaelite" and its noun. Holman Hunt, all through his rather unattractive career, slyly understood how to use his attractively shaped and sounding vocable, for himself. But it wasn't Holman Hunt who overextended it. That has been the work of generations of lazy journalists, collectors, critics, and art historians, who have allowed the word for a naturalistic incident or mode to cover so much of the naturalism and realism of mid-nineteenth-century England.

Because we have so magnified this incident or a movement which its authentic instigators were never powerful enough to transcend, one by one other "naturalists" of purer merit continue to be misstated or misinterpreted, even obscured altogether. Stuffing needs to be taken out of the "great" Pre-Raphaelites, as in the story of the Texas millionaires reduced to dwarfs. They need diminishing. We have to begin to employ "Pre-Raphaelitism" to describe accurately and sensibly at last both a nineteenth-century bout of self-advertising and a rather jejune, garish, angular, moralistic way of setting natural detail against detail in the pictures of a few modestly talented young men.

1978

Black Poems of Like and As

After all, bad poems are not so just a cause for indignation or dismay as one used to think. One can in fairness be indignant if a bad poet's bad poems are elevated. But inevitably such bad poems outnumber good ones. They are even a condition of the good ones.

About "goodness" there are simple, also more subtle criteria. The simplest is "Am I moved?" — an essential test, though deceptive. Poems need a music. I think this has been denied by Ted Hughes, in a claim for his own modernity and independence. But it is true, despite the decidedly dependent attitude of Hughes, and so many pontificators, in spite of a contemporary she who countered my praise of a poet she had not read, the other day, with the complaint that I was only "talking about musical poetry".

Other criteria are deducible from one's experience of poems as diverse, let us say, as those of George Herbert or Trakl or Jacques Prévert. One conviction which experience dictates is that, in spite of all contrary talk, poems do need a poem language, differing as much and as authentically as possible between poet and poet.

Taking his *Remains of Elmet*[1] with these considerations in focus, I am first and last repelled by the extreme ordinariness of the language, the word usage, of Ted Hughes. But, to begin with, I shall ask about the writer's perceptions. They are often peculiar, individual; yet, as well, often perverse, or inverted, to a point of indulgent nastiness, in presenting a wild, savage primal mess for the primitive wriggles of the divine, or a divine to be recaptured, re-experienced.

De Sade's obsessions could push him to the risible — to write of dosing girls with aniseed to add a desired perfume to their farts. Nothing is risible by intention or accident in these obsessive poems centred in the *disjecta membra* of Ted Hughes's native district, the black moorlands of millstone grit, which were part of the old Celtic kingdom of Elmet, west of Deira, north of Mercia, not conquered until early in the seventh century. In these poems, everything, nearly, is hard, black or residual; is elemental; tales, detritus, rubbish for a renewal which is less accented than the state of things.

Even so, two other peculiarities are indulged in. Perceptions

1 *Remains of Elmet* by Ted Hughes with photographs by Fay Godwin.

are enfeebled because in these poems again and again something is proffered as *like* something else (*like* and *as* are some of Ted Hughes's frequent words). Also the mindless, the inert, the rubbish of this Elmet, from rock to moor, is personalized; credited with aim, ambition, achievement — a cause either way of a sentimentality I take to be childish, as well as false, a romanticism *démodé* (though in his ninth Elmet poem I rather like it when the moorland of death becomes a mother, or at least when the "whole scene" of death lifts a cry:

> A solitary cry.

> She has made a curlew.

But that is my sentimentality as well, my curlew sentiment).

The whole perceptive case against the poet in these poems I would put by isolating an image from a later poem, or versicle, in which he is a Pennine child among the mill chimneys, the hard hills, the old women, swallowing the alarm clock, going to school, crawling towards Peter Pan, himself

> the ageless boy
> Among the pulsing wounds of Red Admirals.

Yes, Red Admirals are red. Red Admirals (their name, by the way, a charming corruption of "Admirables") open their wings and shut them, like other butterflies, "pulsing" if you like. But *wounds*? Blood, cut flesh — why?

A use for that perception is imaginable, a valid use — but not this one. That the Admirables are wounds to Ted Hughes in this context seems to me gratuitous. If in another context it might enhance life, in this context it diminishes life: it is depressive. All of us perceive disagreeably as well as agreeably; but there are perceptions we can legitimately and wisely censor or sidestep, not as false, but as heaping muck on life, if we employ them gratuitously or viciously. But, no, life is wild; "beauty" is wounds, wounds are "beauty". Let's invert everything. Let's be elemental (while the hobs run screaming at us out of cracks in the millstone grit).

So much for perceptions, inventions — in which Ted Hughes is prodigal — but perceptions and inventions are not poems; which are words still, or nothing, and structures of words, making a music. These poems of Elmet are hard to describe because, in nearly every way, they exist — if that verb is justified — outside all the possible viable structures of verse. Linked sound, end-rhyme, internal rhyme, assonance, cadence

— avoiding them amounts to a pseudo-modern contempt for memorability.

Like and *as*, I have remarked, are common in this writer's process. *Is* and *the* and *with* in his vocabulary also enfeeble his pronouncement. Cliché abounds: "the great adventure", "it stayed in position", "that came and went", "failed to come back", "heavy silence", "giddy moments", "taking the strain". Think of the space any such dead verbiage occupies in the shortness of a line. Weak compounds also destroy dramatic realities of style, scores of them, "air-stir", "wind-parched", "beautiful-eyed", "time-long", "near-female".

Another item of slackness is this collection's union — or really disunion — of words and photographs, as if photography, however accomplished, was other than the bastard of art (which is which — are the Hughes poems captions to the black Godwin photos or are the photos captions to the poems?)

Literature, like it or not, depends on class — its own class, not yours or mine; verse especially so. It depends on its language, in its own realm, being classy, upmost classy, and not middle class, or common; and vis-à-vis this verbal decency, this verbal good breeding of literature, the words of this poet, in this book, are little else than very common ones sprawling in very common attitudes, if for uncommon purposes. "In the end, one's poems are ragged, dirty, undated letters from remote battles and weddings and one thing and another." Yes indeed, for these poems in *Remains of Elmet*; and the writer of that sentence was — Ted Hughes, in an article some years ago.

Nonsense Verse

It wouldn't be sensible to be too serious or too historical about nonsense verse; or to say, with one's jaw stuck out, that proper word-nonsense is only of one kind or another. We see in front of us a poem. We prepare to read it in the poem way. It looks normal, the shape decidedly announces poem, it is divided into stanzas. We begin. The poem rhymes, it does no violence to syntax, and we discover that

> The common cormorant (or shag)
> Lays eggs inside a paper bag

or that a respectable elderly man in Spithead is opening his window (why not?), but calling out

> Fil-jomble, fil-jumble, Fil-rumble-comm-tumble.

The poem attends inversely to natural history or human habits or human probabilities, and so on.

In nonsense-writing sense may suddenly give way to a nonsense chorus (the simple endearing trick of nursery rhymes). Nonsense adjectives, nouns, verbs, adverbs, animals, individuals, peoples, countries, are invented. Poems or prose (Rabelais, Thackeray, Lear, Christian Morgenstern) are even written in the writer's own useless Volapuk or Esperanto. And then nonsense poems can be situational rather than nonsensically verbal. Sense can underlie nonsense. Nonsense can impart feeling. The many kinds of nonsense can be mixed in a single poem. Whatever the kind or the mixture, the nonsense poem — if it works — refreshes us by surprise, by invention, or by commenting, in what is said or how it is said, on sense taking itself too seriously or being pompous, or in fashion.

The moment literature develops, nonsense literature must be expected as both a counter-genre and an innocent game. So it begins often in parody. But if the parodist is an able poet nonsense in what he writes is likely to take over, and take off. Canning and his literary-political friends in their *Anti-Jacobin* began by parodying the pro-Jacobins and what looked to them like advanced or revolutionary sillybillyism, and then found that they were creating nonsense — years before the first inventions of Lear and Carroll — which had its own nonsensical independence.

A similar thing happened in Russia half a century later. In 1852, under the stifling Russian autocracy, the poet Alexei Konstantinovich Tolstoy and his two cousins invented their ridiculous bureacrat Koz'ma Prutkov: in Prutkov's poems, Prutkov's plays, Prutkov's Collected Works they parodied civil servants' conceit and self-satisfaction and pomposity; and they enjoyed doing it so much that the nonsense took over, suriving its time and the targets the trio had in front of them.

In England we have rather fancied ourselves as the pioneers and developers of nonsense writing. But then as well as Tolstoy in Russia (and later — see below — Daniil Kharms), think of the nonsense poems of Christian Morgenstern in Germany, and in France, long after Rabelais, of *Le Hareng Saur*, the Pickled Herring, by Charles Cros, which hung, *sec, sec, sec*, on the white wall, or the modern nonsense of Robert Desnos.

I doubt if any national literature in the world, once it is sure enough and conscious enough of itself, can fail to develop its nonsense writing, its nonsense verse in particular, doubly fathered by a sense of fun and a sense of the absurd. And remember what Charles Cros said in his *Hareng Saur*:

> J'ai composé cette histoire, — simple, simple, simple,
> Pour mettre en fureur les gens — graves, graves, graves,
> Et amuser les enfants.

Poking fun and giving pleasure. But he wasn't quite telling the truth. I am sure he wrote of his herring as every poet writes: because certain words came to him, and nagged him till he lengthened them into a poem. Lewis Carroll, as everyone knows, was out for a walk in the country, on a hillside,[1] alone, on a bright summer day, when there came into his head, for no discernible reason, the line "For the Snark *was* a Boojum, you see." Then later he completed a single stanza, incorporating that *donnée*, from which grew, or to which he added another 140 stanzas, to complete *The Hunting of the Snark*.

Nonsense poetry, at its best, at its least contaminated, leaves

---

1 I valued a fancy that Carroll might have been walking on Cumnor Hill above Oxford on that bright day, and that he might have run into serious Matthew Arnold with serious non-nonsensical words coming into *his* head and demanding a poem. And I thought of them crossing together in the punt at Bablocke Hythe, arms round each other, in token that poetry is a union of sense and nonsense. But no, Carroll was walking outside Guildford.

parody, leaves satire, leaves the literature against which it is set, for its own freedom, something not to be written for a living, like leading articles, or to a programme. So in nonsense poems, in words and situations, I see as well as an inconsequent, sophisticated playing a special kind of liberated "mirth", much as John de Trevisa, five hundred years ago, wrote of animals that "Some beestis servythe for mannys myrth: as apes and murmusettes and popyngayes." You cannot but see something of the nature of nonsense verse in the nature, shapes and names of its special fauna, oyster, lobster, herring, red herring, pickled herring, owl, pelican, snail, crocodile, kangaroo, dormouse, walrus, llama, etcetera.

Nonsense, in our special sense, has not much to do, I would say, with the rather boring, institutionalized, démodé and now academically studied nonsense of surrealism, which conformed too much to a conscious theory, to a programme; and I wouldn't be happy about much of a shift to a black nonsense, such as informed the extraordinary "mini-stories" of Daniil Kharms, melancholic poet lost under the weight of the Russian Revolution, who so much admired Edward Lear, was a friend of Malevich the painter, and kept in his Leningrad room "a machine for doing nothing", made up of empty cigarette boxes, springs, tins, bicycle wheels and pieces of string. Into black nonsense of his kind creeps a design on the reader; whereas the better non-sensifiers from Bishop Corbet downwards are happy in a corner juggling with their words, and released, for that while, from their melancholy.

Free as it may be (could anything be more free than a perfect, complex spoonerism?), the best nonsense verse — the writing of it certainly — is in danger now because it does demand an accepted idea of the nature of verse in general, a widely shared idea of the ways in which poetry works. Against accepted forms and poetic tricks and poetry language, it plays its own nature and language. Edward Lear, that melancholic, intelligent genius of a poet, needed Tennyson to play against, for instance, although Lear's

Spoonmeat at Bill Porter's in the Hall

or Lear's

Cold are the crabs that crawl on yonder hills,
Colder the cucumbers that grow beneath

are still the man, the nonsense poet, in his own liberty.

I suppose that nonsense set going by writing which is

formless and anarchic won't be much fun. For future nonsense verse which is deeply mirthful we may have to wait, whenever it comes, in whatever shape, for a reasserted common art which is deeply artful. As for now we still have in our heads enough of the older forms of verse to enjoy the older nonsense.

But this is getting too serious. When Maria Edgeworth lifted Samuel Foote's famous nonsense mnemonic about the Grand Panjandrum —

> So she went into the garden to cut a cabbage leaf, to make an apple pie; and at the same time a great she-bear coming up the street, pops its head into the shop, "What! no soap?" So he died, and she very imprudently married the barber; and there were present the Picninnies, and the Joblillies, and the Garyulies, and the grand Panjandrum himself, with the little round button at top; and they all fell to playing the game of catch as catch can, till the gunpowder ran out at the heels of their boots.

— and put it into a chapter of didactic educational fiction, she made the father remark, as the children tried to repeat it without mistake, that "It is sweet to talk nonsense in season."

Good advice, and true. And enough.

1979

What is a War Poet?

The concept of a "war poet" is odd, when you come to analyse it. Does it mean a poet who writes only about a war in which he is engaged, a poet who ceases to be a poet when his war is finished? A poet who is killed in war, as Keith Douglas was killed in the Normandy fighting?

Fighting, or experiencing war, its scenery, its tragedy, its dirt, its inhabitants, the living and the dead, the sprawling, rotting, stinking dead, has sometimes lifted talent — for a while — out of mediocrity, or least ineffectuality. To take an example from painting and from World War One, Paul Nash, an artist of minor talent, was shocked by the sight of pocked and denatured No-Man's Land into painting his one remarkable picture, the famous picture he called "We have Created a New World", in which the moon looks down on shell-holes and ragged stumps of trees. The shock over and absorbed, back Nash fell into his mediocrity.

The question, I am afraid, about Keith Douglas, killed when he was twenty-four, is whether he had any talent; whether he is much more or anything more than a name in a gallery of the shadow-poets of the Second World War — poets who had only the smallest poetic existence. After being wounded — he was a tank officer — in the Western Desert, he wrote an essay on the apparent absence of any poet "who seems likely to be an impressive commentator" on the war. Hell, he said, could not be let loose twice, and it had been let loose in the 1914–1918 war. Now, in 1943, it was only the "same old hell" over again:

> The hardships, pain and boredom; the behaviour of the living and the appearance of the dead, were so accurately described by the poets of the Great War that every day on the battlefields of the western desert — and no doubt on the Russian battlefields as well — their poems are illustrated. Almost all that a modern poet on active service is inspired to write, would be tautological.

That looks sensible, yet re-examined it is nonsense, because every genuine artist of every kind is *sui generis*, seeing or sensing the same things differently. If the case Keith Douglas puts in that essay were true, all art, all poetry would be endless reiteration, endless tautology.

Keith Douglas's biographer has written a surprisingly detailed book.[1] Those few years and the life is over. Yet, between facts and quotations, there is enough to establish both Keith Douglas's nature and the nature of his writing, his milieu and his keepings. Desmond Graham says his own biographic role was negative — "to act at best as a clear glass through which Douglas shows himself, without distortion or absurdity".

He evidently admires Douglas: he does not judge him, he does not exactly explain his admiration. He compiles a Douglas chronicle, the child of divorced parents, his father an ex-officer of no great ability, the boy at Christ's Hospital (described by those who knew him and taught him there as brilliant, cantankerous, difficult and clever), the undergraduate at Merton College, Oxford (where his tutor was the minor poet Edmund Blunden); the soldier in Palestine and the desert, and on leave in Egypt, the writer at all times of poems and more poems.

But I must express my own disappointed conviction that Keith Douglas's poems are almost uniformly bad. Desmond Graham — and it is not his fault — does not find a convincing stanza, a convincing line to quote, let alone a convincing poem. The unconvincingness is partly an absence of fit between word and word and partly an absence of immersion in words and things. Who wrote of poetry that there is no magic horse without a real horse? I find neither the magic nor the reality in Keith Douglas, I find in him no living individuality, his poems transmit no warm, attractive individuality of feeling.

Douglas, I see, was intelligent and inquisitive. But I see also that he was contrary and arrogant, and obstinate in a cantankerous cynicism; which is the poorest equipment for writing — or for writing poems. He seems to have upset some of his leave-time associates in Cairo. One of them wryly recorded, for instance, that "his talk was all of burning tanks and roasted bodies".

War or no war, early death or no, this life of Keith Douglas impressed me as an unwitting study of the third-rate in literature; of the fix of an intelligent man who would like to create but finds, and does not care to admit, that, after all, he has neither the tackle nor the temperament.

I suppose that knowledge of his shortcomings made him the more cynical, oscillating between cynicism, with its tough talk,

1 *Keith Douglas 1920–1944* by Desmond Graham (1974).

and sentimentality. And it fits in with his shortcomings and his realization of them that he kept, in his obstinate way, what was in fact the poorest of literary company.

Would this book have been written if Keith Douglas had been something else than a "war poet", who was killed, and so had a role ready made for him? I doubt it. And before you say, Well, he was killed so young, remember that other poets have written themselves into futurity by their early twenties.

2

From the earlier war descends the problem of the poet, or rather of the poems of, Isaac Rosenberg, who was killed in France on the first of April 1918. Rosenberg reminds me that in the lifelong course of his trade the professional reader — the reviewer, to use a word less exalted than critic — has to ponder so often a mystery of reputation, of acceptance or of rejection.

How is it that a greater writer may come so sluggishly into favour, or can be so quickly dropped? How can the badness of a writer be so invisible to a generation or two of readers? Why can't critics X and Y see "the obvious"? And then to worsen matters, maybe your X or your Y is some grandee of authorship whose work leads you to believe that everything he says is gospel; and here he is, this hero of yours, condemning some other writer you respond to so warmly and judge to be so excellent. Yeats, whose poems I revere, could see and feel nothing in the poems of Wilfred Owen, which I also revere. Extraordinary. He could not feel, he could not hear, the terrible beauty which was born out of Owen's nature when he was caught on the Western Front.

Am I behaving like Yeats when I declare I can see next to no merit in the poems — poems of war and poems of peace — by Isaac Rosenberg? For me here is a prime, indeed fascinating mystery of reputation undeserved. And years and years late here is all of Rosenberg presented, with enormous praise, in a handsome memorial edition,[1] a final edition of poems, prose and letters, fuller than the Rosenberg collection I first read forty-two years ago, in a flush, and then a despondency, of exploration.

Isaac Rosenberg, physically a very small creature, was descended from Jews, child of a Jewish couple from Lithuania who had come to rest in Stepney. He trained as a process

---

1   *The Collected Works of Isaac Rosenberg* edited by Ian Parsons (1979).

engraver, then became a student at the Slade, making a rather slow uncertain entry into adult life, never free of a very real poverty, and hesitant between his poetry and his painting. Then came the war. In the upshot he enlisted — so that a separation allowance should go to his mother — and he was killed, twenty-seven years old, on a night patrol.

How one would like Rosenberg to have been a good poet, and how many people have told us that he was a good poet, when he wasn't. Everything in this fine collected edition seems to me proof only of aesthetic turbulence in an ordinary mind, or a mind which could not express itself verbally. I thought so when I first read his poems in 1937 or 1938, finding a hopeless incoherence in his lines — words not welded to words, words out of the rag-bag of the poetic: maiden, measureless, murmuring, dross, dread, dim, dumb, hurls, curls, unfurls; words not coaxed into rhythm; words and lines and stanzas and whole poems not at all proceeding from acuteness of the senses, from seeing, hearing, touching, scenting.

> They leave their love-lorn haunts,
> Their sigh-warm floating Eden;
> And they are mute at once;
> Mortals by Gods unheeden;
> By their past kisses chidden —

such derived falsity of writing was only a little changed by the sudden terrors and black corruption which Rosenberg, like Sassoon and Owen (and every other front-line soldier), encountered in the trenches.

> The air is loud with death,
> The dark air spurts with fire,
> The explosions ceaseless are.
> Timelessly now, some minutes past,
> These dead strode time with vigorous life,
> Till the shrapnel called "an end!"
> But not to all. In bleeding pangs
> Some borne on stretchers dreamed of home,
> Dear things, war-blotted from their hearts —

that comes from one of the war poems, from "Dead Man's Dump", which Isaac Rosenberg's editor calls "deservedly Rosenberg's most renowned poem". But what stuff it really is — and yet there has been so steady a cult elevating Rosenberg to greatness — a greatness to come, had he only survived, or even to a greatness achieved and inviolate.

I think I see how an involved Keatsian staccato was mistaken for the real thing. It came to the notice of readers, with the added pathos of young death, when the sense of poetry was newly freshened by the discovery of Hardy and Hopkins. It was taken — mistaken — to be of the same family — poems, all the same, which lack what Hopkins spoke of so well as "the roll, the rise, the carol, the creation" of poetry. And cult or no, I do have to add that no one whose judgment *ad hoc* it seems reasonable to value, has ever written a word — so far as I know — in support or denial of Rosenberg's ineffectuality. He belongs, I must conclude, to a special class of poets, those who stay in the reference books, but not in the head.

Even so, there is a second mystery; which is the contrasting and contradictory merit of Rosenberg's paintings, especially his portraits and self-portraits (several of them are reproduced in this book, in colour).

A question of the professional painter who lived to be only the amateur poet? A question of the correcting influence of his time at the art school?

I suppose so. Rosenberg's paintings seem firm and deliberate, and devoid of swank; portraits by him (such as the self-portrait in the Imperial War Museum) are skewed and poised dramatically, and modelled with an apparent simplicity of effective colour. No fumbling. No muddling weakness. Perhaps it was the painter, not the poet, who would have won through, but for that shell or bullet on 1 April 1918.

Aleksandr Blok

The grand stature of poets in other languages than our own, whether we have "acquired" their languages or no, is something we do have to take on trust. Translation can help, of course, but not so much as we believe. It can help us to the startling, illuminating images, to attitudes, it can enable us to observe kinship perhaps with the poetry which we really know because it is written in our own language.

Even so translation is usually very bad. Publishers and academics do obstinately disbelieve in a fact: which is that poetry can be translated — so far as it can be translated at all — only by other poets, and only by other good poets.

Do we know that Aleksandr Blok is one of the grand masters of European poetry in our own century? We may hear that he is, we may believe that he is; but from such translations of him as exist we could not really know anything of the kind. But here we are. Forgetting encyclopaedias and anthologies, we can, now, at last, turn, in two big volumes, to what (we are told) is the only full-scale life of Blok in any language, Russian included.[1]

Blok, tall, handsome, kindly, yet rather remote and silent, died in 1921, after, but not because of the Russian Revolution; and here we learn, with singular pleasure, if we are given to books of the kind, about the keepings of this educated Russian from the minor nobility, who felt the world stirring and greeted the Revolution, in his way, with his world-famous poem *The Twelve*.

We discover his childhood. Avril Pyman's biography opens with some of Blok's at once tender and ironical recollections of a late visit to the country house he grew up in; a white house against the woods, which the local peasants looted after the Revolution.

"We were sitting, all the family, drinking tea under the limes at sunset. Beyond the lilacs the mist was already rising from the gully. The sound of scythes being sharpened came to us."

Yes, but for Blok at least it was too late to indulge such a dream of country living as we can find and enjoy elsewhere in Russian literature, legitimately enough — in the auto-biographies of Aksakov, for instance. Yet much of Blok the

---

1   *The Life of Aleksandr Blok,* Vol. I, *The Distant Thunder 1880–1908*; Vol. 2, *The Release of Harmony* by Avril Pyman (1979 and 1980).

poet must have grown from the mild years lived by Blok the child, with his cultured grandparents and his mother and his aunts, on the small estate at Shakhmatovo; and from his winter life in Petersburg, above the Neva.

In the country, "like any self-respecting Russian child," says his biographer (who is English, and is married to a Russian, and who lived in Russia until three years ago), this small Sasha Blok "knew all the best places for lily-of-the-valley, wild strawberries and the various kinds of mushroom". Life in and round the Shakhmatovo house (from which there was nothing but a rutted track to the railway station) and life in the old Petersburg gave this child a marvellously rich stock of the experience of the senses — out of which he actualized the symbols of his prophetic symbolist poetry.

Elsewhere — in a professorial chair at Warsaw — Blok had a demonic, violent father never really known to him. His parents had parted soon after he was born. He had grandfathering in lieu of fathering, and at Shakhmatovo he would trudge in delightful expeditions with his botanist grandfather (who was Rector of Petersburg University). No doubt, all the same, with his small pretty mother, whom he called Droplet, or Crumb, or "his dearest tiny", and the aunts and the grandmama and the nanny, he was surrounded by too many women for a later balance or peace, a later normality, in his life.

As a poet Blok begins with a *fin-de-siècle* decadence, at least with visions of the Eternal Feminine, of mystical harmony, and symbolic correspondences: but existence does not work out in that way. He lives through the abortive revolution of 1905 (the first volume takes Blok to within nine years of the Revolution which did not fail): he finds his experiences twisting and torturing. He passes through that which makes life "black and terrible", to his overwhelming and very different visions of a Russia shaking itself free of the centuries. And of course to say of Blok either "Russia" or "the Revolution" is to say too little, or to say it wrong.

For Russia we have to read "mankind", in Blok's vision, and for the particular revolution we have to read what, in multaneity, has been happening to all mankind, separating us from what was — or what looked to have been — our once settled and only slow-moving past. In 1918 he ended an article about Wagner by saying that the new epoch was alarming and unstable: "He who will understand that the meaning of life consists in restlessness and anxiety, will already cease to be a common man. He will be, not a self-conceited nonentity, he will be a new man, a new step towards the artist."

Some of the pleasure and authority of the first volume of her life of Blok comes from his biographer's direct knowledge of Russia, of what it is to live in that north of north, where spring is a tremendous release, after the snow-light of winter, and where "for natives of Petersburg the despair of oncoming winter is the natural symbol of all other despairs".

The trouble — and once more the deep trouble, I am afraid — is the Englishing of Blok's poems. Pasternak declared that the real "whirled into poems by Blok like a stream of air". Symbolist or no, there was nothing so quick, nothing so sure, he maintained, as Blok's observation; to look at any one of his poems was to recognize that "it contained a piece of news". It seemed "as if the piece of news had settled on the page of its own accord without anyone's permission, as if the poem had not been written down by anyone".

I wish I could say that Avril Pyman's versions could make English readers feel that news and that newness. Without the rare tackle for translation, she attempts versions in rhyme. That is really the worst thing to have done, and I am sorry for it, having myself met in anthologies and elsewhere no more than two English versions which really suggest great originals — one a version of Blok's prophetic lyric of 1916 about the vulture planing over a desolated Russia and over a cabin where a resigned mother gives her baby the nipple, the other a prose translation of Blok's poem about Ravenna ("You sleep like a child, Ravenna, in the arms of drowsy eternity").

Forgetting what Blok's "harsh candour" in matters of writing would have made of Avril Pyman's unhappy versions, let's go on to the second volume of this book of hers, which is history as well as biography.

Here is Blok in his fame, Blok in the opening years of the Russian Revolution — and Blok on his death-bed in 1921, aged only forty-one.

Tact is one thing displayed by this portrait of a strange, powerful complex man; and by tact I do not mean falsity, I do not mean pretence about the Revolution or pretence that Blok, this poet from the minor nobility, was someone who shuddered away from the huge topsy-turvydom of his age.

Books are written about great Russians which in fact prove to be about politics; sticks or clubs which are only for thumping the Communists or the émigrés. In Avril Pyman's second volume we are made to see the dilemma of every sensitive, creative Russian as the Revolution took shape and as the Revolution hardened.

Russian life, so much of it, had for so long been about revolution, about a new birth, a new future. So much emotion swelled up about leaving an Old World of oppression. If Avril Pyman's extraordinary book is above propaganda, it is not above good and evil; it is about acceptance, doubt, dismay — in, so much of it, Aleksandr Blok's own words, from his diaries especially. He knew that the times were dreadful, that the future was doubtful. But it was the future which mattered, and he hoped; he loves life, he loves the world, his hopes survive; and it is this situation which Avril Pyman handles with such tact.

Enjoyable it is to have this man pictured for us, this exceptional man with his long strong face, his "piercing inhuman beauty". Akhmatova, herself a young woman of uncommon beauty, wrote a poem, which Avril Pyman translates, about her meeting with Blok in 1914.

> I came to visit the poet
> Just at midday. On a Sunday.
> The quiet in the spacious room. . .
> Beyond the windows, frost.
>
> And a raspberry sun shone
> Above the tattered blue-grey smoke. . .
> How unclouded the gaze of my silent
> Host, fixed attentively on me.
>
> He has the kind of eyes
> That everyone ought to remember
> But that for me, a cautious woman,
> It were better not to look into. . . . .

This man with eyes that everyone ought to remember, spoke of writers as men put into the world for those who are hungry in spirit. In a speech in the year of his death he says "We are dying" — the men of his generation, I suppose he means — "but art will remain. It is one in essence and indivisible." He said that though it was scarcely possible to breathe the air of the present, it was still possible "to breathe the air of contemporaneity, that thin air that smells of the sea and of the future".

Regimentation or attempted regimentation of art began, and Blok wrote: "We all know what a difficult thing art is. We know how capricious and whimsical is the soul of the artist and we wish from our hearts that eventually a milieu should come into being where the artist will be able to be capricious and whimsical, as he needs to be, where he will be able to remain himself, without being an official, a member of a collegium, or a scholar."

He felt we were all in the first centuries of what would be seen as a new era. Avril Pyman says of his most famous poem "The Twelve" that it was "the supreme expression of his great and simple idea of a Third Force, a sound from some other shore beyond all the warring and clamour of this agonizing and terrible world". He spoke, as always, "of the free morning, of the green garden beyond the dark corridor".

As with all great writers, the reader comes to feel that he is an instrument through which all human life is speaking — the life of all time. Maybe Russians feel that more strongly — far more strongly — than any other people in the western world, perhaps because they live more in crisis and are momentarily free only in music or in the quiet reading to themselves of a poem. In England, if a writer or an artist has been acclaimed enough or has been around long enough, we may arrange, in the end, a memorial service for him in the Abbey, as for Auden or Eliot, but the funerals we leave them to are quiet and private enough as a rule. The death, or rather the burial, of a Moscow writer or a Leningrad writer, to judge from the biographies, often seems to draw as well as his personal friends, many who were friends of his work.

That was so later with Pasternak, as with Blok. "All day people came", after his death. "Somebody took a photo. A young girl whom nobody knew brought the first flowers, four white lilies." And then, "All the way across Petersburg and the Vasil'evsky Island where he had been born, Blok's friends carried him with the hearse plodding empty and unwanted behind." Afterwards Akhmatova again wrote a poem —

In a silver coffin we bore him,
Aleksandr, our pure swan,
Our sun extinguished in torment.

Maybe there is a lesson for us here. Maybe we are too cynical, or too indifferent. Or too unemotional. Stiff upper lips, without snowy winters.

One detail of the last pages moved me. Aleksandr Blok lies near his death. His mother comes into the room, he recognizes her — and appears "to take her presence for granted". Through her he comes into being, with her beside him he ends. Next morning he died with his wife on one side, and his mother, by his request, on the other side.

Christina Rossetti's Oppositions of Desire

I very much welcome the prospect of having, at last, a proper, well laid-out and well printed edition of all the poems of Christina Rossetti — the major Rossetti — in three volumes, of which this is the first.[1]

The grounds for an extra welcome are two at least. Christina Rossetti's poems are now neglected and undervalued; and one cause of the neglect is that for more than fifty years they have been available only cramped and crowded, poorly printed, meanly published, two columns to a small page. As I wriggle round the turn-over lines, in the Globe Edition of the Poetical Works, unable to see the form of some great lyric in its right individuality, I am tempted to recall how Miss Rossetti's eminent publisher said of himself that he only dealt in books as others dealt in pork and cheese.

In this new edition, from the printed texts and the now scattered but fortunately surviving notebooks, the poems are to be arranged in three categories. First come the collections which were individually published, together with the poems added to each collection in later editions. These will fill volumes one and two. Then in the third volume will come poems printed but uncollected, and poems which have never emerged from manuscript. A chronological arrangement would have been better, helping us to see into Christina's obscured life as well as her art; but how good it will be to read the poems free and clear, on a wide enough page, each one of them, in a phrase used by Christina Rossetti's brother and first editor, William Michael Rossetti, "an observable thing", at last.

What has been most observed, or speculated upon recently, is Christina Rossetti's life, not her poems. Yet nearly seventy years ago Ford Madox Ford in his *Ancient Lights* spoke up for Christina as, in the conditions of 1911, a modern writer. He contrasted her scrupulosity and purity of style, her seriousness, with the triviality and faded romanticism of that more famous brother who changed his Christian names from Gabriel Charles Dante, to Dante Gabriel. But then as always — as, for an extra instance, between Gwen John and Augustus John — biography

1 *The Complete Poems of Christina Rossetti* edited by R.W. Crump, vol 1 (1980).

shouts down the quietness of creativity. What chance — in the biography market or the television market — have melodies of love and agony against mistresses and wombats and drugs and the exhuming of stained manuscripts from Highgate Cemetery? Misjudgments of Christina's poems spring from that contrast in lives, as well as from the meat-packing of her work.

Taking the life of this writer nearly as far as the poems require, or perhaps a little further, here is a girl, born in 1830, a Bloomsbury Londoner tucked out of sight in a dark square from which she does not want to emerge. In looks she is by no means unattractive; in her teens, at least, she is vivacious. Very soon, as William Rossetti explains in his memoir of Christina, the poles of her life become defined as love and salvation: here is the girl who begins her poet's life, a student of the poems of George Herbert, divided between natural and spiritual desires which she cannot, as her experience teaches her, reconcile and combine; the girl of strong will and strong appetite who dreams of adding extra-familial love to the close family love between the Rossettis, and to religious love and sternness, and then falls for a young painter who is variable, and by no means at ease, in his beliefs. He changes and changes back, this young James Collinson, this talented friend of Gabriel Charles or Dante Gabriel. She is eighteen when they become attached to each other, in 1848, and only twenty, or thereabouts, when she says no to him, having once declined his proposal and once accepted it.

Christina's poems are well dated, so to some degree, some probability, the poems and the experiences of this very reticent girl can be equated. We may take as Collinson poems of early vintage four celebrated lyrics, "When I am dead, my dearest" (12 December 1848), "Oh roses for the flush of youth" (6 February 1849), "An End", beginning "Love, strong as Death, is dead" (8 March 1849), and "After Death" (28 April 1849).

William Rossetti states that her up-and-down love relationship with Collinson lasted till the end of 1849 or into 1850. He also insists that her experience with Collinson was "a staggering blow" to her peace of mind from which she took years to recover. She wrote on and on through her twenties; but, as one might expect, with lessening intensity, less melody, except in a few poems, retrospectives all of them. Some of these are "Echo", the great December lyric of 1854 ("Come to me in the silence of the night"), "Unforgotten" (1855) and the poems of 30 June and 27 August 1857, in which she writes that her life is like a broken bowl, and that she will lean no more "on child of man", that she longs to be stirred in her depth. "You call me with a puny call," she exclaims not of Collinson, but of those around her; "You talk, you smile, you nothing do: / How should I spend my heart on you, / My heart that so outweighs you all?" And instead as a High Anglican zealot she sets course to union with the divine.

Then, suddenly, in the November of this 1857, the spirit of this girl, who has already known illness and more illness of the body as well as of the emotions, jets into that famous poem "A Birthday" — "My heart is like a singing bird/. . .Because the birthday of my life/Is come, my love is come to me".

This is where we must begin to sense the deeper obscurity of Christina Rossetti's life. It is not possible to suppose that "A Birthday" was in fact an earlier Collinson poem, now rediscovered or revised and entered in her notebook of the time. Something had happened; and something which goes on to some years — the final years in her excellence — of extra-ordinary creativity; years which continue and end in expressions of hope killed and cold, yet insatiably remembered. Christina, reticent yet by no means debarred from stimulus of the mind, was now a week or two short of twenty-seven. Had someone new entered her life? So it has been supposed. But in 1857 it would have been too early for sudden ecstasy over the second man who is known to have been entangled with her, the reclusive, timid scholar, Charles Cayley. Christina's brother gives the years of warm involvement with Cayley, the years in which it is conceivable that she might have married him, had he as well not been religiously wanting, as the close of 1862 to the opening of 1867.

Had Collinson come back? That too has been supposed, or hinted; and seems the likelier solution — Christina soon faltering, soon rejecting in extra-finality, perhaps in particular because Collinson had re-entered her life from his own marriage.

Poems follow of a return which proved no return, of a heart-shaking revulsion and remorse and yet unsatisfiable longing. In the long poem "From House to House" (19 November 1858) Christina speaks of the "one night" which turned all her summer back to snow, asseverating that she would not, if she could, rebuild her "house of lies", in which she had joyed to live.

Then in the spring of 1859 she swept or attempted to sweep the table clean in writing "Goblin Market", that poem of deliverance from the effects of having eaten the sweet vicious fruits of the goblin marketeers. Superior persons suggest that in

writing "Goblin Market" Christina was ignorantly mastered
by sexual fantasies, by her subconscious; but it seems to me
that this extraordinary woman knew to a T what she was
stating, and rejecting — and accepting. Before the summer of
1859 was over she had composed the desolate, resolute "Up-
hill", that one of the half-dozen or so poems by her known to
everyone — back to the up-hill journey, to the end. And in
December 1860 (how many of her best poems belong, as the
years go by, to that winter month), she wrote "Passing away
saith the World, passing away"; in October 1861 (she is still
only thirty):

> Too late for love, too late for joy,
>   Too late, too late!

(in "The Prince's Progress").

Obscurity, though, still succeeds obscurity. To whom are
we to attach the powerful despondency, or half-despondency,
of "Twice", which came from Christina in the summer of
1864, all of five years later? How are we to explain
biographically the succeeding February and March of more
poems of renunciation and longing and dead hope which
welled from Christina, the poems of 1865?

> I took my heart in my hand
>   (O my love, O my love).

Who also takes it in his hand? Who sets it down, so that it
breaks? The third stanza of "Twice" clearly refers back to the
coming of the love who had made her heart like a singing bird:
she has not often smiled since this breaking of her heart

> — nor questioned since,
> Nor cared for corn-flowers wild,
>   Nor sung with the singing bird.

The answer should be her absent-minded Charles Cayley —
if William Michael Rossetti was wrong in his dates, and if the
image of Cayley which has come to us is in fact caricatural. But
it does not sound like Cayley; and if it was not until 1867 that
she firmly rejected that mild agnostic lover as a husband, how
are we to explain Christina writing on 17 February 1865, in the
second part of "Memory", that she has a room no one enters
but herself — "There sits a blessed memory on a throne. / There
my life centres"? And does it fit with Cayley that she writes
three days later, on 20 February, "If I might only love my God
and die!", which she follows on the next day with the two

poems "Shall I forget on this side of the grave", and "Amor Mundi", with its adjuration to turn back from the world — "Turn again, O my sweetest, — turn again, false and fleetest"?

She is looking backward and backward; and in March of this year she will write "Dead Hope" — how "Hope newborn one pleasant morn/Died at even"; in September, "A Daughter of Eve", in which she says she had been a fool to pluck her rose too soon, and a fool to snap her lily, "Stripped bare of hope and everything"; in November, "Young Death":[1]

Her hair a hidden treasure,
Her voice a lost pleasure:
Her soul made void of passion,
Her body going to nothing,

and later in the month (21 November) "A Dirge" — "Why were you born when the snow was falling" — which it seems just possible to relate to the hope reborn in that earlier November of 1857 when Christina's heart was like a singing bird, which so quickly died and remained dead, yet was unforgotten and unforgettable. Perhaps we must suppose a conflation of Collinson and Cayley, in regret and dismay, in the past, and the present.

Still what we cannot miss in Christina's most remarkable poems, standing as they do by themselves without requiring revelations of biography, is the continuing circumstance of tragedy from which they emerge. She is caught between flesh and spirit, between two kinds of love, one of them coupled with sin and punishment; and we realize that poems have come into being by that process which Donne describes in "The Triple Fool". Like Donne she has been drawing her pains through the vexations of rhyme to allay them, she has been taming or trying to tame the grief of love in the fetters of verse.

Swinburne soon after her death had harsh things to say of the effects of "theolatry" on such a fine nature as Christina's, and we may echo his strictures, while seeing that the poems come out of the clash of loyalties; also observing ironically that in her verse it is defeated love which wins, or makes the better poems, and her dictatorial piety which loses. For all her Anglican aspiration, her fears and uncertainties, all, as her brother lists them, "her perpetual church-going and communions, her prayers and fasts, her submission to clerical direction, her oblations, her practice of confession", it is Christina Rossetti's devotional poems (and the devotional

1   In the *Poetical Works,* 1904, page 244.

addenda to her love poems) which are weak. We may recall, as a last word on her life, how greatly Christina admired Elizabeth Barrett Browning, for her *Sonnets from the Portuguese*; and we may ask what would have resulted if Love, in the shape of someone as resolved as Robert Browning, had drawn Christina Rossetti backward by the hair? Fewer great lyrics, certainly; or great lyrics of a different kind.

In esse it is now to the lyrics, to the words-in-order, that we have to attend, helped by this lucid new edition (which has textual notes, but no introductory chatter).

When all the poems are free and clean of that meat and cheese packing in which they have been squashed, it will be easier to reverse the grotesque misjudgments of Christina Rossetti which are current; we shall more easily see in her poems what criticism is never well equipped to explain. *Dans le poète l'oreille parle, la bouche écoute.* I think no poet of stature since her day has ever doubted that it is the ear which speaks in Christina Rossetti's poems, in a music delicate, subtle, and exceptional, yet not too separated from speech.

What we have to understand — or relearn — in these public poems drawn out of private vicissitudes is appreciation of the right forming, the right saying, the right hearing of such a line as "In the bleak mid-winter", of such a conclusion as

> Speak low, lean low,
> As long ago, my love, how long ago.

Christina Rossetti is one of those who could have said *Toutes choses autour de moi étaient simples, et pures: le ciel, le sable, l'eau.* We would do well to discover how it is in a complex of simplicity that the ear of this poet speaks, allowing next to nothing extravagant or bizarre; for instance, how in her poems rhyme links cadence into wholes with never too much insistence on itself.

In other words, here is a poet unaffined to the poetic of today who could do much — all imitation rejected — to correct a today's type-poet (or type-critic) in the unchanging fundamentals.

The Morbid Tennysons

Poets known to me in my lifetime, and many more poets known to history in different cultures and countries, have been drawn from the strangest families, have had the strangest parents, brothers, sisters, ancestry, have been odd in their keepings. We peer more into their lives, it is true; but that doesn't explain all that we find. Are we to deduce that there are genetic and biochemical peculiarities which run to the making of verses rather than to the elaborations of novels or paintings? I shall not attempt to answer, or more than to suggest that a lassitude of great awareness may be involved, a habit of inconsequence and of long pauses in life, five minutes or ten between putting on one sock and then putting on the other.

Tennyson, all the same. There is the poet who is so far, and who promises to remain, our prime exemplar in this mystery. We learn more of his own oddity, and of the pool of oddity in which he floated, with each new book. The newest life of Tennyson, *Tennyson: The Unquiet Heart*,[1] has much to reveal (not very sympathetically, but then it is by an American and Americans are dabs for hygiene) about grubby grandeur, Tennyson in undarned socks, Tennyson in dirty shirts, etcetera, making more piquant the view we have of him — and the view we shall certainly retain of him — through the gleam and grandeur of his rhetoric. For me, though, the Tennyson book is the book of the Tennyson brothers — six of them — and the Tennyson sisters — four of them — given to us in 1974 by Sir Charles Tennyson and Mrs Hope Dyson.[2] R.B. Martin emphasized for us a Victorian family, odd certainly, but in many ways not untypical in a Victorian pretentiousness, piling up the imaginary turrets of descent. The earlier book showed us a population of Tennysons mooning between idleness and the madhouse. To say that these Tennysons are threaded on a string of morbidity would be summarizing a delightful book in a cold way. Let's begin with Septimus, No. 7. Septimus once rose to greet Dante Gabriel Rossetti with the words: "I am Septimus, the most morbid of the Tennysons." I am not sure he was quite the most morbid, but he certainly declined into depression and unshakeable indolence.

1 *Tennyson: The Unquiet Heart* by R.B. Martin (1980).
2 *The Tennysons: Background to Genius* by Sir Charles Tennyson and Hope Dyson (1974).

A year older than Septimus, Arthur took to drink and
indolence. As a child he was found under the dining-room
table, trying, he said, to find God's legs (as a result of
Cowper's hymn "God moves in a mysterious way"?). As a man
he is on record as having pointed, during a supper party, to a
bowl of trifle and to have asked for "some more of that angels'
vomit". The Tennysons, all or most of them, shared a gift of
words.

Horatio, Number Eleven, contemplated some angel panels
of a reredos which a woman artist was painting, and he
remarked in a faraway voice. "After all, angels are only a
clumsy form of poultry." He tried farming in Tasmania.
Without success.

Charles, the cleric, became the grey opium addict of his
lonely vicarage, and wrote his rather attractive accomplished
sonnets, such as the one about little Phoebe killed by a fall of
the cliff when she was out collecting shells —

She took the homeward path that led
Beneath yon dark-blue ridge, when sad to tell,
On her fair head the gloomy lias fell

— or the sonnet which preserves the now forgotten noise of
the Steam Threshing Machine —

The fly-wheel with a mellow murmur turned

and others on the Hydraulic Ram, the Telegraph Cable to India
and the South Foreland Electric Light.

Then Edward Tennyson and Frederick Tennyson. Edward
was committed to Lincoln Asylum. He was nineteen, and he
stayed there till his death nearly sixty years later.

Frederick, eldest of the family, as an undergraduate was
"sinister in aspect and terrific in manner, even to the
discomfiture of elderly dons". He remained (Edward
FitzGerald's description) "a gigantic child", took against the
clergy of orthodoxy and their sermons ("the frowsy diatribes
of black men with white ties — too often the only white thing
about them"); became a British Israelite and a Swedenborgian,
and indulged in spiritualism, communicating with the dead in
the dead of night "by means of a kind of electric ticking".

Living as an old man in Jersey, he was once heard to shout,
as he raged up and down the stairs, "Where are my trousers,
where are my trousers? I have forty pairs, and I can only find
thirty-five". One of his unpublished poems has this engaging
couplet:

I had a vision very late
After a dinner of whitebait.

And one of his published poems, quoted in this book, ought to
be better known. He remembers (in, I imagine, elderly
autumn) a spring morning, in an "old carven room", where
the girl he is in love with begins to sing:

The open casement quivers in the breeze,
    And one large muskrose leans its dewy grace
    Into the chamber, like a happy face,
And round it swim the bees; . . .

She stays her song; I linger idly by;
    She lifts her head, and then she casts it down,
    One small, fair hand is o'er the other thrown,
With a low, broken sigh;

I know not what I said; what she replied
    Lives, like eternal sunshine, in my heart;
    And then I murmur'd, Oh! we never part,
My love, my life, my bride!

And then, as if to crown that first of hours,
    That hour that ne'er was mated by another,
    Into the open casement her young brother
Threw a fresh wreath of flowers.

In fact, he married an Italian girl, not the girl of the poem.
    So the notes of this notebook go on, the record of a
Victorian family whose economic and social insecurity was
complicated by mental insecurity, or the other way round. The
villain is old George Tennyson, the more or less self-made
wealthy grandfather of "the strange brood", who took
violently and viciously against his eldest son, the learned
Tennyson father, and disinherited him, an act which stirred the
black, heated turbulence of the son and the son's children. A
letter from that brutal (and morbid) old George Tennyson, that
country solicitor rising to manorial gentleman, and anxious to
found a county family, gives his tone:

Sir, You are a man of leisure and I am not, and have no time
for peevish and ill-tempered correspondence. . .

Extracts from the record of Tennyson's table talk kept by his
son show the great Alfred's delight — his rather Victorian as
well as Tennysonian delight — in events, items and stories of
sick eccentricity, such as the story of a daughter who tied her

mad father to a tree and beat him, or the pig which "ate a man's face and nose to the bone while he lay drunk in a ditch".

One curious note in this exceptional book tells us something of English churchyards in the last century, as well as something of the great Alfred himself: "A.T. walking through Didcot churchyard found a young girl's shin bone stuck in the heel of his boot."

How did he know it was the shin bone of a young girl? Did he pick it out and get it identified by one of his medical friends? I expect so.

How Many Sprigs of Bay in Fifty Years?

Do we have major poets alive and at work? Do we have as many middling poets as we should have? In poetry can we reasonably look forward to a decade or so of the valuable and the vigorous? If no seems the right answer, the conclusion I work towards is "So much the worse for all our present and immediately future writing, prose no less than poetry".

I am on record as saying that literature is always in a bad way (like mankind or like politics or government). But then bad can be either worse, or less bad. Anthony Thwaite not long ago wrote one of these uncommon poems in which a proposition is laid, or at least inferred. He listed poet after contemporary poet, and concluded that most of them — though he was not so blunt or so absolute — must at best be fabricators of the indifferent.

Perhaps he had been reading Swift, or Edward Young, or Pope, from a time when poets spoke out on poetry and were not expected or disposed to think of bad poets as "colleagues" who were therefore immune to attack or demolition.

Peri Bathous; or The Art of Sinking in Poetry, by Swift and Pope, is, though brief, a classic text poets should never be unfamiliar with. *The Dunciad,* too. We should stop complaining of Pope's cruelty, we should insist, when we can, on Pope's verity and everlasting usefulness. There is Dryden to be read and re-read —

Fools change in England; and new fools arise,
For though th'immortal species never dies,
Yet ev'ry year new maggots make new flies.

And on the way back to Dryden (and Shadwell in Pissing Alley) there is Swift to be remembered on poets and poetry — Swift asking if Britain could ever boast "Three poets in an age at most" and continuing:

Our chilling climate hardly bears
A sprig of bay in fifty years:
While ev'ry fool his claim alleges
As if it grew in common hedges.

Who is to say that the rate of the occurrence of good poets has gone up since Swift's day, or the rate of middling poets?

Our population is bigger, certainly. Many more people undergo an education. That should mean an advance in the number of good and middling poets in fifty years. But then how irregular and odd are the genetics of art. All we can be sure of is that the number of bad poets increases, in spite of indifference to verse, with increased population.

Swift warned us not to be peevish when we come to be old; but I had better begin now to set out my own conviction (reminding readers at the same time that by my age I have become inoculated against scream and counter-charge). After looking and sifting and then repeating the process, my conviction is that since Eliot and the leading poets (now dead) of my own Thirties generation, there have been no major poets, no "good" poets at all; and perhaps only six middling poets worth attending to — six poets in England (and as far as long or short sight tells me, fewer still in the United States).

And the bad poets? *Circumspice* one might say to dons and critics and reviewers and editors and then call on rude Mr Pope (with his Great Dane to defend him):

Some have at first for wits, then poets passed,
Turned critics next, and proved plain fools at last.

I count up to forty or fifty poets, now published, discussed and praised — or allowed at any rate — whose work requires to be called inept, which is a portmanteau adjective covering, according to fit, amateurism, plagiarism (a little transposed French modernism, a little Guillevic or Ponge is the latest trick), tediousness, silliness, blandness, nastiness, pretentiousness, pseudo-modernism, violence, and plain nothingness.

Names? — whether of the middle few, or of those forty to fifty? Here I guard myself, not just because I lack the nerve. I have to allow for charity (not too much of that in this matter of bad verse or any other kind of bad writing), and for uncertainties (Eliot once remarked to me in his grand *Criterion* days how difficult it had become for him to recognize the merits of new verse). I have to allow for poets I have not heard of. I have to remember that bad can — but seldom does — become less bad.

Still I think history suggests that my figures are unlikely to be far wrong: no "good" poets, i.e., major poets whose formal melody is life, medicine and pleasure for us; only those half-a-dozen or so middling poets, and those forty to fifty shockers to whom we are subjected by the kindly innocence, if that is the word, of publishers, and the folly of advisers and critics and reviewers.

How many of these gentlemen and ladies are possessed by characteristics of our time, by a marked uncertainty (as we dwindle modernistically from a pronounced and prolonged modernism), by a proletarianization or democratization of art, coupled with a powerful simple-simonism imported from America and for some reason — for several reasons — actually encouraged by some of our new meinie of university critics? If the gross fathering figure was Pound, blown up — as we may now see it — by Eliot's peculiar praise of him, in misguiding gratitude, as *il miglior fabbro*, other fathers have been subsequent American masters of writing without labour, subsequent fabricators of those too easy poems which lack both the qualities required in art for our human condition, our brief duration, and that necessary impingement of the "outside" — of everything that is made imaginatively available to us by our senses.

Of course, other literatures show a related infection. I suppose that Marguerite Yourcenar, that remarkable writer we so neglect in England, had some French as well as English and much American poetry in mind when she told one interviewer recently (*Magazine littéraire*, October 1979) that modern poetry had gone wrong in rejecting that rhythmic repetition which remains necessary to poems. She said that for herself a poet is "quelqu'un à travers qui passe un courant — quelqu'un 'qui est en contact' ", through rhythms and repetitions which have a hallucinatory effect, and which impose themselves on the subconscious. "Une poésie qui n'a pas ce rythme là n'établit pas ce contact nécessaire. La forme émane du fond."

To see things reversible or reversed in the now so common way: mustn't that be a peculiar rejection of the better poetry of all peoples and all previous ages — an insolence? An empty, presumptuous philistinism? Who do we think we are, to break off poetic relations with the past, and push *semper aliquid novi* or not so *novi*, so far?

In the 1930s, Pasternak, who felt "entitled to his own egoism", was writing of those who live beneath a sky which "covers them with the meaning of one common date". In the 1950s he wrote that in life he had seen something that had some connection with great men, he wrote of gratitude to the past, of memories "fed by all the juices of the earth, gradually spread by the flow of time", of poetry *needing* to contain painting, meaning and music.

Does it matter if for a while — how long we don't know — poetry, so much of it, is out of contact, in Marguerite Yourcenar's sense? A turn or two, and an owl-light (which was Thomas Lovell Beddoes's description in the 1840s of a poetry slump between Wordsworth and Coleridge and the emergence of Tennyson and Arnold), and new poets will come and lights go up — and a new clique will form around them, poets will again be introduced and warranted by poets, not by the fiat of whoever will then be holding the Nancy Mitford Chair of English Literature at the University of Trumpington or Tintagel.

But meanwhile the bad way, the more than usually bad way, of poetry contributes to a general badness in literature. Few people bother about poetry, or buy it, or read it (though so many write it)? Yes. Few novelists read it? Yes, but I maintain a conviction that health in literature does depend, and more than we realize, on health in poetry; a conviction that the writing of poems has been, and remains, and will always remain the primal initiatory art of words. An effective novel can be written badly. But not an effective poem. In the brevity of the poem's lines and stanzas, cliché — for one thing — shows up too much. Fiction can survive bagginess or looseness (though it is never the better for it); whereas by those dropsical infections poetry is drowned.

Popular or no, the "good" poem, then, provides always the best exemplar for its time of the art of words, language in that good poem being purified and concentrated to its essence; and it is therefore the good poem and the rare revitalizing good poets — if they exist — setting standards like this, who raise the tone of any period in literature. Against vulgar belief nothing helps more or is worth more than the clique in which the good combine, with enough of the fresher middling poets as their lieutenants; or the clique which forms around one such leader if there is one only. Those who hate cliques or groups should remind themselves of what Sainte-Beuve had to say, with a side-swipe at the professors, about the way the young talents find each other out, and form groups — talents

> non pas précisément semblables et de la même famille, mais de la même volée et du même printemps, éclos sous le même astre, et qui se sentent nés, avec des variétés de goût et de vocation, pour une oeuvre commune.

However, the absence of some such vital group or of good poets does not leave us without resource, or without some possible degree of leadership, or corrective leadership, without some stringencies to be encouraged and some possibility of detecting and reversing silly-billyism.

I should like to see literary editors ceasing to treat poetry quite so obviously as the least vital or necessary of literary arts. I want to see poems included by the page, and not singly as occasional and convenient stopgaps in a corner. I want to read no more omnibus reviews of new books of verse. If such a new book has merit, it should be reviewed on its own, like other books of importance. If it is fit only for an inch or five inches in an omnibus review, it is fit for nothing and no one.

I would like to see fewer little magazines. There is no excuse for such a magazine unless it promulgates the strong message of a new clique or group.

Let other things happen as well. Let history be consulted more. Let human nature and needs be more considered. Let the sneer of élitism be eliminated. Let those who write about writing be more decisive (a modish cowardly kind of reviewing, especially of verse, is marked by the sentence in the middle which begins "And yet —". *And yet* the virtues described are not so very virtuous. *And yet* the vices objected to are not so vicious. We take it all back, or half of it back. We insure ourselves. We call ourselves judicious).

But, more importantly, the need is to recognize writers as the best authority on writing — new writing, new verse in particular. The history of the matter does show that the few who most wisely and successfully helped new poetry to find its readers have been other poets in their critical role: authority without pedantry, and with enthusiasm; the lively in sympathy with living.

1980

The Most Popular Poem
in English?

From the huge collection of Edward FitzGerald's letters, over a thousand of them previously unpublished, are we likely to discover a man, or a writer, more exceptional than we knew him to have been already?[1] As long ago as 1947 the co-editor of these letters, the late Professor Terhune of Syracuse University, published a life of FitzGerald (the second attempt at a full biography), which half explained him, though without asking or answering, or even approaching, the one question of human and literary concern; which, naturally, is how an amateur author of such flaccid abilities came suddenly to write, and almost as suddenly to forget, a poem so extraordinary as the hundred and one stanzas of his *Rubáiyát of Omar Khayyám*?

In the second of these four volumes, we reach and pass by the Suffolk-cum-Persian preliminaries to the poem, its private and quasi-secret publication on Fitzgerald's behalf by Quaritch the bookseller (in 1859), and the famous episode of its delayed "discovery" or at least celebration by Rossetti, a younger man and poet-chaser of the pleasures or some of the pleasures of sensation, the poet least likely among the Victorians to be upset by its distanced epicureanism. Clues, faint at first, and never very direct or strong or unevasive — unevasive vis-à-vis FitzGerald himself — begin to appear. They accumulate; but even so each reader will need to be fascinated enough to tie them into an explanation.

The evidence of the letters — of FitzGerald's life and character — is both positive and negative. The letters begin at the close of his years at Cambridge, FitzGerald well off, independent and unsure, undecided on a calling; half English, half Anglo-Irish (his father Edward Purcell had taken his wife's name, FitzGerald), and more than half-rooted in East Anglia.

About this young man, and the middle-aged man, and the old man he became, there is very much half and half. When he was old, Charles Keene drew FitzGerald huddled at his organ, back view; the sketch seems to say as much as (and more than) the sketch of FitzGerald, young and prim, by his in some ways unlikely, yet close friend Thackeray. Thackeray's sketch (reproduced in Volume I) suggests withdrawal as if from the

1 *The Letters of Edward Thomas Fitzgerald* edited by A.M. and A.B. Terhune (1980).

smell of average life. Keene's drawing (reproduced in Lionel Lindsay's *Charles Keene*, 1934) seems to say — after-interpretation as this may be — "Well, it is all but over," and, head down, face invisible, hair long, shoulders drooping, but favourite notes coming from the organ, "What have I done, after all?"

From Thackerary's sketch it is a step back to school and university, to the first and later friends FitzGerald made and kept. At that remarkable East Anglian institution Bury Grammar School (which he loved) FitzGerald made friends of James Spedding, who was to be Bacon's editor, and Kemble the Anglo-Saxon scholar, and W. B. Donne, who became head of the London Library. Superior mediocrity of that kind, and correct orthodoxy, marked most of his slightly distant intimates — dons, parsons, scholars, and the like. Thackeray, encountered when they were undergraduates, was an exception — an exception of extra significance? — and so were the eccentric Tennysons, Frederick and Alfred.

The letters — as well as the *Life* by Professor Terhune — show (however much Professor Terhune would have objected) a lazy, easy-going, well-to-do individualist, retreative, and bedded — with slight or not too persistent, or at all public questioning and unease — in the defensive and respectable orthodoxy proper to someone born in 1809 and so in his un-ambitious forties and fifties at the critical time. It is no good imagining secrets — or at least secrets of action and event. It is no good asking what FitzGerald was up to — young, and less young, bachelor dilettante, in London, in Paris, so much on his own (he wasn't one for associating much with his family, brothers, sisters, parents; he wasn't given to introducing parents to friends, or friends to parents). The answer to what he was up to is surely nothing.

Yet as we read the letters, and especially the letters to young Edward Cowell, who instructed him in a dilettante's Spanish and then, in the 1850s, in a dilettante's Persian, a small flame of possible illumination or revelation begins to strengthen; we begin to glimpse a possibly growing strength in FitzGerald, despite himself, of unacted and nagging desire, exploding in the *Rubáiyát* — and then subsiding for ever with age and quiescence.

First we have to understand — and in this Volumes One and Two of the letters afford plentiful instruction — how FitzGerald valued himself as writer, as poet in particular. He valued himself not at all. Here he was ambling in curves as slow and blind as a Suffolk river, amiable, kind, and middling. Again and again he says, and he means it, and he shows it in his intermittent verse, I am no writer, I am no poet. "I have not the strong inward call, nor cruel-sweet pangs of parturition, that prove the birth of anything bigger than a mouse," he wrote in 1842, to Cowell. Then to Cowell again in 1849, seven years or so before he was first attracted at all to Omar Khayyám, "You know how little I think of my verses. I never wrote more than twenty good ones in my life." In a letter of 1851 to Cowell's wife (with whom he seems to have been dimly in love at one time) he says, "I am no Poet, but a good Critic."

As the letters go by, he seems less a good critic than an erratic appreciator. He comes on Blake (by way of Benjamin Heath Malkin, his old headmaster at Bury?), and on Vaughan, and is no more than superficially entranced. Comments on one modern and another, though perhaps currency of his generation, strike one even as rather nasty as well as impercipient. He does not care for Hawthorne or George Eliot. He refers always to Wordsworth abominably as "Daddy Wordsworth". "I have rather a wish to tie old Wordsworth's volume" — the 1820 volume which includes among the Duddon sonnets one of Wordsworth's supreme poems — "about his neck and pitch him into one of the deepest holes of his dear Duddon". He extended a dislike of Victor Hugo, whom he called the beginner of the "Gurgoyle School", to Browning, "The great Prophet of the Gurgoyle School"; and it is ironic — seeing what Rossetti did for his fame — to find him asking Tennyson, "Is Mr Rossetti a Great Poet like Browning and Morris? So the Athenaeum tells me. Dear me, how thick Great Poets do grow nowadays." Crabbe's poems he loved, though not without a degree of patronage. Even so his pious book of selections from Crabbe is no sufficient guide to Crabbe's strength and felicities.

And Tennyson? Worshipful as he was of Tennyson he disliked almost all Tennyson's verse after the earlier poems. (He said of *In Memoriam*, when it appeared in 1850, that it contained "fine things", but was monotonous, and had "the air of being evolved by a Poetical Machine of the highest order".) Setting Tennyson and FitzGerald together points to a nearly entire lack in FitzGerald of any sensuous relationship to the physical world. About as much in the perception line as FitzGerald can manage is a complaint about "the same level meadow with geese upon it always lying before my eye; the same pollard oaks with now and then the butcher or the washerwoman trundling by in their carts", or "The Chestnut trees are in their usual glory at this season, crowned over with blossom; and I never saw the fields so rich."

Really there is little to contradict the summary of himself written to his early intimate John Allen: "I have no strength of mind and very little perception."

When and how — and why — does the seedling of *Omar Khayyám* appear? What happens, what stirs in this languid, moneyed Suffolk poetaster and dilettante, whose later tranquillity — according to his friend Spedding — was to seem "like a pirated copy of the peace of God"?

The happening is the languid attraction to the study of Persian, proposed to him by his friend Cowell, Ipswich merchant's son and scholar of languages, who had already encouraged him in his reading of Spanish and of Calderón's plays.

The letters indicate how things went, step by step. Cowell urged, in effect, why be idle, why not do something else, why not try Persian, with me as instructor? That was at Christmas 1852, Cowell (his junior by seventeen years) then a late-coming twenty-six-year-old undergraduate at Oxford. Cowell found his Omar Khayyám manuscript in the Bodleian in 1856, and copied it out for FitzGerald, just before leaving for a professorial job at Calcutta, where he stayed until 1864.

Early in 1856 FitzGerald writes to Tennyson that he is still "puddling away faintly at Persian". Later in the year, writing again to Tennyson, just before Cowell went out to India, he mentions that he and Cowell are reading "some curious Infidel and Epicurean Tetrastichs by a Persian of the eleventh century — as savage against Destiny, etc., as Manfred — but mostly Epicurean Pathos of this kind — 'Drink — for the Moon will often come round to look for us in this Garden and find us not'". He goes on asking the absent Cowell about points of interpretation of this "curious infidel", not at all sure that serious Cowell will approve of his continued interst — "You would be sorry to think that Omar breathes a sort of Consolation to me! Poor Fellow, I think of him, and Olivier Basselin, and Anacreon; lighter shadows among the Shades, perhaps, over which Lucretius presides so grimly" (1857). He does not quite approve of his own concern and interest — to Crabbe's son, George, Suffolk vicar and neighbour: he hasn't been reading much, "only looking from time to time at a poor little Persian Epicurean, who sings the old standing Religion of the World: *Let us make the best of To-day, — who can answer for To-morrow?*" Then to George Borrow, a month later, in June, he is calling Omar "the best Persian I have seen". He is coming round. To Tennyson in July: "I have really got hold of an old Epicurean so desperately impious in his recommendations to live only for Today that the good Mahometans have scarce dared to multiply MSS of him. . . . One of the last [?best] things I remember of him is that — 'God gave me this turn for Drink, perhaps God was drunk when he made me', which is not strictly pious. But he is very tender about his Roses and Wine, and making the most of this poor little Life."

In August he writes to Cowell that he sees "how a very pretty *Eclogue* might be tesselated out of his scattered Quatrains: but you would not like the moral of it". The poem is progressing; and by January 1858 it exists, in its first version; and rather timidly he sends thirty-five not too objectionable stanzas to *Fraser's Magazine*, which neither accepts nor declines them. He recovers the stanzas after a year or so, and with stanzas added, he has the poem, the "eclogue", printed for him by Quaritch the bookseller, and published — Victorian moralism and religiosity or no — price one shilling, 250 copies, — without his name.

What followed is well known — how the pamphlet-poem went unnoticed, how in the end it was "discovered" in the penny box outside Quaritch's shop in what afterwards became a portion of Charing Cross Road, on the Leicester Square side, and how it was preached by Rossetti, Swinburne, Morris, Meredith and the rest of them. The discovery was in 1861. By that time FitzGerald had abandoned his Persian studies. He had given away a very few copies of the *Rubáiyát*, kept a few, tossed the rest of them to Quaritch, and by 1861 had more or less forgotten these "very little affairs".

A reading of the letters, previously unpublished or published only in part, confirms in my judgement that explanation already suggested. When he was taking more and more to his "poor little Persian epicurean", impious, yet tender, FitzGerald was very much feeling the inconsequence and lassitude of his own existence. He was nearly fifty. Friends were dying off. FitzGerald (in 1856) had made his dutiful, yet bizarre match with ugly and dull Lucy Barton, after seven years of an impersonal engagement from which she would not release him. They parted after eight months, in that year when FitzGerald also lost the Cowells, such dear and necessary friends, to India. He was seeing much of Thackeray, who lived with an epicurean or hedonistic freedom for which one may suspect FitzGerald had an underlying inclination, mainly censored in himself; and now, at a last moment, early balding, fat, grey-haired, he was himself celebrating a defiance, which soon died away, under the romantic cover of a Persian poet of centuries past, unknown either to his own eminent and less eminent friends (except Cowell, to whom he wrote in so gingerly a way about Omar Khayyám's lack of the strong weave of Victorian morality and piety) or any readers his poem might find.

In a letter to Cowell, some two months after his *Omar Khayyám* was printed, he speaks rather wearily of death and doing one's best and rounding things off with print, and his "own stupid Decline of Life".

He had once written, when he was an undergraduate, of taking the coach from Cambridge to London and dozing off to visions of the "Lady of Shalott", which he had read in an MS copy, — "really, the poem has taken lodging in my poor head". Now it is as if that youth and that early absorption in Tennysonian poetics had risen in him again, in his rich quatrains of the pathetic and the passing of days, as if a strong, brief resurgence of the suppressed fundamentals of his life, a strong regret, now accounted for the sudden timbre of his pseudo-Persian, or semi-Persian quatrains.

There it is; and assuredly his Omar Khayyám remains almost the sole interest of these letters, more than 2000 of them, which go on and on till his last year (he died in 1883, when he was seventy-four). We do learn a scrap or two about Tennyson, his look, his walk, his taste in the classics. He clings to Tennyson — from a distance; and debases himself in his annual letters to his "dear old Alfred", who does not bother to reply, leaving answers to Mrs Tennyson. But then Tennyson must have been bored by his old friend's repeated declarations of how superior Tennyson was to vulgar cockney Browning, and by the way he harps on the virtues of "my eternal Crabbe", whose poems Tennyson liked, after all, as much as he did.

FitzGerald's worshipful humility towards Tennyson-on-his-throne was such that he had never sent the Tennysons — never dared to send them — a copy of Edition One or Edition Two of the *Rubáiyát*; and how surprised he was to discover, in 1867, that Tennyson admired his stanzas so much — surprised, too, that Tennyson had ever come across them. In 1872, when he was contemplating Edition Three, he rather fearfully asked the Great Man whether it had been Edition One or the enlarged Edition Two he had encountered. For that enquiry all he had from His Majesty was a short note both dismissive and gratifying: Tennyson didn't know whether it had been Edition One or Two, he had mislaid his Omar. Yes, he admired it; but he coupled admiration with a complaint that FitzGerald had stolen one line from his "Gardener's Daughter". Tennyson, we may think, had never quite forgiven him for liking only his early poems. (How would he have taken to FitzGerald's remark apropos the inferiority of "Lucretius" of 1868 to "Locksley Hall" of 1842: "But once get a name in England, and you can do anything"?)

The truth is that FitzGerald's merit as a letter-writer has been much exaggerated. In that role he fitted the Age of Essays, but his letters are not intimate, valuably introspective, or expressive, or more than slightly illustrative or informative. In himself FitzGerald condemns a "visionary inactivity" and his failure to grow up, but the vision is vague; except in that contradictory breakthrough to a sonorous, unforgettable poem which will always be read, in spite of changes in taste and value.

1981

Edward Thomas Again

There are various questions which could be asked about the poems of Edward Thomas. Are they really much read? (But that is a question which can be asked about most poets.) Are they sensibly read? Why in some snooty or dictatorial corners is Edward Thomas considered "respectable" and safe (for undergraduates) to read? Excessive praisers and explicators of the Cantos of Ezra Pound, perhaps even of John Ashbery, can be found to give a pat, if a little pat, to Edward Thomas, which they withhold from any other more or less modern who is incautious enough to mention nettles or broken willow-pattern or cherry blossom. Some of Thomas's poems — not many, but some of them, if fewer than are to be found among the poems of his friend and trigger-puller, Robert Frost, who survived him into a T.V. dotage — are sentimental, undeniably. Why isn't this held against him, as you might imagine?

I wish I could be naif enough and confident enough to say that these and some other questions about Edward Thomas are subsumable in the one answer that he wrote his poems well, when writing well is so often the slowest way to acceptance. In addition to writing well, perhaps mystery and convenience were scented by keen noses in Edward Thomas himself. He was over, but not done with. He had delivered himself only of a small oeuvre of 144 poems. He could be handled, and it could be remarked that he rose (as Frost noted) above a circle of inferiors, whose inferiority could be shown up, by contrast, to characterize that tame era into which Hardy and then Eliot erupted. As for the scarcely readable prose Edward Thomas wrote — out to the dust cart with it all, all the essay stuff, all the Eleanor-Farjeonry, the tramping of ridgeways etc.

So much for one party. For another party of readers, those who adore wood engravings of barn and plough, those in whom the soft essay-mind survives, here is a poet whom "modernists" admire and whose success has contradicted all that modernist guff. We are right, after all. Reynolds Stone for us — and him; not Bonnard or Matisse or the blue half-abstract pools of David Hockney.

Comforting for both parties, yet surely dangerous for the writer himself. For one thing — witness this exhumation of Edward Thomas's book about the Icknield Way[1] — too much

1 *Edward Thomas. The Icknield Way* introduced by Shirley Toulson (1980).

metal-detecting over the prose word-heaps seems likely to
bring up much that was better undisturbed, much rather base
and ordinary metal. There is a recipe here for detraction. And
as for praise and acceptance, have we in two score English
faculties to wade through all that tiresomeness in search of
clues? So there could be, and perhaps there is, a clash of soft
and sharp around Edward Thomas in which his poems will be
the loser, in the end.

Sentimentality again: there is a pivot on which, I would say,
he can be discussed. Question: Is Edward Thomas
remembering Adlestrop more sentimental than Philip Larkin
walking down Cemetery Road arm in arm with Old Toad, or
Geoffrey Hill cheeping about God? How many sentimental
poems do even the severer among us enjoy? Sentimental —
"expressing or tending to rouse foolish or exaggerated feelings
of tenderness, pity, etc." — I must myself enjoy at least not too
foolish or too exaggerated feelings of tenderness and pity,
because at the word sentimental a dozen poems at least jostle
into pleasurable recollection — among them Mörike's famous
poem about the strange girl he loved and had parted from.
(What would it be if he opened the door and there she was
again, on the doorstep — *da bin ich wieder/Hergekommen aus
weiter Welt*); or Marceline Valmore's "Qu'en Avez-Vous Fait"
to the man who has left her, and perhaps will come back some
day — when it is too late:

Vous viendrez rêvant,
Sonner à ma porte;
Ami comme avant
Vous viendrez rêvant.

Et l'on vous dira:
"Personne! . . . elle est morte"
On vous le dira:
Mais, qui vous plaindra.

Or (coming nearer, in time anyhow, to Edward Thomas) Alice
Meynell's "Letter from a Girl to her own Old Age" (which I
once asked Sir Francis Meynell's leave to reprint. His reply:
"Why on earth do you want to reprint my mother's most
sentimental poem?").

Of course there isn't the clearest division between arousal of
feeling and arousal of excessive feeling. Some can take more,
others less. I find myself that I can put up happily enough with
Edward Thomas's poem on what he will give to his elder
daughter —

If I should ever by chance grow rich
I'll buy Codham, Cockridden, and Childerditch

— or with his "Adlestrop", both poems sentimental in
movement and content, the point being, if I have taken so long
to reach it, that a poem stirring us to any emotion of tenderness, pity, etc, must by that token at least be skilled in poetic
processes. "Adlestrop" is skilled, so I can take it, I remember
"Adlestrop", I incline to say "Adlestrop" to my wife if we pass
that station site along the Fosse Way; and it does not upset me
if I find Edward Thomas, in turn, liking other men's sentimentality — "O Blackbird, what a boy you are" etc, or if I
contemplate, once more, the sentimental, and, as I say, there is
plenty of it, not so well handled, in the sound and movement
and substance of poems by his friend Robert Frost. How high
on the sentimentality scale do you find "Two roads diverged in
a yellow wood", or, if you assess it properly, that rather ill-
written poem "Dust of Snow"?

Which party of admirers includes Edward Thomas's editor,
R. George Thomas?[1] The countryside party. "This sense of
oneness with man in his natural surroundings is the nub of his
enduring appeal to late twentieth-century readers." Whether
that seems nonsense or only half-nonsense rather depends on
the identity and nature of the late twentieth-century readers,
who are not a body with identical responses. There are poems,
and images and reports in various poems, which are about our
surroundings, of course, but which do not expand much in
symbolic meaning. They give delight — I think of "A Tale"
(the apparently cancelled version), of "Tall Nettles", and
"Thaw", or of the lines

Bluebells hid all the ruts in the copse.
The elm seeds lay in the road like hops

or

. . . walking among the nunneries
Of many a myriad anemones

but to value Edward Thomas too much in that mode is to
diminish the Edward Thomas who writes best about man —
about himself or about us, analogically — nipped in the steel
vice or circumstances. "Beauty", yes, and wood anemones like
nuns and elm seed like hops; but what of not-loving, lost-
loving, and other-loving and impossible loving?

The unifying quality about Thomas's poems, countryish or

1 *Edward Thomas: Collected Poems* edited by R.G. Thomas (1980).

sentimental or rooted in sad relationship, is that high quiet violin playing of his lines and his whole poems, which approaches something Haydnesque in my scale of values. So the worst fault remains that prating of countryman Thomas which celebrates the poet who is so honest about what is delightful yet insufficient, yet so obscures the poet of the deep issues; from which, for this tortured man and father and ex-lover, no escape can be contemplated or justified except — at the age of thirty-nine — going away into khaki, in defence of a country he certainly loved.

Edward Thomas then — by the country party — is under-estimated, and more than that, concealments are made. Too much, I am pretty sure, is said of his melancholia, over-advanced defensively to excuse or conceal essences of poems (and behaviour), about which the truth, it if hasn't been told, may by now be unknowable. There are poems about which Professor Thomas is (carefully?) silent in his notes, such as "Go Now", "After You Speak", and "Some Eyes Condemn"; and there is one more such poem — one about which — I wish to put this strongly —Professor Thomas persists in being ridiculous, to the detriment of his hero, whom he serves well enough in most ways. This poem is "No One so Much as You", which says:

> Scarce my eyes dare meet you
> Lest they should prove
> I but respond to you
> And do not love.

and continues:

> I at the most accept
> Your love, regretting
> That is all: I have kept
> A helpless fretting

> That I could not return
> All that you gave

and concludes — with what emotional force — that:

> sometimes it did seem
> Better it were
> Never to see you more
> Than linger here

> With only gratitude
> Instead of love —
> A pine in solitude
> Cradling a dove.

Who is the dove? His wife Helen Thomas? Oh no, it is about his mother, says Professor Thomas, who is well aware that this identification depends on the quick interjection of Helen Thomas, in a broadcast interview, that the poem was not about herself, but her mother-in-law. We can understand and sympathize with her denial. We can excuse her unreadiness to admit in public that her marriage ever came to that piteousness of failure — and to the production of poems about it — on her husband's side. It is Professor Thomas who canot be excused for his unadorned acceptance, and for smothering the obvious, without a hint. He deceives readers by first deceiving himself. Those who are left in doubt should compare with "No One So Much as You" Edward Thomas's ending of "Last Poem" which is about the greater sorrow of "less love" which does not know "tempest and the perfect scope/

> Of summer, but a frozen drizzle perpetual
> Of drops that from remorse and pity fall
> And cannot ever shine in the sun or thaw,
> Removed eternally from the sun's law.

That was written two days after Edward Thomas had said a last goodbye to his family, en route to his howitzers and the Somme — and death.

I am not leaving myself much to report on the resuscitation of *The Icknield Way*, which seems to me so unnecessary, the run of it is so thin and ordinary, a money job pushed through in Edward Thomas's later time of exceptional distress. Here it is, anyhow, introduced in a faintly foolish, childish or old-fashioned manner, asseverative about country pleasures — "And so this book is a tribute to men's persistence as travellers, and a treasure for anybody who, on foot or in imagination, likes to follow the old highways of this country."

And the book or booklet by Andrew Motion?[1] If *The Icknield Way* is for the country party, Andrew Motion's accountant's examination of the poems vis-à-vis the life allows country party stuff to mix with the sterner stuff of the quadrangle or lecture room. The book says nothing, or practically nothing, about the verbal and cadential substance of Thomas's poems. A

1 *The Poetry of Edward Thomas* by Andrew Motion (1980).

kind of vanishing or evaporative liquor seems to fall on the poems, leaving only a dull semi-abstraction of "what they are about", in five chapters which cannot be read certainly with pleasure:

> The opening lines of "Digging" inaugurate a fine sensuous catalogue which affirms that scents are stimulatingly regenerative.

> The cautious balance of optimism and resignation which ends "Wind and Mist" depends on the assumption that isolation from nature is the result of particular circumstances. But discussions of his place in human society lack potential consolation.

Hell, Hell, Hell, and dust. Mr Motion lectures in English at Hull — I nearly wrote Hell a fourth time. Am I to suppose this is how he talks to his students, poor sods?

I wish I could be sure that the multiplication of often arrogant English faculties (in which teachers begin and continue their ascent by books similar to this one) isn't going to be a thumping, numbing blow to the enjoyment of literature — especially if literary editors persist in employing poor, harassed, untalented old and young clerks to interpret literature to the rest of us in reviews as if we were their students. "Later in the poem these images of integration are gradually modified into images of stasis" — who is going to read that again after he has taken his degree and found his job in advertising?

The Poetry of Edward Thomas is not worse — and it is shorter — than a score of other books of the kind which come out every season, recession or no. And I will compliment Mr Motion on seeing through that nonsense of finding Mrs Thomas Senior instead of Mrs Thomas Junior in "No One So Much as You", in Edward Thomas's wonderful conclusion of himself and herself as a "pine in solitude/Cradling a dove".

1981